Study Manual on the Bases of Russian Law

Study Manual on the Bases of Russian Law

By

Anna V. Shashkova

Cambridge
Scholars
Publishing

Study Manual on the Bases of Russian Law

By Anna V. Shashkova

This book first published 2015

Cambridge Scholars Publishing

Lady Stephenson Library, Newcastle upon Tyne, NE6 2PA, UK

British Library Cataloguing in Publication Data
A catalogue record for this book is available from the British Library

ISBN (10): 1-4438-7121-4
ISBN (13): 978-1-4438-7121-1

CONTENTS

PREFACE

INTRODUCTION TO THE MANUAL

Aim of the Manual

The objective of this manual is to meet the needs of professionals, teachers and students in comprehensive study material on bases of Russian Law.

The intention of the author is that after reading the material, people from different backgrounds will understand the basic principles of Russian Civil & Corporate Law and how such principles interact. The author considers necessary to set as well a Chapter on Essential Elements of the Russian Legal System to give an overall and profound understanding of the process of the creation of business entities in the legal environment of the Russian Federation.

After reading the book you will be able to:

- Analyse and evaluate situations from a legal perspective
- Identify the essential elements of the Russian legal system and the main sources of law and explain their operations
- Demonstrate the ability to apply to an appropriate court in the Russian Federation
- Understand and apply Russian contractual law
- Distinguish between alternative forms and constitutions of business organisations
- Explain the main legal principles relating to the exercise by foreign individuals and legal entities of their rights in the sphere of Russian business law in the Russian Federation
- Recognise the legal implications relating to companies in difficulty or in crisis
- Demonstrate an understanding of governance and ethical issues relating to business
- Explain the nature of, and legal control over money laundering.

The manual is directed mainly to undergraduate and postgraduate law students, as well as to Russian and foreign lawyers, heads of legal entities, financial directors, chief accountants and auditors using English, and to any person interested in Russian Law.

The authour has tried to state the law accurately as of 1 October 2014, though a number of changes known to be taking effect later in 2014 have been included in the text.

The author would appreciate any suggestions and comments on the manual, which you can e-mail directly to a.shashkova@inno.mgimo.ru.

List of Abbreviations for Major Terms Used

BD	Board of Directors (Supervisory Board)
CEO	Chief Executive Officer (Sole Executive Body)
GM	General Meeting of Shareholders or Participants
J-SC	Joint-Stock Company (Company Limited by Shares)
LLC	Limited Liability Company (Company Limited by Stakes)
Management Board	Collective Executive Body
RF	Russian Federation

CHAPTER ONE

ESSENTIAL ELEMENTS OF THE RUSSIAN LEGAL SYSTEM

Part I. A Definiton of Law

Law has been defined as the written and unwritten body of rules, derived from custom, formal enactment and judicial decisions, which are recognised as binding on persons who constitute a community or state, so that they will be imposed upon and enforced among those persons by appropriate sanctions. Russian law can be classified as national (domestic) or international, public or private, criminal or civil.

During the last 20 years rapid legal, economic and political reforms were implemented by federal and municipal bodies of the Russian Federation. However, the legal, economic and political systems in Russia were greatly influenced by seventy years of socialism. Communism lasted longer in Russia than anywhere else, and influenced it more completely. Moreover, in contrast to the Czech Republic or Poland with their traditions of free-market democracy, Russia was never such a democracy, and had patterns of communal ownership long before 1917.

The President, the Federal Assembly, the various Federal Ministries, and regional and municipal government authorities have enacted massive amounts of legislation and regulations since the dissolution of the USSR, some of which are inconsistent with or contradict legislation issued by other Russian governmental entities. Many laws and decrees are also vague and unclear, permitting varied interpretations by Russian authorities. Legislation in the RF has been implemented vigorously, partially or not at all, depending on the nature of the legislation and on the political leanings of government officials charged with its implementation. Disputes exist among various Ministries as to which Ministry is empowered to regulate particular areas. In short, the study of the legal framework in Russia is a perpetual and demanding task.

Branches of Law

Juridical provisions composing the laws of the RF are tightly interconnected, conformed and compose a single system. This system can be subdivided on large component parts; the law branches.

A branch of law is a separate complex within a major system of similar legal norms and legal institutions regulating one field of relations.

Strictly speaking, Russia has constitutional, administrative, civil and criminal branches of law. However, as the business turnover (negotiation) grows the list of the major branches becomes longer.

The law system in Russia includes the following major branches:

- Constitutional law
- Administrative law
- Financial law
- Customs law
- Civil law
- Business law
- Corporate law
- Family law
- Labour law
- Land law
- Housing law
- Ecological law
- Criminal law
- Civil procedural law
- Criminal procedural law
- Criminal executive law
- Arbitrazh procedural law.

A branch may be divided into smaller complexes - sub-branches such as tax law deriving from financial law, or immovable law deriving from civil law, etc.

Part II. Classification of Laws

Public and Private Law

There are two major areas within the Russian legal system:

- Public law
- Private law.

Public law regulates relations between an individual and the state. These are relations of power-subordination. Constitutional, administrative, financial, criminal, criminal procedural law and criminal executive law are parts of these relations.

Private law regulates relations between subjects of law on the basis of their mutual obligations, where the participants of relations are equal. These relations include civil, labour, family and other branches of law.

The following characteristics are typical for private law: the object of private law is relations based on legal equality of participants, autonomy of their will and their proprietary independence (possessing set-apart property). Application of "residuary" norms is typical for private legal relations (for example, the Civil Code stipulates that parties may conclude a contract either in the form set by law and/or other legal acts or in other form).

Civil law is one of the branches of private law. The Civil Code stipulates legal foundations of private law:

- Equality of participants to proprietary relations
- Inviolability of property
- Contractual freedom
- Inadmissible arbitrary interference into private affairs (Privacy of contract)
- Necessity to freely exercise civil rights and guarantee their protection in court.

Substantive and Procedural Law

Substantive law regulates social relations directly. Examples of branches of substantive law are the following:

- Civil law
- Criminal law
- Administrative law.

Procedural law regulates the order and the cover of the law regulation of substantive branches. Examples of procedural branches are the following:

- Civil procedural law
- Criminal procedural law
- Arbitrazh procedural law.

Civil and Criminal Law

An important distinction must be drawn between the areas of criminal and civil law. A crime is any conduct which is prohibited by law. Criminal prosecutions are brought by the state. The state prosecutes because it is notionally the community as a whole which suffers when criminal law is infringed.

Civil proceedings have as their object the resolution of disputes between individuals and the compensation of those who have been wronged under the civil law. The main areas of civil litigation comprise company law, the law of contracts, torts, labour and family law.

A Tort

A tort has been defined as a civil wrong arising from a breach of duty created not by agreement but by operation of law. A civil wrong is one which gives rise to civil proceedings as opposed to a criminal prosecution. It is defined as a civil wrong (other than a breach of contract or a breach of trust) for which the normal remedy is an action for damages.

Attempts are often made to define the tort by contrasting it with other distinct areas of law such as contract law. A contract exists where there has been an agreement between parties and where the parties intended to create legal relations and have supported their agreement with consideration. The contractual relationship is denoted by the concept of privity, which means that only a party to a contract or interested person can sue on it. The law of torts exists outside the confines of the doctrine of privity of contract, and therefore a contract is in no way a prerequisite for a successful tort action. However, a breach of contract may also amount to a tortious act, for example the selling of a car with faulty brakes. A plaintiff is free to sue for breach of contract and in tort in the same set of proceedings.

Part III. Sources of Law

A source of law serves as the basis for deciding (ruling) on juridical matters.

Russian law derives its validity from the Constitution of the RF. The Russian legal system is broadly similar to the legal systems which exist in most European countries, whether part of the E.U. or otherwise.

The Russian Law Family

Russia belongs to "Romano-German" law family. Usually "Romano-German" law family countries are called continental law countries. Russia is a civil law jurisdiction. In a civil law jurisdiction an attempt is made to codify or put into legislative form all laws applicable in that country. The laws are contained within the statutes passed by parliament. In this way we may distinguish our legal system from those which exist in the United Kingdom, Ireland, the United States of America and other "Anglo-Saxon" law family countries. These countries are common law jurisdictions and the judicial precedent is the most important source of law in such countries. Usually "Anglo-Saxon" law family countries are called precedent law countries.

The Sources of Russian Law

The main sources of Russian Law are the following:

- Statute Law
- The acts of Executive Bodies
- International Law
- Customs of Business Turnover
- Judicial Precedent / Rulings of the Constitutional Court of the RF.

Overview of the Statute Law of the Russian Federation (RF)

The statute law is the main source of Russian law. The structure of the statute law in the RF is very complex, because Russia is a federal state and has statute law both in the RF and in the Subjects of the RF. The structure of the statute law is the following:

- The Constitution
- The Constitutions and the Charters of the Subjects of the RF
- Federal constitutional laws of the RF
- Federal laws of the RF
- Laws of the Subjects of the RF
- Laws of the former USSR and RSFSR.

The Constitution of the RF

The Constitution of the RF is the supreme normative legal act, holding the highest juridical power (establishing general principles and regulations), superiority and direct action on Russian territory. All laws and other legal acts adopted in Russia must comply with the Constitution. Thus, the Constitution of the RF has the following notions:

- The highest juridical power
- Superiority
- Direct action on Russian territory.

The RF enacted the current Constitution on 12 December 1993. The Russian Constitution, approved by state referendum, is the basis of Russian constitutional law, and the most important source of domestic law. The Constitution provides for a federal state and introduces the concept of the separation of powers. The Constitution provides for the separation of executive, legislative and judicial power. The legislature is structured as a parliament. The main legislative body, the Federal Assembly, is composed of two chambers – the Federation Council (the upper house) and the State Duma (the lower house). The Constitution deals with such matters as the national territory, the President, the legislature, the executive, the judiciary of the RF and, of course, the fundamental rights, which are contained in the 2nd chapter of the Constitution.

It is commonly said that the executive branch consists of the President, elected directly by the people for a six-year term, and the Government. However, the President of the RF remains separate to the executive power. The President is the guarantor of the Constitution[1] and possesses some executive, legislative and judicial powers.

The Government is responsible before the President and is headed by the Head of the Government (unofficially called the Prime-Minister), who is nominated by the President and confirmed by the State Duma.

Amendments to the Constitution

The Russian Constitution is rigid when considering the complex procedure of adopting Constitutional amendments. The Constitution itself, and the Law on Amendments to the Constitution establish the procedure and conditions for making, adopting and approving amendments to chapters 3-8 of the Constitution of the RF, as well as their entry into force. The Constitution cannot be modified by the State Duma alone.

---

[1] Constitution, Article 80.2.

According to the Amendments to the Constitution of the RF the terms of the President of the RF and of the State Duma of the RF were increased from 4 years for each to six and five years respectively[2].

The Statute Law

A "statute" denotes that a body of law is enacted by the parliamentary process. Statutes are, as a source of law, subject only to the Constitution and always prevail in the event of a conflict with other normative acts of the RF.

Laws possess the following characteristics:

- They are adopted by representative bodies (the Federal Assembly) or by public referendum (source of adoption)
- The law is adopted in accordance with a certain procedure which ensures the adoption of laws regarding significant issues only, and thorough consideration of laws prior to their adoption (specific order of adoption)
- Laws hold supreme power in comparison to other normative legal acts (legal supremacy).

Federal Constitutional Laws

Laws of the RF are divided into:

- Federal constitutional laws and,
- Federal laws (not attached to the constitutional laws).

Federal constitutional laws cover issues that are directly foreseen by the Constitution. Federal constitutional laws are enacted in the most important areas of constitutional law, such as referendum, government and human rights. They include the following laws: Law on Referendum, Law on Government, Law on Judicial System, Law on Constitutional Court, etc. Changes to the above laws would also require the adoption of a federal constitutional law, e.g., the specialised Arbitrazh court – the Intellectual Rights court was introduced by federal constitutional law[3].

---

[2] Law of the RF on Amendments to the Constitution of the RF No.6-FKZ, dated 30 December 2008.

[3] Federal Constitutional Law No.4-FKZ "On Introduction of Amendments to the Federal Constitutional Law: 'On the Judicial System of the RF'".

According to the Constitution, constitutional laws enjoy a higher status than ordinary statutes, as it provides that federal laws may not contravene federal constitutional laws[4].

The procedure for adoption of federal constitutional laws is more complex than the procedure for adoption of federal laws; federal constitutional laws require the adoption of the qualified majority of both the State Duma and the Federation Council.

Federal constitutional laws differ from federal laws on the following criteria:

- Legal force
- Competence
- Procedure for adoption
- Powers of the President on application of its suspensive veto.

Federal Laws

Federal laws are adopted by the supreme representative body – by the Federal Assembly. Laws can also be adopted directly by the people through referendum.

Among the laws one may emphasise codified laws (e.g. the Civil Code, the Tax Code, the Criminal Code, etc). Norms of other legislative acts of the RF shall comply with the Civil Code[5]. However, in the case of a contradiction between a Code and a special federal law, a special federal law shall prevail.

The RF has enacted a Civil Code, which is intended to repeal most Soviet era civil law rules and establish a market-oriented system. Part I of the Civil Code, which deals with general principles of civil law, property rights and rules, governing obligations and contract, entered into force on 1 January 1995. Part II, which deals with rules for specific types of contracts and torts came into force on 1 May 1996. Part III, which deals with inheritance and private international law, came into force on 1 March 2002. Part IV, which deals with intellectual property, has been in force from 1 January 2008. Drastic changes to the Civil Code came into force on 1 September 2013.

Federal Laws and Laws of the Subjects of the RF

Russia is a federal state and laws adopted in it include:

---

[4] Constitution, Article 76.3.
[5] Civil Code, Article 3.2.

- Federal laws (adopted by the Federal Assembly) and
- Laws of the Subjects of the RF (adopted by the bodies of the legislative power of the Subjects of the RF).

Jurisdiction of the RF or the Subjects of the RF is divided into:
- Jurisdiction of the RF
- Joint jurisdiction of the RF and the Subjects of the RF and,
- Jurisdiction of the Subjects of the RF.

Laws of the Subjects of the RF are subordinated to the jurisdiction of the RF or the joint jurisdiction of the RF and the Subjects of the RF. Laws of the Subjects of the RF may not contradict federal laws. According to the general rule, in case of contradiction between a federal law and another act adopted in the RF, the federal law has the juridical supremacy[6]. The rule of supremacy provides the unity of the law regulation system in Russia.

Federal laws of the RF, together with the Constitution, hold the supreme power over the entire territory of the RF, and the highest juridical power when compared to other regulatory legal acts adopted in the RF on issues in the exclusive jurisdiction of the RF or in the joint jurisdiction of the RF and its Subjects[7].

Laws have direct force within the territory of the RF [Constitution, Article 76.1]. Federal laws concerning issues in joint jurisdiction of the RF and the Subjects of the RF are adopted together with laws and other acts of the Subjects of the RF[8].

The Relationship between Statute Law and the Constitution

The relationship between statute law and the Constitution can be summarised as follows:
- Under Article 125 of the Constitution the President, the State Duma, one-fifth of the members of the Federation Council or deputies of the State Duma, the Government and the Supreme Court of the RF[9], the bodies of legislative and executive power of the Subjects of the RF can apply to the Constitutional Court[10] with a request concerning compliance of federal laws, normative acts of

[6] Constitution, Article 76.5.
[7] Constitution, Articles 71, 72.
[8] Constitution, Article 76.2.
[9] http://www.supcourt.ru/
[10] http://www.ksrf.ru/

the President, of the Federation Council, of the State Duma and of the Government with the Constitution
- Litigants before the Constitutional Court may assert that legislation is unconstitutional.

Example

The Constitutional Court of the RF has found part of Article 446 of the Civil Procedural Code not to be corresponding to the Constitution of the RF and therefore such provision has been abolished[11].

According to the version in the dispute of the above article, only the real property of a natural person may be recovered by creditors, though mortgaged property may not be. The Ruling of the Constitutional Court of the RF has held the provision concerning specifics of mortgaged property unconstitutional, making the recovery of such property possible not only by banks, but by ordinary creditors as well.

Stages of the Legislation Process

The Legislature

The legislature is the function which initiates legislation on behalf of the people. Like most countries, the legislature of the RF comprises two houses: the State Duma and the Federation Council, through which most legislation is debated and enacted, all within the overall framework of the Constitution and international treaties to which the State has committed itself.

As the Russian system is highly dependent on statute law, the legislature has a central role in creating law. However, law making does not begin and end with the actions of these government organs. The system permits legislation to be enacted through a hierarchical structure that includes regional governments and public and municipal bodies that are enabled to create legislation within their respective terms of reference.

Law cannot always evolve at the pace required to keep up with changes in society. The decision making of government and subordinate bodies is complemented by the powers of the President to make decrees and orders, and to a limited degree the application of analogy in courts to resolve legal dilemmas or lacunas.

[11] Ruling of the Constitutional Court of the RF No.11-P, dated 14 May 2012.

Which State Body Adopts Federal Laws

Before a piece of legislation becomes a law it is known as a draft law. Federal laws are adopted by the Federal Assembly: the State Duma and the Federation Council.

Notes

Draft laws and discussions thereof shall be published at www.regulation.gov.ru.

The Legislative Initiative

The legislative initiative is a right to submit draft laws for the consideration of the State Duma. According to the Constitution the right of the legislative initiative belongs to:

- The State Duma
- Deputies of the State Duma
- The Federation Council
- Members of the Federation Council
- The President of the RF
- The Government of the RF
- The legislative (representative) bodies of the Subjects of the RF
- The superior courts (the Constitutional Court, the Supreme Court) on issues concerning their jurisdiction[12].

Preliminary Consideration

Preliminary consideration includes forwarding the draft law to an appropriate committee of the State Duma. At the same time, the draft law is forwarded to commissions, committees and deputies associations, to the President, to the Government, etc.

Readings in the State Duma

First reading in the State Duma means the discussion of the concept of the draft law. The major provisions of the draft law are considered and assessed. On the basis of the results of the first reading the State Duma may decline the draft law or accept it. The State Duma may also accept the law in the first reading and continue working with it. In this case a special

---

[12] Constitution, Article 104.

committee in charge is appointed to study and summarise the amendments. At the beginning of the second reading the work of the committee is discussed. The draft law may be adopted at the second reading, and then it is forwarded to the committee in charge in order to eliminate possible discrepancies with participation of the Legal Department of the State Duma. In the majority of cases the draft law is adopted in the third reading.

Adoption of the Law

A federal law is deemed adopted if more than half of the deputies of the State Duma (at least 226 deputies) have voted for it[13]. When a draft law is passed by the State Duma it is sent to the Federation Council where it is further considered and may be amended. It has to be approved by a majority of the members of the Federation Council within 14 days.

Draft laws on introduction or abolition of taxes, on exemption from tax payment, on issuance of state loans, on changes in the financial obligations of the RF and other draft laws that stipulate expenses covered by the federal budget may be submitted for the State Duma's consideration after the Government's conclusion (approval) exclusively.

The Consequences of Non-Consideration of the Draft Law by the Federation Council within 14 Days

Within five days after a law is adopted by the State Duma, it is to be transferred to the Federation Council for further consideration and approval. If the Federation Council does not consider the draft law within 14 days and the draft law is not subject to the compulsory consideration by the Federation Council, the draft law is deemed to be automatically approved by the Federation Council.

Federal laws adopted by the State Duma shall be considered by the Federation Council on a mandatory basis if such laws deal with the issues of:

- The federal budget
- Federal taxes and levies
- Financial, monetary, credit and customs regulations and money emission
- Ratification and denunciation of international treaties of the RF

[13] Article 95.3 of the Constitution states that the State Duma consists of 450 deputies.

- The status and protection of the state border of the RF
- War and peace.

Special stage - eliminating discrepancies between the Federation Council and the State Duma (a conciliatory commission is set up in the event of the Federation Council declining draft laws approved by the State Duma).

Promulgation (Signing) of the Law by the President of the RF

The draft law is then sent to the President who must sign it within 14 days, unless the President uses his suspensive veto rights to decline the law in case of disagreement. In case of a decline, the State Duma examines that law again, and either amends it according to the remarks of the President, or leaves the law in its old version. In the second case, the State Duma may override the veto of the President, if not less than two-thirds of all the members of both the State Duma and the Federation Council vote for the adoption of the law. Afterwards, the President must sign the federal law within seven days[14].

The date of adoption of law is the date of its promulgation by the President of the RF.

Does the President Have Veto Rights to Decline a Federal Constitutional Law?

Article 108 of the Constitution provides that, after adoption of the federal constitutional law by at least the two-thirds of the State Duma and three-quarters of the Federation Council, the President signs the federal constitutional law within 14 days. Therefore, no suspensive veto rights may be used by the President in this case.

Official Publication and Enactment

The laws are published within seven days from the date they are signed by the President of the RF[15].

The law must be published in one of the official newspapers of the RF: “Rossiyskaya Gazeta”, “Sobranie Zakonodatelstva”. The general rule is that the law enters into force 10 days after its publication in the official

[14] Constitution, Article 107.3.
[15] Law on Entering into Force of Federal Legal Acts, Article 3.

newspaper or magazine of the RF[16]. The statute itself may provide the term when it enters into force.

Notes

The official publication shall also be considered the first publication at the "Official Internet Portal of Legal Information" www.pravo.gov.ru[17]. Within 10 days after adoption of the acts they shall be posted on the internet.

Validity of the Normative Acts in Time

Unless the statute contains express words to the contrary, the following presumptions apply:

- A statute does not alter the existing law nor repeal other statutes
- By general rule legislative acts are not retroactive and shall be applied towards the relations, which had arisen after they were put into force.

The operation of law shall be extended toward the relations, which had arisen before it was put into force, only in cases, directly provided for by law.

Example

Article 10 of the Criminal Code states that a criminal law which excludes a crime, absolves the criminal liability for a crime or otherwise improves the conditions of the person who has committed a crime, shall have retroactive effect.

Regarding to relations which had arisen before the statute was put into force, the most recent normative act shall be applied towards the rights and duties which have arisen after its being put into force.

There are certain situations when a statute can have a retroactive effect:

- When a statute benefits all the people or the parties involved and does not infringe interests of any other third parties
- When a statute simply interprets (construes) other statutes and does not infringe rights of any other third parties.

[16] Law on Entering into Force of Federal Legal Acts, Article 6.
[17] Decree of the President of the RF No.1505, dated 17 November 2011.

General Principles of Law Implementation

The usefulness and necessity of laws reveal themselves solely in the course of the implementation of those laws; their embodiment. Implementation of law provisions is the practical execution of instructions included in those provisions, when a rule, displayed in a law provision in general form, is embodied in people's deeds. The forms of law implementation are the following:

- **Accomplishment** (use)

Accomplishment of law is active realisation by the subjects (e.g. individuals, legal entities, state bodies) of opportunities included in the law. It is generally accepted in Russian law that actions that do not cause harm to others and are not forbidden by law, are permitted. Some laws prescribe the actions that individuals and legal entities may take and the manner of accomplishing them. Accomplishment of law is restricted by rights of other subjects of civil turnover[18].

Example

An owner of property may sell it, present it or bequeath it, etc. An owner of property may even destroy the property, but only if it does not violate rights and lawful interests of other third parties.

State bodies, accomplishing their rights, simultaneously execute their obligations (e.g. courts when practicing justice, tax bodies when executing tax examinations).

- **Execution**

This term refers to the discharge of the legal obligations of individuals and legal entities as laid down in legislation. Execution means the embodiment of obligatory provisions (e.g. fulfilment by individuals of their constitutional obligations, such as tax payment, obligatory military service, etc). Another example is the fulfilment of obligatory returns in the form of statutory records, including registration of births, marriages and deaths or formation or reorganisation of companies.

---

[18] Article 17.3 of the Constitution states that the execution of one's rights and liberties shall not infringe the rights and liberties of another person.

- **Observance**

This term refers to compliance with the limits laid down in relation to the activities of individuals and legal entities. Observance is the realisation of the forbidding provisions or non-execution of actions that may inflict harm on an individual, society or the RF. It is a more negative concept in that it involves not taking certain actions that are forbidden by law. Prohibitions may be set, for example, by provisions of criminal or administrative law. The restrictions on the active capacity of minors is an example of observance. Parties to most types of contracts shall observe certain legal provisions, and even outside the scope of contract law they can be held accountable if by their actions they inflict loss or harm on others. Legal entities are also constrained by their own constituent documents, which under the provisions of law must lay down specified parameters within which they may act.

Example

A person keeping from crossing the road when red lights are on.

- **Enforcement**

A special form of law realisation is its enforcement. A peculiarity of the given form is that it is executed by the competent bodies and is aimed at a restricted number of persons or one person. An act of law enforcement is an individual act of an authorised body of power that is based on norms and determines particular rights, duties or liability. Non-observance of such acts is punished. The courts are integral players in enforcing the law, such as in matters requiring the resolution of contractual disputes and confirmation of the entitlements of citizens (such as payments from the State or from their employer).

Legal entities incur certain obligations in the course of economic activity. One example is the enforcement of the rights of creditors when the sums due to them become payable, such as on maturity of the debt, on default by the debtor, on reorganisation or insolvency.

Major requirements to such acts are the following:

- Strict compliance with legal provisions
- An act must be issued within the limits of powers of the law enforcement body or an official
- An act must be substantiated (the court bailiff takes the decision on institution of the executory process, which shall be then approved by the senior court bailiff)

- An act must have all the required characteristics of an official document.

Law enforcement acts are not sources of law since they do not contain any general rules of conduct but ensure the application of certain law provisions with respect to a particular case or person. Unlike normative legal acts, acts of law enforcement are supposed to be applied once only.

Law enforcement is required in different cases, when implementation of law is impossible without the interference of the state, its bodies or officials, such as:

- Relations in the sphere of the state management (e.g. appointment of a Federal Minister)
- Relations in the area of distribution of social benefits (e.g. pensions or state welfare payments)
- Relations arising in solving law disputes (e.g. the court's decision)
- Relations arising under juridical prosecuting, imposing and executing the punishment (e.g. the ruling of the criminal investigator to initiate a criminal case).

A Gap in a Law (A Law Lacuna)

A law-enforcement process is also executed in case of a gap in a law. A gap in a law is the absence of a necessary provision regulating public relations that are to be regulated by law. A gap in a law arises when the law does not provide a satisfactory reference point for the resolution of an issue. This is inevitable, as the law cannot accommodate every situation that will arise in the future.

A gap in a law can be resolved in several ways. The relevant law-making body can lay down a law specifically to address the situation, thereby removing any ambiguity. This can be done at any level, subject to the powers of the law-making body.

At the very highest level, the President is empowered to issue a decree to eliminate the law lacuna.

Alternatively, the court may apply a provision applicable to a similar situation if appropriate, or resolve the issue with reference to the general meaning and purpose of the legislation as it exists by application of analogy of law or analogy of legislation.

Application of Analogy of Law

If there is no written law, the courts may have to resort to analogy whereby they consider similar circumstances in which a law actually exists.

Alternatively, the court has to consider the existing legislation and apply a decision that is consistent with the purposes and principles of the legislation.

The role of the courts in resolving a law lacuna is quite common in codified legal systems such as that of the RF. This is inevitable, as it is unlikely that the legislative process can ever keep up with the pace of change in the commercial environment and society as a whole.

In this case a gap in a law is eliminated by the application of a law provision, regulating similar relations (such law provision serves as a law basis for the court decision).

Example

In case of a dispute between participants of an LLC on the possibility to vote at the General Participants' meeting by appointing a representative under a power of attorney, the court shall rule under the LLC Law. Due to lack of relevant provisions thereof, the court shall give a judgement under a similar law, e.g. the J-SC Law – application of analogy of law.

Application of Analogy of Legislation

In the absence of a law provision regulating similar relations, the law-enforcer eliminates a gap in a law in accordance with general principles and the meaning of the legislation.

Analogy of law and analogy of legislation take place in Russian civil law-enforcement practice, but are prohibited in administrative and criminal laws.

Other Normative Legal Acts

The current situation in the RF is that a law often contains gaps, which executive bodies of the RF issue acts to fill. Both laws and acts of executive bodies of the RF are equally binding as sources of law, but may not contravene the Constitution. On the grounds of, and in the execution of the Civil Code and other laws, legal relations are also regulated by acts of the executive bodies of the RF and the Subjects of the RF, containing norms of civil law.

The hierarchy of normative legal acts in Russia is the following:

- Decrees and Orders of the President of the RF
- Rulings and Orders of the Government of the RF
- Normative acts of the federal executive bodies
- Acts of the bodies of power of the Subjects of the RF
- Normative legal acts of local self-government bodies[19].

The system of regulatory legal acts of local self-government bodies is relatively independent: local self-government bodies are not included into the system of state bodies of the RF. Such acts are adopted by the municipalities, by the councils and heads of self-government territories (cities and villages), and also by the population directly.

Such acts are obligatory for the population of the territories and organisations located there (e.g. local regulatory act, introducing advertising tax and an advertising tax rate).

The Hierarchy of Normative Legal Acts

As for the legal meaning of the hierarchy of legislative acts, it is the following:

- The lower (from the point of view of hierarchy) legislative acts may be issued by the relevant state bodies for means of implementation of the higher legislative acts and may also contain details of general provisions stipulated in laws, but;
- The lower legislative acts must not contradict the higher ones and in case such contradiction arises the provisions of the higher legislative act should prevail, and the relevant provision of a lower act may be considered invalid.

Thus federal laws shall prevail over laws of the Subjects of the RF and statutes shall prevail over acts of the executive bodies of the RF.

[19] Local self-government bodies are referred to in certain Articles of the Constitution (Articles 33, 40, 46, etc.). They are not included in the system of state bodies of the RF. Local self-government bodies adopt legal acts within the limits of their powers and with respect to issues of local significance.

Conflict of Laws

Law Implementation

The following rules shall be applied to the implementation of laws:

- In the case of a contradiction between provisions of a general and a specific act of equal levels (e.g., the Civil Code and the Law on Bankruptcy), a specific legal act shall be applied – horizontal conflict of laws
- In the case of a contradiction of normative legal acts issued by bodies of different levels (e.g., a law and a decree of the President of the RF, an instruction of the Tax Service and an order of the Government of the RF), the higher one shall be applied (the hierarchy principle) – vertical conflict of laws
- In the case of a discrepancy between regulatory legal acts issued by one body (e.g. between laws), but on different dates, the most recent normative legal act shall be applied, even it does not stipulate that directly.

International Law

International law may be divided into:

- **Universally recognised principles and norms of international law**

Universally recognised principles and norms of international law are official guidelines and fundamental regulations of international law, admitted by all subjects of international law. Such regulations do not allow deviation. In particular, such regulations concern governments' sovereignty, forceful actions or threat with force, territorial unity of states, inviolability of their borders, peaceful settlement of disputes, non-interference of internal affairs and respect of human rights and freedoms.

- **International treaties of the RF**

The RF has concluded several thousand international treaties concerning a wide range of issues - political, economic, social, etc.

Prevailing Force of International Law

Article 15 of the Constitution states, that the universally recognised principles and norms of international law and the international treaties of the RF form, in conformity with the Constitution, an integral part of the legal system of the RF. International treaties of the RF are directly applied towards legal relations, with the exception of cases in which a corresponding international treaty provides for a special intra-state act to be issued. If an international treaty of the RF stipulates other provisions than those stipulated by the domestic law, the provisions of the international treaty shall prevail.

International treaties have supremacy over federal laws, laws of the Subjects of the RF and other normative legal acts, regardless the date of their adoption – whether before or after an international treaty was adopted.

One of the most important acts of Russian legislation in this area is the Law on International Treaties. It is based on provisions of the Constitution and on universally accepted provisions of contractual law stipulated in "The Vienna Convention on the Treaties between the States and International Organizations and between International Organizations", dated 21 March 1986, and in "The Vienna Convention on the Law of International Treaties", dated 23 May 1969.

The International Treaties Signed by the USSR

The Law on International Treaties is also effective with respect to international treaties, with the RF acting as the successor of the USSR[20].

Will the International Treaty Be in Force in the Territory of the RF Automatically after Signing?

The above notwithstanding, Article 14 of the Law on International Treaties provides that ratification and denunciation of international treaties of the RF must be adopted by consideration of both the State Duma and the Federation Council on a mandatory basis. Article 125 of the Constitution also states that international treaties of the RF may not be enforced and applied if they violate the Constitution.

Therefore, an international treaty of the RF does not come into force before the ratification of such a treaty. Sometimes, the ratification of an international treaty by the Parliament can take years.

---

[20] Law on International Treaties, Article 1.3.

Example

"The Convention on Prevention of Major Industrial Accidents (Convention No.174)" was signed in Geneva on 22 June 1993, but ratified by federal law only on 30 November 2011[21].

The Lawful Custom

A lawful custom can also be deemed a source of law in the RF. The word 'custom' denotes rules of conduct which, by virtue of long usage, have the force of law. A valid custom must eventually be recognised by the state to be obligatory. It must be certain, reasonable and not contrary to statute law. The lawful custom is rarely used in most branches of the Russian legal system. However, the lawful custom is more commonly used in Marine law.

At the same time, Russian law admits and applies customs of business turnover as a source of law in cases where it does not contradict the Russian legislation or terms of contract.

Example

Customs value of goods may be assessed under customs of business turnover – similar customs transactions[22].

The Judicial Precedent

A judicial precedent is a decision of a higher court that becomes a model for future decisions of lower courts on similar cases. A given decision acts as an obligatory rule for those judges who examine similar cases in the future. It does not act as a recommendation.

Judicial precedent is one of the major sources of law in Anglo-Saxon law family countries. Romano-German (continental) law family countries, including Russia, reject the judicial precedent as a law source. Although there is no formally developed equivalent to judicial precedent in Russian law, the decisions of the courts are documented and serve as a source of reference for judges presiding over current cases. This is particularly important for the Arbitrazh courts which deal with matters relating to entrepreneurial activity. To this extent, therefore, there is some reliance on the previous decisions of courts as a source of law.

---

[21] Federal Law No.366-FZ, dated 30 November 2011.

[22] Resolution of the Federal Arbitrazh District Court No.A32-30626/2010, dated 11 January 2012.

Rulings of the Supreme Court of the RF play an important role in the application of the Russian law.

Notes

Since 1 January 2012 it is directly stated in the Russian Civil Procedual Code that decisions of the ***European Court of Human Rights*** *stating infringement of the European Convention on Human Rights by the Russian court decision, shall constitute the grounds for appealing the decision of the Russian court on the basis of discovering new circumstances.*

The Supreme Court of the RF periodically publishes information letters on the court practice in certain particular areas of Russian law.

Rulings of the Constitutional Court of the RF

In the Constitutional Court individuals may challenge federal laws which contradict the Constitution, in the areas of property rights, freedom of economic activity and the regulation of liability. If the Constitutional Court decides that the federal law does contradict the Constitution, the contradictory part of such a law will not apply. Rulings of the Constitutional Court of the RF have binding force and enter into force from the moment such rulings are held.

Example

The Constitutional Court recognised as not corresponding to the Constitution, Article 107 of the Criminal Procedural Code[23].

Notes

Rulings of the Constitutional Court may not abolish decisions of other courts under law. Therefore the Constitutional Court shall not verify the legality of court practice norms.

Part IV. The Court System

Judicial authority in Russia is implemented through constitutional, civil, administrative and criminal court proceedings. Another judicial branch, arbitrazh (economic) proceedings, is under reformation at present. The civil courts of general jurisdiction deal primarily with legal relations between individuals in the areas of contract, tort, property and family law.

The Law on the Judicial System establishes and regulates the RF's judicial system, establishes the hierarchical format of the judicial system,

[23] Ruling of the Constitutional Court No.27-P, dated 06 December 2011.

determines the basic principles for the exercise of judicial authority, the status of judges and the procedure for the establishment and abolition of courts.

The parties to an action are called the plaintiff (the person filing a suit) and the defendant (the person being sued), and if there is an appeal the person appealing is called an appellant and the other person the respondent.

The parties are informed of the process via post, sms or email.

The Court System of the RF

The court system of the RF consists of:

- The Constitutional court
- The Courts of General Jurisdiction
- The Arbitrazh courts and the specialised Arbitrazh courts – the Intellectual Rights court[24].

Notes

Under the Federal Constitutional Law of the RF No.2-FKZ on Amendment to the Constitution "On the Supreme Court and the Prosecutor's Service of the RF", dated 5 February 2014, the High Arbitrazh Court of the RF is merged with the Supreme Court. Thus the Supreme Court of the RF becomes the crowning instance for both the courts of general jurisdiction and the arbitrazh courts.

The structure of courts in the RF is consistent with the judicial systems of other European civil law countries. However, Russian judges lack experience in most commercial cases. Disputes involving individuals are resolved in the courts of general jurisdiction, while economic disputes between legal entities are resolved in the Arbitrazh courts. In addition, parties may, by an agreement, provide for the arbitration of disputes in Russia or abroad. Russian law allows parties contractually to choose the application of foreign law, with some restrictions. Parties to international agreements may also agree to have disputes resolved in a foreign jurisdiction, either in the court or by arbitration. If the parties agree to have a dispute resolved in a foreign jurisdiction by arbitration, a Russian court will not consent to hear the dispute.

---

[24] Under the Federal Constitutional Law No.4-FKZ "On Introduction of Amendments to the Federal Constitutional Law "On the Judicial System of the RF" the specialised Arbitrazh court – the Intellectual Rights court shall be formed not later than 1 February 2013.

The USSR (and Russia as a successor of the USSR), on 22nd November 1960, acceded to "The United Nations Convention on the Recognition and Enforcement of Foreign Arbitration Awards", dated 10 June 1958. Russian legislation requires the enforcement of foreign court judgments when a separate treaty provides for reciprocal enforcement. Russia has entered into treaties on the reciprocal enforcement of foreign court judgments with a number of countries (mostly of Eastern Europe), though decisions of the highest Russian courts provide for the possibility of the execution of the decisions of the foreign courts even without such an agreement[25].

The Superior Courts

There are two Superior Courts in the RF:

- The Constitutional Court of the RF
- The Supreme Court of the RF

The System of the Constitutional Courts

As republics of the RF are the only Subjects of the RF where constitutions of the republics exist, constitutional courts at the level of the Subject of the RF may exist only in those republics of the RF as well.

In all other Subjects of the RF, charter courts form the system of constitutional courts.

The System of Courts of General Jurisdiction

Other courts of a limited and local nature are known as inferior courts. Other Federal Courts, which constitute the system of courts of general jurisdiction, are:

- Courts of general jurisdiction of the Subjects of the RF (the Supreme Courts of the Republics of the RF; Areas, Regions and Cities of federal importance (Moscow and St. Petersburg), Autonomous Regions and Circuit Courts of Autonomies)
- The Municipal Courts
- The Justice of the Peace
- The Specialised Military Courts.

---

[25] Ruling of the High Arbitrazh court of the RF No.5-G02-64, dated 7 June 2002.

The System of the Arbitrazh Courts

Federal Courts, which constitute the system of the Arbitrazh courts, are:

- The Federal Arbitrazh Circuit (District) Courts – high instance courts of cassation
- The Arbitrazh appellate courts
- The Arbitrazh courts of the Subjects of the RF – the initial level.

The Constitutional Court

The jurisdiction of the Constitutional Court is the observance over compliance of federal laws, decrees of the President of the RF, acts of the Federation Council, of the State Duma, of the RF Government, Constitutions of the Republics of the RF and a number of other normative legal acts with the Constitution of the RF. The Constitutional Court may rule on legal matters when it is stipulated by the Law on the Constitutional Court.

Among persons that may file their claims to the Constitutional Court are the President of the RF, the State Duma, one-fifth of the members of the Federation Council or deputies of the State Duma, the Government of the RF, the Supreme Court of the RF, the bodies of legislative and executive powers of the Subjects of the RF, individuals, groups of individuals and legal entities. The named persons may file their claims to the Constitutional Court in case their constitutional rights and freedoms were infringed by a law enforced or to be enforced in a particular legal case.

While filing a personal or joint complaint to the Constitutional Court one should keep in mind the following peculiarities of jurisdiction of this court:

- Firstly, it must be a law and not other legal acts that infringes or has infringed rights and freedoms of the plaintiff. Here the law is understood as federal constitutional laws, federal laws, constitutions and statutes of the Subjects of the RF. Normative legal acts of Ministries are appealed against in courts of general jurisdiction.
- Secondly, it must be constitutional and not other rights and freedoms that are infringed by the law.
- Thirdly, the law appealed against has been enforced in a particular legal case already considered.

Jurisdiction of Courts of General Jurisdiction

Jurisdiction means the power of a court to hear and determine a case. There are three forms of jurisdiction:

- A court has original jurisdiction if a case can be completely heard before it
- If a court hears appeals from a lower court it is said to have appellate jurisdiction
- If a court can be consulted by another court on points of law it is said to have consultative jurisdiction.

In particular, individuals and legal entities may defend their rights in courts of general jurisdiction in case these individuals and legal entities are parties to a disputable legal relationship. The following cases are considered in courts of general jurisdiction:

- Cases and claims arising from civil, family or labour relations, if at least one party is an individual, unless otherwise is directly provided for in the legislation
- Disputes arising from public legal relations based on power subordination of one party to another with an individual being the subordinated party
- Contest by an individual (or a group of individuals) of normative legal acts, if the compliance with constitutional norms of acts being contested shall not be verified by other courts (including the Constitutional Court)
- Contesting refusals to register mass media, to issue licenses to these bodies; contesting decisions to declare licenses issued to these bodies as null and void or decisions to terminate or suspend the activity of mass media
- Disputes of public or religious organisations (associations) with bodies of state power or state officials; disputes between public and religious organisations themselves or disputes of these organisations with other organisations[26]
- Cases and claims arising from administrative legal relations
- Cases and claims arising from transportation agreements
- Cases and claims of special jurisdiction directly provided for in the Civil Procedural Code
- Cases in which a party is a foreign citizen, unless otherwise provided for in an international treaty or convention

---

[26] Civil Procedural Code, Article 26.

- Other cases and claims.

Notes

A resolution of an application on dispute of a non-normative legal act of a federal executive body is subject to the jurisdiction of a Municipal court[27].

Cases on creation, reorganisation and liquidation of non-commercial legal entities (e.g. political parties, public funds, etc.) which do not have the deriving of profit as a chief goal for their activity, are subject to the jurisdiction of courts of general jurisdiction[28].

The above list may be continued: courts of general jurisdiction may also consider other disputes. Having the largest capacity, the jurisdiction of these courts is determined first of all on the basis of Article 46 of the Constitution, according to which "each person is guaranteed to have judicial protection of their rights and freedoms", while "decisions and actions (inaction) of bodies of state power, of bodies of local self-government, of public organisations or officials of these bodies and organisations may be appealed against in court". Therefore, the scope of issues considered by courts of general jurisdiction may only be determined by the method of exclusion – i.e. courts of general jurisdiction consider all disputes except those that pertain to jurisdiction of the Constitutional Court[29] or of Arbitrazh courts[30]. Still, there are general criteria for determining which cases are considered by courts of general jurisdiction - that is depending on who the participants of the disputes are. The general rule implies that courts of general jurisdiction consider disputes with at least one party - an individual (providing the given dispute is not related to entrepreneurial activity of an individual entrepreneur). Courts of general jurisdiction have the broadest spectrum of cases.

The Supreme Court of the RF

The system of courts of general jurisdiction consists of three levels: supreme, medium and major. The Supreme Court of the RF is the court of the supreme level. The Supreme Court of the RF acts as a court of first instance with respect to criminal cases of extra complexity and civil cases, described below. The Supreme Court may consider appeals and court rulings either in the course of planned supervision or in the event of the discovery of new case circumstances. This court is the court of final appeal on decisions of two subordinate levels of court.

---

[27] Ruling of the Supreme Court of the Russian Fedration No.88-G04-1, dated 14 April 2004.

[28] Ruling of the Supreme Court of the RF No.63-G04-2, dated 24 February 2004.

[29] Constitution, Article 125.

[30] Arbitrazh Procedural Code, Chapter 4.

The Civil Colleague of the Supreme Court of the RF has full original jurisdiction in all matters, so no action may be excluded from the Supreme Court. Its jurisdiction is unlimited.

The Presidium of the Supreme Court of the RF shall consider review appeals submitted within 3 months from the date of entering into force of the appeal or cassation appeal rulings, in case such rulings were held by the Supreme Court of the RF.

The Supreme Court of the RF comprises of 170 members. Court Colleague on Economic Disputes is formed. It is located in Saint Petersburg.

Jurisdiction of the Supreme Court of the RF as the Court of First Instance

The Supreme Court is the court of first instance for the following cases, e.g. of putting into dispute legal non-normative acts of the President, legal non-normative acts of the chambers of the Federal Assembly and legal non-normative acts of the Government.

The Supreme Court of the RF supervises all courts of general jurisdiction, including the Specialised Military Courts. The Supreme Court also gives explanations concerning court practice. The Supreme Court of the RF consists of 170 judges and executes its activity in the form of the Presidium of the Supreme Court, Appellate Colleague, Diciplinary Colleague and Court Colleagues on Administrative, Criminal, Civil and Economic Cases and on the Affairs of Military Persons[31]. The Presidium of the Supreme Court of the RF consists of 13 members and is the highest body of the court system of general jurisdiction in the RF. The Plenum of the Supreme Court of the RF is to be called at least once every four months.

Courts of the Subjects of the RF (Supreme Courts of the Republics of the RF; Areas, Regions, Cities of Federal Importance (Moscow and St. Petersburg), Autonomous Regions and Circuit Courts of Autonomies)

These courts belong to the medium level. Courts of the Subjects of the RF may act as courts of first instance when considering specific categories of cases deemed to be of particular importance to society. In general cases they are deemed to be courts of second instance (courts of appeal), i.e.

---

[31] Resolution of the Plenum of the Supreme Court of the RF No.2 "On Approval of the Reglament of the Supreme Court of the RF", dated 7 August 2014.

they shall consider cassation appeals and other appeals, and check the compliance with law and the validity of decisions and other court rulings not enacted yet. Such courts have a supervisory role in that they assess the validity of lower court decisions and determine whether such decisions are compliant with the law.

A cassation appeal is considered by the Presidium or by the correspondent Colleague of such a court. The cassation appeal must be submitted within 6 months of the date of the court ruling entering into force, and only if the person(s) applying for cassation has(have) taken all possible steps to appeal the court ruling before its entering into force.

The appeal must be submitted within 30 days of the date of the decision of the first instance court, which has not yet come into force.

Notes

Since 1 January 2012 the appellate instance has been deprived of the right to resubmit a case for new consideration to the court of original jurisdiction[32].

From March 2014 there are 85 Subjects of the RF: the territory of the RF is divided into 85 circuits. Courts of the Subjects the RF are the second instance for those who appeal the decision of the Municipal Court.

Jurisdiction of Courts of the Subjects of the RF as the Courts of First Instance

Courts of the Subjects the RF are the first instance courts for the following cases, most of which are connected with the corresponding Subject of the RF, e.g. on disputing legal normative acts of the state bodies of the Subjects of the RF, infringement of rights, freedoms and lawful interests of individuals and legal entities, or connected with state secrets.

Rulings of the courts of the Subjects of the RF come into force immediately after holding.

Presidiums of the courts of the Subjects of the RF are the highest body in such courts. Presidiums of courts at this level act as supervising bodies, whose functions include the checking of compliance with law, validity of court decisions already enacted and reconsideration of cases whether in the course of planned supervision or in the event of the discovery of new case circumstances.

[32] Federal Law No.353-FZ, dated 9 December 2010.

The Municipal Court

The Municipal Court is the most major level of court in the RF. According to established rule, the Municipal Courts are the courts of first instance with respect to the majority of cases for consideration, both criminal and civil. Article 26 of the Civil Procedural Code directly states that the Municipal Court considers all cases, except for the cases considered by the Arbitrazh Court, by the justice of the peace, by courts of the Subject of the RF or by the Supreme Court of the RF.

In the RF there are several hundred court areas, in Moscow alone there are 33 Municipal Court areas. The Municipal Courts are presided over by the President of the Municipal Court. The Municipal Court has very wide jurisdiction under the Civil Procedural Code, it deals with all actions where a party is an individual (excluding the cases directly provided for by the Arbitrazh Procedural Code) involved in issues of tort or contract law (and other issues). The Municipal Judge can hear the case alone, if both the claimant and the defendant agree to it. There are certain cases where the Municipal Judge must hear the case with two assessors.

Appealing the Decision of the Municipal Court

The decision of the Municipal Judge can be appealed to the corresponding court of the Subject of the RF. The jurisdiction of the Circuit Court when hearing an appeal from the Municipal Court is not the same as an original Municipal Court action, but in the interest of the judgement the appellate court may control the decision of the court of the first instance in full volume.

The general rule is that the decision of the Municipal Court enters into force 30 days after holding if it has not been appealed. Both parties may appeal and the appeal takes the form of a check of the procedural and material grounds of the Municipal Judge to uphold such a decision. It is a final appeal, questioning both fact and law. Either party may then, within one year from the date of the decision of the corresponding court of the Subject of the RF, apply to the Presidium of a corresponding court of the Subjects the RF (supervisory court) to abolish the decision already entered into force.

Notes

The supervisory court is not entitled to determine actual circumstances of the case other than those that the courts of the first and cassation instances did[33].

---

[33] Ruling of the Supreme Court of the RF No.51-V03-20, dated 23 December 2004.

The Justice of the Peace

The justice of the peace considers minor cases and is a court of first instance for the following cases, e.g.:

- Criminal cases with the maximum punishment of three years of imprisonment
- Property disputes, if the sum of the claim does not exceed 50,000 roubles as of the date of filing the claim.

If there are several claims in the case, one of which refers to Municipal Court and others to the justice of the peace, the claim shall be subject to the jurisdiction of the Municipal Court.

The Specialised Military Courts

The Specialised Military Courts' jurisdiction is similar to the jurisdiction of the Municipal Courts and other courts of general jurisdiction. The particularities in the jurisdiction of the Specialised Military Courts are that one party to the case must be an actual or former military person. On matters not concerning military service a military person can apply, at his discretion, to the Specialised Military Court or to the Municipal Court. The decision of the Specialised Military Judge can be appealed to the Military Colleague of the corresponding court of the Subject of the RF.

The Federal Arbitrazh Circuit (District) Court

Federal Arbitrazh Circuit Courts are deemed to be courts of second (appellate) instance for Arbitrazh courts of the Subjects of the RF. Federal regions each include numerous Subjects of the RF; there are 10 regions altogether.

The Federal Arbitrazh Circuit Court is the first instance court for the following cases, e.g. disputing normative legal acts of the President, the Government and federal executive bodies, concerning rights and legitimate interests of an applicant in the area of business and other economic activities.

The Presidium of the Federal Arbitrazh Circuit Court is the highest body of the Federal Arbitrazh Circuit Court.

The Arbitrazh Appellate Court

At present there are 20 Arbitrazh appellate courts in the RF[34]. Certain Arbitrazh circuits have 2 Arbitrazh appellate courts (e.g., Moscow Region Court Circuit; Severo-Zapadny Court Circuit).

The composition of the Arbitrazh appellate court is in line with the composition of other Arbitrazh courts at a higher level:

- Presidium
- The court colleague on consideration of disputes deriving from civil and other relations
- The court colleague on consideration of disputes deriving from administrative relations.

Jurisdiction of the Arbitrazh Appellate Court

The main function of the Arbitrazh appellate court is to examine the lawfulness and sufficiency of court acts which are not yet in force, regarding cases which were considered by the Arbitrazh courts of the Subjects of the RF. This is done by reconsidering the case.

The Arbitrazh Court of the Subject of the RF

Arbitrazh courts of the initial level, unlike courts of general jurisdiction, are not district courts, but courts of the Subjects of the RF. There are 81 Arbitrazh courts at present. According to the general rule, these courts are deemed to be courts of first instance in consideration of economic disputes.

The Arbitrazh court of the Subject of the RF is a state court specialising in commercial cases, and it extends its jurisdiction to any cases on commercial disputes. It also extends its jurisdiction to cases concerning the exercise of business and other commercial activities, where both parties are business entities or individuals engaged in business activities without forming a legal entity and having the status of an individual entrepreneur obtained in the procedure established by law. In this particular case it does not matter what kind of legal relations serve as the basis for dispute arisen: civil, administrative or otherwise. Cases between the RF and the Subjects of the RF are subject to the jurisdiction of the Arbitrazh court as well. Arbitrazh courts do not consider disputes that,

---

[34] Article 33.1. Federal Constitutional Law No.1-FKZ "On the Arbitrazh Courts of the RF", dated 28 April 1995.

although relating to economic relations, pertain to the criminal sphere of legislation.

It is advisable to emphasise that Arbitrazh courts do not consider disputes whose parties are individuals not registered as individual entrepreneurs, if otherwise is not provided in the Arbitrazh Procedural Code.

Jurisdiction

The jurisdiction of the Arbitrazh court of the Subject of the RF is the following:

- Economic disputes, arising from administrative and other public legal relations, and other cases concerning the exercise by legal entities and individual entrepreneurs of business and other commercial activities, such as:
    - On disputing normative legal acts concerning rights and legitimate interests of an applicant in the area of business and other commercial activities
    - On disputing non-normative legal acts of the state bodies of the RF
    - On administrative offences where federal laws refer their consideration to the jurisdiction of Arbitrazh courts
    - On the recovery from legal entities and individual entrepreneurs, engaged in business and other economic activities, compulsory payments and sanctions, unless federal laws provide for another procedure for the recovery thereof.

The following cases and claims are considered as arising from economic relations:

- Misunderstanding of a contract
- Introducing changes/dissolution of a contract
- Undue fulfilment and non-fulfilment of obligations
- Acknowledgement of rights on property
- Demand of property from one's illegal possession (the replevin)
- Violation of property rights of the owner or another legal possessor, not connected with deprivation of property (the negatory)
- Reimbursement of damages and losses
- Collection of fines from legal entities and individuals by state bodies, local self-government bodies and other controlling bodies, if federal law does not stipulate such collection without

recourse to court or without notifying a legal entity or an individual (maximum 50,000 roubles from a legal entity and 5,000 roubles from an individual entrepreneur)
    - Other cases, directly provided for in the Arbitrazh Procedural Code.
- Cases on establishing facts of legal importance for arising, changing and terminating the rights of legal entities and individual entrepreneurs in the area of business and other economic activities
- Cases on disputing decisions of tribunals of arbitrators and on issuing writs of execution concerning compulsory execution of tribunals of arbitrators' decisions
- Cases on recognising and executing decisions of foreign courts and foreign arbitration awards, concerning disputes arising in the exercise of business and other economic activities
- Special jurisdiction of Arbitrazh courts, which includes the following cases:
    - On insolvency (bankruptcy)
    - On disputes related to the establishment, reorganisation or liquidation of commercial legal entities[35]
    - On disputes related to the denial of the state registration or evasion of the state registration of legal entities and individual entrepreneurs
    - On disputes between a shareholder and a J-SC, between participants of other economic partnerships and companies arising from activities of economic partnerships and companies, except labour disputes
    - On protection of business reputation in the area of business and other economic activities
    - Other cases, arising in the exercise of business and other economic activities provided for by federal laws.

Notes

A dispute between a participant of an LLC (who has filed an application of withdrawal from that LLC) and the LLC itself (on transactions of the LLC concerning transfer of property seized to satisfy the execution of the court decision on payment of the stake of the withdrawing participant) is a result of the business activity of the LLC and is therefore subject to the jurisdiction of the Arbitrazh

---

[35] The court practice states that this provision shall refer to commercial legal entities only.

court[36].

The given list is not exhaustive. Besides the aforementioned disputes, Arbitrazh courts consider cases relating to the ascertaining of facts that have juridical meaning in the sphere of economic relations and others.

Disputes with the participation of foreign legal entities, foreign citizens and persons without citizenship are considered both by courts of general jurisdiction[37] and Arbitrazh courts[38]. The decision on what jurisdiction corresponds to any given case shall be made depending on the composition of the parties to the dispute and on the nature of the disputable issue.

Example

An individual entrepreneur "Sidorov" was driving home from his friend's house at night when his car collided with a truck owned by a transport organisation. The truck driver was at fault, and Sidorov decides to claim damages from the transport organisation in court. In this case he would have to apply to the court of general jurisdiction. Although both participants of the car accident were either business entities or individual entrepreneurs, the accident occurred after working hours for Sidorov and therefore the dispute cannot be deemed as arising from entrepreneurial activity of his. This fact is sufficient for the dispute to be resolved in the court of general jurisdiction rather than in the Arbitrazh court.

Had Sidorov been involved in the accident while moving some merchandise from a warehouse to a supermarket, the dispute would be within the competence of the Arbitrazh court. In this case the dispute would have arisen from the entrepreneurial activity of both parties.

Notes

Administrative cases commited by independent entrepreneurs or legal entities shall still be in the jurisdiction of Arbitrazh courts in case such independent entrepreneurs or legal entities terminated their status[39].

Two main criteria are applied by the Arbitrazh court in consideration of a given case:

- The appropriate type of legal relations, i.e. disputes concerning economic activity
- The appropriate composition of subjects of the case, i.e. legal entities or individual entrepreneurs.

---

[36] Ruling of the Presidium of the High Arbitrazh Court of the RF No.2999/04, dated 8 June 2004.

[37] Civil Procedural Code, Article 22.2.

[38] Arbitrazh Procedural Code, Article 27.5.

[39] Ruling of the Plenum of the High Arbitrazh Court of the RF No.73, dated 17 November 2011.

The decision of the Arbitrazh court of the Subject of the RF enters into force 30 days after holding, as long as it is not appealed, and if otherwise is not provided by law. There are certain cases when the decision of the Arbitrazh court of the Subject of the RF enters into force immediately.

Within 2 months after the decision enters into force either party can file a cassation appeal (or second appeal) to the Federal Arbitrazh Circuit Court. The term "cassation" is derived from the French "to quash" (to shake violently).

Notes

Although appellation and cassation have very much in common there are two major differences between them. Firstly, appellation may be initiated only before the decision of the first instance Arbitrazh court comes into force (the term of appellation is one month). Cassation is effected in respect of decisions already in force, either if the appellation did not take place within the established term or if one of the parties for some reason is not satisfied with the decision of the appellate court (the term of cassation appeal is two months). Secondly, appellate courts reconsider each case for a second time with the revision of evidence produced in the first instance and examination of newly produced evidence. In contrast to appellation, cassation implies a check-up of the decisions from the viewpoint of the due application of norms of substantive and procedural law.

Tribunals of Arbitrators

Tribunals of arbitrators, which are non-state arbitral committees, are not indicated in the Law on the Judicial System, and are not included in the court system of the RF. Tribunals of arbitrators execute their activity under a separate federal law[40].

The parties may provide for the tribunal of arbitrators at a competent court by:

- Application of a provision concerning the tribunal of arbitrators to be put into the contract
- Conclusion of a separate agreement on transfer of the dispute to the tribunal of arbitrators. The parties may conclude such agreement at any stage of the Arbitrazh or court process before reaching a decision.

---

[40] Federal Law of the RF No.102-FZ "On Tribunals of Arbitrators", dated 24 July 2002.

Notes

Only a dispute arising from civil relations may be transferred to a tribunal of arbitrators.

Application of a provision on the competence of the tribunal of arbitrators into the contract with a consumer is illegal and deprives the consumer from his right to apply to court[41].

The International Commercial Arbitration Court under the Russian Chamber of Commerce and Industry refused to consider a case as the plaintiff had not presented enough evidence of the presence of the arbitration clause between the plaintiff and the defendant[42].

Territorial Jurisdiction of Courts

The judicial system consists of several levels, each level having numerous courts, but territorial position is a factor in the question of which court will consider a particular case.

After cases are distributed between basic levels of the judicial system (i.e. between courts of general jurisdiction and Arbitrazh courts), they shall be distributed between numerous courts of one judicial level. The basic principle in determining a court's jurisdiction in this case is the geographic position of the court.

The rules of determining a court's jurisdiction are the following:

- **In personam jurisdiction**

A lawsuit on property dispute is considered at the location of the defendant (a legal entity or an individual)[43]. The jurisdiction over bankruptcy procedures is decided similarly: after the bankruptcy procedures are initiated, all claims addressed to an organisation - a debtor - are considered by a court at the location of the debtor[44].

Example

A dispute between a creditor (plaintiff), situated in Moscow, and a debtor, situated in St. Petersburg is considered by the Arbitrazh court of St. Petersburg in case the creditor submits a claim on recovery of a debt – the place of location of the defendant.

---

[41] Resolution of the Presidium of the High Arbitrazh Court of the RF No.3364/13, dated 19 September 2013.

[42] Ruling of the International Commercial Arbitration Court under the Russian Chamber of Commerce and Industry No.63/2003, dated 25 May 2004.

[43] Arbitrazh Procedural Code, Article 35; Civil Procedural Code, Article 28.

[44] Bankruptcy Law, Article 33.

- **Alternative jurisdiction**

Alternative jurisdiction is also given under law: the Civil Procedural Code or the Arbitrazh Procedural Code. One part of the alternative is always the place of location of the defendant. These are examples of most common alternatives given:

- The jurisdiction over a lawsuit against a defendant whose residential location is unknown holds either a court at the location of the defendant's property or a court at the defendant's last known location.
- The rule of alternative jurisdiction also covers contractual disputes: these disputes are ruled either at the location of the defendant or at the location of the execution of the contract (if the contract stipulates such a location)[45].
- In case of an accident, one of the alternatives is the place of the accident itself.
- In case a legal entity has branches or representative offices it is possible to sue either at the place of location of the legal entity or at the place of location of one of its branches.

Examples

A seller of goods based in Moscow, delivered faulty goods to Yekaterinburg. Under the terms of the delivery contract the transaction is deemed to be executed by the seller at the place of delivery, i.e. in Yekaterinburg. A customer is situated in Donetsk. In this case the customer may choose whether to address the Arbitrazh court of Moscow or the Arbitrazh court of the Sverdlovsky Region – the place of location of the defendant, or the place of execution of the contract.

A Moscow construction firm performed construction works in Yekaterinburg for its customer located in Chelyabinsk and infringed the contractual terms. In this case the customer may choose whether to address the Arbitrazh court of Moscow or the Arbitrazh court of Yekaterinburg – the place of location of the defendant or or the place of execution of the contract.

- **In rem jurisdiction**

This rule covers immovable property disputes - either disputes concerning ascertainment of the right of ownership or lawsuits on

[45] Arbitrazh Procedural Code, Article 36; Civil Procedural Code, Article 29.9.

infringement of the right of ownership. Claims of this type are tried exclusively in the territory where the immovable property is located[46].

Example

A claimant, based in St. Petersburg, owning a building situated in Moscow, files a claim to a defendant, based in Ryazan, to the Arbitrazh court of Moscow – the place of location of the real estate.

- **Agreed jurisdiction**

The parties may determine a court's jurisdiction by their mutual consent, where stipulated in an appropriate contract[47] (except for jurisdiction over disputes on immovable property and other exclusive jurisdiction according to Article 38 of the Arbitrazh Procedural Code).

Example

A seller of goods, based in Moscow, delivered faulty goods to Yekaterinburg. Under the delivery contract the transaction is deemed to be executed by the seller at the place of delivery, i.e. in Yekaterinburg. A customer is situated in Donetsk. The parties to the contract may agree in the contract that a court's jurisdiction is the Arbitrazh court of Leningradsky Region – the place directly agreed.

---

[46] Arbitrazh Procedural Code, Article 38; Civil Procedural Code, Article 30.

[47] Arbitrazh Procedural Code, Article 37.

Chapter Roundup

1. The main sources of Russian Law are the following:

- Statute Law
- Acts of the Executive Bodies
- International Law
- Customs of Business Turnover
- Judicial Precedent / Rulings of the Constitutional Court of the RF

2. The hierarchy of the statutory law of the RF is the following:

- The Constitution of the RF
- Federal Constitutional Laws of the RF
- Federal Laws of the RF / Law of the Former USSR and RSFSR
- Law of the Subjects of the RF

3. A gap in a law shall be eliminated by:

- Law
- Decree of the President
- Courts:
    - Analogy of Law
    - Analogy of Legislation

4. The following rules shall be applied to implementation of laws:

- Horizontal conflict of laws - a specific legal act shall be applied
- Vertical conflict of laws - the higher one shall be applied
- Discrepancies between regulatory legal acts issued by one body - the most recent normative legal act shall be applied

5. The court system of the RF consists of:

- The Constitutional court
- The Courts of General Jurisdiction
- The Arbitrazh courts.

6. Hierarchy of courts of general jurisdiction is the following:
CONSULTATIVE

- The Supreme Court of the RF – *Review Appeal*

APPELLATE

- The Supreme Courts of the Republics of the RF; the Areas, Oblasts, Cities of Federal Importance (Moscow and St. Petersburg), Autonomy Oblast and Autonomies' Circuits Courts - *Cassation Appeal & Appeal*

ORIGINAL

- The Municipal Courts
- The Justice of the Peace

7. The hierarchy of courts of Arbitrazh is the following:
CONSULTATIVE

- The Supreme Court of the RF – *Review Appeal*

APPELLATE

- The Federal Arbitrazh Circuit Courts – *Cassation Appeal*
- The Arbitrazh Appellate Courts - *Appeal*

ORIGINAL

- The Arbitrazh Courts of the Subjects of the RF

8. Criteria to apply to Arbitrazh courts is the following:

- Appropriate Type of Legal Relations
- Appropriate Subjects of the Case

9. Territorial jurisdiction of courts:

- In Personam Jurisdiction
- Alternative Jurisdiction
- In Rem Jurisdiction
- Agreed Jurisdiction

Questions

1. A person may be deprived of their rights only under which of the following circumstances?

- Under the court decision
- Under their own agreement
- Under the decision of the executive power state body
- Under the decision of the municipal body in case of necessity for municipal needs

2. Under the Constitution of the RF the civil legislation is under the jurisdiction of which of the following?

- Of the RF
- Of the subjects of the RF
- Of the subjects and municipalities of the RF
- Of the city and rural municipalities of the RF

3. In case of a contradiction between the Decree of the President of the RF and the Civil Code of the RF, which the following is applied?

- The Decree of the President
- The Civil Code of the RSFSR
- The Civil Code of the RF
- The Civil Code and the Labour Code

4. A law comes into force after the relations between the parties have arisen. Such a law is applied to the relations between the parties at which point?

- Before the law comes into force
- After the law comes into force
- After the law comes into force and under the agreement between the parties
- After the law comes into force and under the demand of one of the parties

5. Which of the following applies to the universally recognised norms and principles of international law?

- Part of the legal system of the RF
- Not included into the legal system of the RF

- Included into the legal system of the RF only in cases when a special legal act is needed to implement them on the Russian territory
- Not included into the legal system of the RF in the cases provided by the legislation of the RF

6.

(a) Explain the purpose, functions and structure of the courts of arbitration.

(b) Discuss the extent to which the decisions in cases heard previously in the courts will affect decisions in current cases.

7. Trukhina filed a suit to the All-Russia Blind Society on reimbursement of damages in May 1990. She suffered, at the fault of her employer, injury of both hands in 1956, 1962, 1975 and 1983 and lost 20% of her earning capacity. However, the Administration refused to pay her compensation for the lost part of her earnings.

The Court of Permskaya Oblast held the decision in 1995 to recover, in favour of the plaintiff, a commutation payment from May 1987 until February 1995 to the amount of 1,375,422,00 roubles, and monthly payments for life from 1 March 1995 in the amount of 13,762,00 roubles.

The defendant in the cassation appeal asked to abolish the decision of the Court of Permskaya Oblast on the grounds that the court held to recover the injury for three years before filing a suit to the court under Article 208 of the Civil Code of the RF and not under Article 43 of the Rules on Reimbursement of the Injury to the Employee, dated 24 December 1982, which provides that the injured, in case of the omission of a three year term to apply to the court, is entitled to the reimbursement of the injury from the date the injured applied to the Administration or to the court.

Required:

(a) Which act shall be applied in the case of the provisions of the Civil Code contradicting the provisions of other legal acts of the civil legislation of the RF which entered into force before the entering into force of the Civil Code of the RF?

(b) Resolve the case, providing potential arguments of the parties involved.

Further Readings

1. Special report. Trading with Russia Today. International Maritime Bureau, London, 1995.
2. Yakovlev E. and Zhuravskaya E. Reforms in Business Regulation: Evidence from Russia.
3. Зинченко С., Лапач В., Газарьян Б. Новый Гражданский кодекс и предпринимательство: проблемы регулирования // Хозяйство и право. 1995. № 10.
4. Зинченко С.А., Шапсугов Д.Ю., Корх С.Э. Предпринимательство и статус его субъектов в современном российском праве. Ростов н/Д, 1999.
5. Лаптев В.В. Предпринимательское право: понятие и субъекты. М., 1997.
6. Предпринимательское право в XXI веке: преемственность и развитие. М., 2002.
7. Пугинский Б.И. Коммерческое право России. М., 2000.
8. Ровный В.В. Понятие и признаки предпринимательства. Иркутск, 1998.
9. Ровный В.В. Проблемы единства российского частного права. Иркутск, 1999.
10. Семеусов В.А., Тюкавкин А.А., Пахаруков А.А. Правовые проблемы предпринимательской (экономической) деятельности. Иркутск, 2001.
11. Хозяйственное право. Учебник / Под ред. В.К. Мамутова. Киев, 2002.
12. Хоскинг А. Курс предпринимательства. Практическое пособие / Пер. с англ. М., 1993.
13. Шашкова А.В. Предпринимательское право РФ, курс лекций. – М., 2007.
14. Шашкова А.В. Financial & Legal Aspects of Doing Business in Russia. – М.: Аспект Пресс. 2011.
15. Шершеневич Г.Ф. Учебник торгового права. М., 1994.

CHAPTER TWO

THE LAW OF OBLIGATIONS

Part I. Overview

A contract is an agreement which is given legal effect. It creates rights and obligations which are recognised by law. People enter into simple contracts every day of their lives. Such contracts can range from straightforward transactions such as buying a pint of milk in the local shop, to more complex arrangements such as buying shares in a company.

The Definition of a Contract

The contract is (or should be) the only written evidence of the bargain between the parties, and is the result of negotiation. The success of negotiation depends upon the negotiator having a very clear idea in his or her mind as to the relevant points, implementing the proper negotiating technique and drafting a clear statement of the "bargain". Clarity of thought process demands a comprehensive knowledge of the points which should be at issue; points which are based upon learning, upon experience, upon common sense and upon reasonable foresight. This is really the starting point. You can negotiate; create and record your contract by covering all of these points.

Freedom to Enter into a Contract

The Russian legislation interprets a contract as:

- The agreement
- Concluded by two or by several persons
- Under which civil rights and obligations arise, modify or cease to exist.

One of the major principles of Russian law is the freedom of conclusion of contracts and freedom to enter into a contract itself, which means that the parties to the contract may stipulate in the contract any conditions they agree, not contradicting the legislation of the RF.

The parties (individuals and legal entities) are also free to conclude contracts or not, with the exception of the cases when the duty to conclude the contract has been stipulated by:

- Law, or
- A voluntarily assumed obligation.

The parties have the right to conclude a contract, both stipulated and not stipulated by law or by other legal acts, or to conclude a contract, which has elements of different contracts, stipulated by law or by other legal acts (a mixed contract). Therefore, contracts exist which are listed in law (e.g. sale and purchase contracts), but there are also unlisted contracts, the types of which are not provided by law.

Contract terms (provisions) may be defined at the discretion of the parties, with the exception of the cases when the content of the corresponding terms has been stipulated by law or by other legal acts.

Contracts rarely duplicate each other, every contract will almost always be different. Differences may be absolutely fundamental; they may be minor or peripheral. It is impossible to have a "model" form of a general contract for all purposes. Nonetheless, there are many general principles; general negotiation and drafting points which are common to a large number of contracts.

Part II. Preliminary Agreements

The signing of a letter of intent or a memorandum of understanding as a preliminary expression of a commitment to enter into, or continue negotiating, a particular transaction is to many foreign investors a typical and non-binding step in the process of reaching an agreement on the terms of a transaction. However, under Russian law, in certain circumstances a letter of intent may constitute a binding agreement which gives rise to a mutual obligation to enter into a further binding contract (referred to below as a "principal contract") in the future.

The Civil Code contains the concept of a "preliminary contract" under which an obligation arises to conclude in the future a principal contract concerning, e.g. the transfer of property, performance of work or rendering of services[1]. Such obligation should arise only if a letter of intent or a similar document contains the criteria necessary to establish it as a

[1] Civil Code, Article 429.

preliminary contract under the Russian law, i.e. the "essential" terms of a principal contract. In addition, to qualify as a preliminary contract, such a contract must be in a form which would be applicable to the principal contract (e.g. if the principal contract would require notarisation, the preliminary contract would also need to be notarised).

The Russian courts have examined to a limited extent what constitutes "essential terms" for the purposes of determining whether a document is a preliminary contract under Russian law. Essentially, if a contract contains terms which provide a sufficient basis for the conclusion of a principal contract, it may be deemed a preliminary contract. Under the court practice of the RF the existence of price terms in a contract is not a crucial determinant of whether such a contract constitutes a binding preliminary agreement[2].

Terms contained in letters of intent and memorandums of understanding should not be considered components of a preliminary contract under Russian law, such terms are merely expressions of intentions of the parties, rather than commitments or promises to take future action. In any case, it is generally possible to provide that the law of a foreign jurisdiction (under which such a document would not be binding) will govern the interpretation and application of such a letter of intent or memorandum of understanding. Language reflecting the preliminary nature of the intentions of the parties should be expressly drafted into the document, and additional drafting precautions may also be taken, such as the insertion of express disclaimers of the binding nature of the document or the obligations of the parties to conclude future agreements.

In case one of the parties intends to introduce into the principal contract provisions lacking in the preliminary contract, such a party should apply to the court[3].

Example

A contract of surety, providing surety for execution of an obligation which will arise in future, a credit agreement, stipulating an obligation of a bank to provide the borrower with the credit, are examples of preliminary contracts.

---

[2] Document No.16781.

[3] Information Letter of the Presidium of the High Arbitrazh Court of the RF No.14, dated 5 May 1997.

Part III. The Form of Contracts

Types of Transactions

The following types of transactions may be distinguished:

- Unilateral, bilateral and multilateral
- Real and consensual
- Onerous and gratuitous
- Under condition and abstract transactions.

Note

A special type of contract is a contract of adhesion, where basic conditions of a contract are provided in standard forms and which may be accepted by another party only by adhesion to the contract as a whole, e.g. contracts on provision of electric or heat power, gas, retail sale and purchase contracts, insurance contracts, contracts providing a subscription service (information services on networks), etc.

Unilateral, Bilateral and Multilateral Transactions

Transactions may be bilateral or multilateral and unilateral. Agreements (contracts) are deemed to be bilateral or multilateral transactions.

Unilateral transactions are concluded in the cases provided for by law or by the agreement between the parties (by bilateral or multilateral transactions).

Note

Drawing a will or a promissory note and issuance of a bank guarantee are unilateral transactions, provided for by law. Writing sums off an account of a legal entity without acceptance is a unilateral transaction, provided for by the mandate to the bank under the banking account contract.

A unilateral transaction creates duties for the person who has effected such a transaction. A unilateral transaction creates duties for other people only in cases established by law or by an agreement with these people.

Unilateral transactions are regulated by the same provisions of law as agreements.

Consensual and Real Transactions

Consensual contracts enter into force from the moment of conclusion of such contracts (e.g. a contract for services).

Contracts are considered real when a contract itself is not enough for bringing the deal into force: the transfer of the subject-matter of the contract is a necessary condition. Examples of such contracts are the following:

- A loan contract
- A donation contract
- A banking deposit contract
- A contract of transportation, etc.

Transactions under the Condition

Transactions may be concluded under a condition:

- Under the suspensive condition, if the parties have made the commencement of rights and duties dependent on the (unknown) circumstance, of whether it will, or will not, take place
- Under the subsequent condition, if the parties have made the termination of rights and duties dependent upon the (unknown) circumstance, of whether it will, or will not, take place.

If the arrival of the condition has been obstructed in bad faith by the party, for which the occurrence of this condition is undesirable, the said condition shall be recognised as having taken place.

If the arrival of the condition has been obstructed in bad faith by the party, for which the occurrence of this condition is desirable, the said condition shall be recognised as not having taken place.

Forms of Contracts

Generally speaking, simple contracts are not required to be in any particular form and may be made verbally or in writing. However, there are certain contracts which must be evidenced in writing, the absence of which will deprive them of legal validity. Under Article 158 of the Civil Code certain contracts may not be enforceable unless they are in a particular form. Examples of such contracts include contracts between legal entities, contracts for the lease of land, etc. There are also certain contracts which must be registered with the state government bodies or municipal bodies. Absence of registration will incur voidance of those contracts. Examples of such contracts include contracts for the sale of immovable property, or the lease of immovable property for the term of more than one year.

They distinguish between verbal forms, written forms and special forms (notarial with or without further state registration).

Contracts may be concluded:

Orally

The contract, for which no written form has been stipulated by law or by the agreement between the parties, may be effected verbally.

The transaction, which may be made verbally, shall be regarded as having been effected also in the case, when the behaviour of the person clearly testifies his will to effect the transaction.

Is Silence Recognised as "Yes" or as "No"

Silence shall be recognised as the expression of the will to effect the transaction in the cases, directly stipulated by law or by the agreement between the parties.

Note

Silence does not constitute acceptance[4].

A contract may be regarded valid under "concluding actions", when the behaviour of the person clearly testifies to their will to conclude the contract, e.g. when the goods are dispatched after the payment is received under the invoice; retail purchase of goods.

In written form

The transaction in written form must be effected by way of compiling a document expressing its contents, and the signature thereof by the person or persons who are effecting the transaction (or by the persons properly authorised by them to do so).

Qualified Written Form

The law, other legal acts and the agreement between the parties may stipulate additional requirements to which the form of the deal shall correspond (it should be made in the form of a definite kind, certified by a

[4] Decision of the Supreme Court of the RF No.GKPI01-1369, dated 6 November 2001.

seal, stamp, etc.), and also the consequences of not satisfying these requirements (qualified written form). If such consequences have not been stipulated, the consequences of not observing the simple written form of the deal shall be applied. So, the parties would be deprived of the right to refer to the testimony for the confirmation of the deal and of its terms, but it would not deprive them of the right to provide the court with written and other kinds of proofs.

The Electronic Digital Signature

The law specifies two types of electronic signature:

- Simple electronic signature, and
- Enhanced electronic signature, which can be unqualified and qualified. Information, signed by a qualified signature shall be regarded as an electronic document with the same legal force as the document written personally[5]. Such a signature gives the right to claim any statutory or municipal services.

Note

In case of the submission of information to the Financial Monitoring Service on monetary control, such a submission requires the enhanced electronic signature.

Cases of Substitution of the Personal Signature

If an individual, as a result of a physical defect, illness or illiteracy cannot put down his signature himself; another individual may sign the contract upon his request. The latter's signature shall be certified by the notary or by another official person possessing the right to perform such kinds of notarial action, with the indication of the reasons, by force of which, the person effecting the transaction was unable to sign himself.

Obligatory Written Form

Article 161 of the Civil Code provides that the written form is obligatory for the following contracts:

- Contracts of legal entities between themselves and with individuals
- Contracts of individuals between themselves to a sum exceeding 10,000 roubles, and in the law-stipulated cases - regardless of the sum of the transaction.

---

[5] Federal Law No.63-FZ "On Electronic Signature", dated 6 April 2011.

In the cases directly provided for by law or in the agreement between the parties, the non-observance of the simple written form of the transaction shall entail its voidance.

Non-observance of the simple written form in a foreign economic transaction shall entail its invalidity.

In written notarised form

Article 163 of the Civil Code provides that certain types of contracts must be notarised.

The notarial certification of the transaction shall be performed by making upon the document the certifying superscription by the notary or by another official person possessing the right to perform such kinds of notarial action. According to the Civil Code modifications which are in effect from September 2014, the Notary Public shall verify the legality of the transaction.

The notarial certification of contracts is obligatory:

- In cases stipulated by law
- In cases stipulated by the parties' agreement, even if this form is not required for the given kind of transactions by law.

Examples

A will is not valid unless it is certified by a notary and signed by the testator or written by a notary from the testator's words[6].

A power of attorney issued by an individual entrepreneur to the representative before the Federal Tax Service shall have notarised form[7].

Non-observance of the notarial form of the contract entails its invalidity. Such a contract is regarded as null and void.

If one of the parties has executed, in full or in part, the contract, requiring notarisation, while the other party has been evading such certification of the transaction, the court shall have the right, upon the claim of the party which has executed the contract, to recognise the transaction as valid. In this case, no subsequent certification of the transaction shall be required.

In the state registration form

---

[6] Civil Code, Article 1125.

[7] Letter of the Federal Tax Service No.ED-4-3/18527@, dated 16 October 2013.

Note

There are three types of state registration form:

- State registration of transactions with immovable property. In this case the state registration is a mandatory characteristic of a transaction, and the transaction is in force between the parties from the moment of the conclusion of that transaction.

Examples

Under Article 551 of the Civil Code the transfer of the title to immovable property to the buyer under the contract of sale of real estate shall be subject to the state registration.

Transactions with land and with other immovable property are subject to state registration and shall be in conformity with the Real Property Rights Registration Law.

- State registration of property rights on immovable property, e.g. a servitude. In this case the state registration concerns execution of the transaction, and legal results shall arise from the moment of the state registration of rights.

- State registration for statistic purposes, e.g. the state registration of motor vehicles. The law may stipulate the state registration of transactions with movable property of certain kinds. In this case the state registration does not effect rights of persons, but plays a significant role in the realisation of such rights.

Article 164 of the Civil Code provides that certain types of contracts must be registered with the corresponding state bodies, e.g. a licensing agreement on transferring the title to the invention shall be registered in the Rospatent.

Non-observance of the notarial form of the contract and of the requirement for its state registration shall entail its invalidity. Such a contract is rendered void.

Note

A contract which is subject to state registration enters into force from the date of the state registration of the contract[8].

---

[8]Ruling of the Constitutional Court of the RF, dated 5 July 2001.

If the contract, requiring state registration, has been made in the proper form, but one of the parties is evading its registration, the court shall have the right, upon the claim of the other party, to hold a decision on the registration of the deal. In this case the deal shall be registered in conformity with the court decision.

Thus the lack of state registration of the transfer of title shall not be grounds for finding the transaction invalid.

Note

Only a party to a sale and purchase contract may claim registration of the transfer of title by filing a suit to the corresponding court. A court bailiff, preparing property of the debtor for sale, is not entitled to claim registration of the transfer of title to the property[9].

The party, groundlessly evading the notarisation or the state registration of the transaction, shall be obliged to compensate the other party for losses inflicted by the delay in the effecting, execution or registration of the transaction.

Note

State registration of real estate shall be conducted via electronic registration as well[10]. In this case a qualified electronic signature is required. A Certificate on the State Registration of the Rights or an extract from the Register of the Unified State Register of Rights on Real Estate and Transactions with it shall certify the registered title.

Part IV. Essential Elements of a Binding Contract

The contract shall be concluded by the forwarding of an offer by one of the parties and by acceptance of this offer by another party.

The essential elements of a binding contract may be outlined as follows:

Agreement

The parties must be in full agreement. The parties must have reached an agreement *ad idem* (as to the essential point). The courts will use the

[9] Ruling of the High Arbitrazh Court of the RF No.6518/04, dated 21 September 2004.

[10] Federal Law No.250-FZ, dated 23 July 2013.

concepts of an offer and acceptance in order to determine whether the parties are agreed *ad idem*.

Offer

An agreement is reached when one party makes an offer to another, which is accepted without qualification by that other, at the moment this acceptance is received by the offerer[11]. An offer is the initial step in bringing a contract into existence.

An offer is a clear and unequivocal statement of intent by one party that it is willing to be bound by the terms of the offer should it be accepted by the party to whom the offer is made. Therefore, to be valid an offer must:

- Be precise and unambiguous
- Be addressed to one or more certain persons
- Contain the essential conditions of the agreement
- Express an intention to conclude a contract with the party to whom the offer is made.

Example

A father promised to release his son from an obligation to pay on a promissory note "if the son would stop complaining". The court held – the contract was not legally binding, as the offer was too vague.

The offer must contain the essential terms of the contract in order to be capable of acceptance. Therefore, an offer to sell a "black Lada car in reasonably good condition" is vague and probably incapable of acceptance. However, this communication can form the basis for those reading it to make an offer. It is in the interest of the offeror to make the offer as comprehensive as possible, by setting out the proposed terms in detail. For example, in a sale of goods situation the offer should include not only a description of the goods, proposed payment terms and price, but it should also express the mode of acceptance required and the time limit for acceptance if relevant.

An offer must therefore be something which will be converted into a contract once accepted. For example, the statement: "I will sell my Audi to Elena Issaeva for 720,000 roubles", is a clear and unambiguous offer to Elena Issaeva which is capable of becoming an agreement on Elena's acceptance of the terms of the offer.

---

[11] Civil Code, Article 433.

The offer should be capable of being interpreted as representing the intention of the offeror to be bound if the offer is accepted.

In most cases, the offer must be communicated to the offeree. An exception to this is where offer and acceptance take place simultaneously, such as a purchase of goods in a shop.

Invitation to Treat

An offer must be distinguished from what is known as an invitation to treat. Not all communications may be regarded as offers. For example, a general representation that goods are for sale is an advertisement and would not be binding if accepted. Some refer to this as an invitation to treat. The effect of an advertisement or other inducement to buy is that the communication is not an offer but an invitation to others to make an offer. An invitation to treat typically lacks the detail that would normally be set out in an offer. In addition, it is addressed to the public or a section of the public and not to specified persons. An invitation to treat is not an offer, it is simply a method of making others aware that you are willing to listen to offers, which you may then decide to accept or reject. For example, an advertisement which states: "Audi for Sale", is an invitation to treat. The party making the statement is simply expressing an intention to listen to offers for his Audi. He does not intend to be legally bound by the statement.

However, the doctrine sets the difference between an invitation to treat, which is addressed to an indefinite number of people, and offers which are addressed to any and all people. If an invitation is addressed to an indefinite number of people and is made under conditions according to which the seller might find that the offer is accepted by a number of different people when he has only one item in stock, it is an invitation to treat, but not an offer. In case the invitation is addressed to any and all people, the invitation can be accepted by one person only and can be terminated before a new acceptance is made, the invitation has the legal force of an offer.

Advertisements

The Civil Code explicitly provides that advertisements and other invitations to treat, which are addressed to an indefinite number of people, are mere invitations to treat and not offers capable of acceptance[12]. If one

---

[12] Civil Code, Article 437.1.

were to treat advertisements as offers, then they would be capable of acceptance by any reader, which would result in grave difficulties for the advertiser.

Rewards

One exception to the general rule that advertisements are invitations to treat is the case of rewards. Such advertisements are capable of acceptance and are therefore not considered to be invitations to treat, but offers, e.g. an advertisement stating "Lost Dog – will pay a reward of 2,500 roubles to the person who returns the dog safely." While this is an advertisement, it is clear that it is intended to be binding, and is capable of only creating one valid contract – the person who finds the dog will be rewarded with 2,500 roubles.

Example

The defendants advertised their goods (a "smoke ball") which had medical purposes. They claimed that any person using the product would not contract influenza. They offered to pay $100 to any person who used the product and still contracted influenza. The company deposited $1,000 into a bank account for payment of the reward, as an evidence of its sincerity. The plaintiff used the "smoke ball" and subsequently caught influenza. The plaintiff sought payment of the reward. The defendants argued that the offer was not intended to be a valid offer and was just a "sales gimmick" and was therefore incapable of acceptance. The court held – the advertisement did constitute a valid offer. In particular, the reference to the bank account indicated the seriousness of the defendants' intentions.

The Public Offer

The public offer is the proposal:

- By a commercial legal entity
- Which contains all the essential terms of the contract
- Which displays the will of the person who is making the proposal, to conclude the contract on the terms indicated in the proposal with any responding person.

Items on Display

Unlike in most European countries, items on display at places of sale (like supermarket shelves or shop windows) are considered in Russia as a public offer[13]. Items on display are considered as an offer even if all the essential terms and conditions of the contract are not provided. The seller is contractually bound to a number of people, who accept the offer, in case it is not explicitly provided that the goods are not for sale.

Auctions

Announcements to hold an auction are considered as public offers. A sale by auction is complete when the auctioneer announces its completion by the fall of the hammer; the person offering the highest price wins. It is the bidder who makes the offer, which is accepted or rejected by the auctioneer. The contractual relationship between the auctioneer and the participant at the auction arises only from the concluded contact[14].

Tenders

The advertisement to take part in a tender constitutes a public offer[15]. The person offering the most favourable conditions, wins.

Notes

The suit on declaration of the auction as invalid shall not be subject to satisfaction unless the rights and interests of the claimant were infringed.

The auction shall be declared invalid in case of absence of the notification from the auction of the information, provided by Article 448 of the Civil Code, i.e. on the date, time and form of the action, on the subject-matter and the procedure of the auction, on the initial price, etc.

The auction shall not be declared invalid in case of violations by the court bailiff while arresting the property of the debtor.

Transactions concluded under the results of the auction shall be declared invalid if: they are not corresponding to legislation, the subject-matter of the transaction is property restricted in civil turnover, or they are under the results of the auction itself declared invalid[16].

---

[13] P.8 of the Ruling of the Government of the RF No.918, dated 21 July 1997.

[14] Ruling of the Federal Arbitrazh Court of the Moscow Region, dated 23 February 2000.

[15] Ruling of the Federal Arbitrazh Court of the Moscow Region No.KG-A40/4076-99, dated 15 December 1999.

[16] Information Letter of the High Arbitrazh Court of the RF No.101 "The Judicial Review on the Resolution by the Arbitrazh Courts of the Cases, Concerning Public Auctions within the Framework of the Executory Process", dated 22 December 2005.

Gaming and Betting

According to Article 1063 of the Civil Code the invitation to take part in gaming or betting must include the terms of when the game will take place. It shall be addressed to an indefinite number of people and constitutes a public offer.

Termination of an Offer

Prior to acceptance, an offer may be terminated. Once properly terminated, an offer is no longer capable of acceptance. Examples of such terminations are as follows:

- Rejection
- Lapse of time
- Death (Liquidation)
- Revocation

Rejection

An offer may be rejected where the other party refuses to accept it. A party may reject an offer by making a counter offer.

Note

A contract signed with a protocol of disagreement shall not be deemed concluded.

An answer, indicating the consent to conclude a contract on the terms other than those indicated in the offer, shall not be regarded as an acceptance. Such an answer is actually a refusal of the offer and instead, takes the form of a new offer.

Examples

Maria offered Elena a farm for 1,000,000 roubles. In response, Elena said she would offer 950,000 roubles. Maria refused to sell at this price. Elena then purported to accept Maria's original offer of 1,000,000 roubles and sought to enforce the contract. The court held – Elena's offer of 950,000 roubles amounted to a counter offer, which had the effect of rejecting Maria's original offer resulting in its termination. Elena could not therefore enforce the contract.

Moscow Unitary Entity "Mosvodocanal" sought DEZ "Preobrazhenskoe" to enforce the contract concerning provision of portable water. The court stipulated that "Mosvodocanal" offered DEZ to conclude the contract on certain conditions, in response, DEZ refused the offer and offered other conditions. The court held that DEZ's refusal of the offer and the offering of other conditions is not an acceptance, but a refusal of the offer and therefore a counter offer.

Lapse of Time

An offer may expire with the passing of time. It would be unrealistic and impractical to keep an offer open for eternity.

Example

A offers to sell oranges to B, and B does not accept the offer for two years, at which stage he purports to do so. It can be said that A's offer has lapsed with the passage of time and B cannot bring an action to enforce the contract.

What Time Must Pass before an Offer Must Be Accepted

It is advisable to state the deadline for the offer. Where the offer does not specify a date by which it must be accepted, then the offer must be accepted within a reasonable time. What amounts to a reasonable time will depend on the circumstances of the following case:

Examples

The defendant made an offer in June to purchase shares in the plaintiff's company. The company made no response until November when it purported to accept the offer. The court held – the offer had lapsed, as it had not been accepted within a reasonable time.

In that case the passage of a couple of months in the volatile world of the stock market was considered to be sufficient to cause the lapse of the offer.

The claimant asked the court to find the defendant a participant of the LLC on the grounds that the defendant had paid the share in the share capital of the company, which must be considered as though the defendant had purported to accept the offer. The court held that when the defendant paid the money, the offer had lapsed, as the offer had not been accepted within the term stated in the offer.

Death (Liquidation)

It would appear that death (liquidation of a legal entity) of either of the parties brings the offer to an end, if it is not directly provided that the offer is subject to succession.

Revocation

The person who has forwarded the offer, shall commit it, from the moment of its receipt by the addressee.

The offer is irrevocable under Russian law[17]. The offer, received by the addressee, shall not be revoked during the time set for its acceptance, unless otherwise stipulated in the offer itself or following on from the substance of the proposal.

Russian legislation does not provide that an offer may be revoked or withdrawn at any time before it is accepted. However, the U.N. Convention on the Contracts of the International Sale of Goods, Vienna, dated 11 April 1980, provides for such a revocation of an offer. A party making an offer may revoke or withdraw it at any time before it is accepted. This is true even where the offer states it will remain open for a definite period of time, as such promise is not legally enforceable in the absence of consideration.

However, if the offer is immediately withdrawn and the other party is notified of this before or at the same time as receipt of the offer, any acceptance shall be regarded as not obtained.

If the offer states that it may be withdrawn at any time during a period in which it may be considered, then this too is regarded as a valid revocation of the offer. However, if there is no such stipulation, then the time limit for acceptance remains open to the offeree to either accept or decline the offer.

Example

> Roman agreed to sell his horse to George. The offer was to remain open for six weeks. Within that time period Roman withdrew his offer. The court held – Roman was entitled to do so.

A revocation is only effective once it is communicated to the offeree. To be effective a revocation may be communicated by the offerer or another person.

---

[17] Civil Code, Article 436.

Example

The vendor of a house offered in writing to sell the house, promising to keep the offer open until Friday, June 12th. On Thursday, a third party told the purchaser that the house may have been sold to another. The purchaser then purported to accept the vendor's original offer. The court held – the purported acceptance came too late: the purchaser had known that the offer made to him had been revoked before he purported to accept it.

Revocation is the technical term for the cancellation of an offer and occurs when the offerer withdraws their offer. The rules relating to revocation are as follows:

- An offer is irrevocable unless otherwise stipulated in the offer
- Revocation is not effective until it is actually received by the offeree. This means that the offerer must make sure that the offeree is made aware of the withdrawal of the offer, otherwise it may still be open to the offeree to accept the offer
- Communication of revocation may be made through a reliable third party. Where the offeree finds out about the withdrawal of the offer from a reliable third party, the revocation is effective and the offeree can no longer seek to accept the original offer
- In relation to contracts where one party promises something in return for some action on the part of another party, revocation is not permissible once the offeree has started performing the task requested.

Acceptance

Acceptance is necessary for the formation of a contract. Once the offeree has accepted the terms offered, a contract comes into effect. Both parties are bound: the offerer can no longer withdraw the offer, nor can the offeree withdraw the acceptance.

An acceptance must be full and unconditional. An acceptance is a final, unqualified assent to the terms of the offer, communicated to the offeree. If the purported acceptance attempts to vary the terms of the offer in any way this will amount to a rejection of the original offer and is a counter offer. Partial acceptance does not form a valid contract. Therefore, if the offeree communicates acceptance of the offer subject to modification of one or more of the terms and conditions, this is not an acceptance. A modified acceptance has two effects:

- Firstly, it cancels the original offer, which is not capable of acceptance unless resubmitted by the offeror

- Secondly, the modified acceptance becomes a new offer, which the original offeror can choose to accept or reject. This is sometimes referred to as a counter-offer.

Counter-offer is a common feature of commercial bargains when the two parties have to decide on price or other terms and conditions. There can be several counter-offers between the parties, each cancelling the previous offer.

Silence

Silence is not regarded as acceptance unless otherwise following from law, customs of business turnover or former business relations between the parties [18].

Examples

The acceptance must be communicated to the offerer. Silence cannot be taken as acceptance, save, in exceptional circumstances where performance constitutes acceptance ('concluding actions')[19].

Fedor offered to buy his nephew's horse in a letter which stated "If I hear no more about him I consider the horse is mine at that price." His nephew did not reply and the auctioneer sold the horse to another party. Fedor sued the auctioneer. The court held – as the nephew had not communicated his intention to accept Fedor's offer there was no contract between them.

Where Performance Constitutes Acceptance

In some circumstances, the offeree's conduct will imply acceptance. For example, an offer of reward is capable of acceptance by performance, i.e. performing the required task.

Example

If the offeree, within the term stipulated in the offer for its acceptance, performed actions concerning fulfilment of the conditions, provided for by the offer, it is considered as acceptance, if otherwise is not provided by law or by the offer.

---

[18] Decision of the Supreme Court of the RF No.GKPI01-1369, dated 6 November 2001.

[19] Ruling of the Federal Arbitrazh Court of the Ural Region, dated 20 March 2003.

Where Acceptance Is Made by Post

Unlike in most countries, and due to Russian specifics of communication lines, the Civil Code provides that a letter of acceptance creates a valid contract only from the moment it reaches its destination.

Generally, an offeree may accept an offer in any way that he pleases, i.e. if an offer is made by post, then it may be accepted by post. However, if the offerer expressly prescribes a method of acceptance then an acceptance will only be valid if it is made in that manner.

Example

Pavel made an offer, stating that the offer was only to be accepted using a telegram. The plaintiff purported to accept by letter. The court held – there was no contract as no valid acceptance had taken place.

Special Cases of Acceptance

If the party accepting the offer sent its acceptance notification in due time, but the other party received it late, the acceptance is nevertheless regarded to have been received in time (unless the party that has forwarded the offer immediately notifies the other party about late arrival of the acceptance)[20].

If the party which has forwarded the offer immediately notifies the other party about the obtaining of the acceptance of that other party, which has come with a delay, the contract shall be regarded as concluded.

Place of Conclusion of a Contract

In case the place of conclusion of the contract is not indicated in the contract, the place of execution of the contract is deemed to be the place of residence of the individual – the offeror – or the place of location of the legal entity – the offeror.

Mandatory Conclusion of a Contact

In case the conclusion of a contract is mandatory for the offeree under the Civil Code or other laws of the RF, the offeree is to forward to the offerer the acceptance or the refusal to accept within 30 days from the date of receipt of the offer[21].

---

[20] Civil Code, Article 442.
[21] Civil Code, Article 445.

Example

Under Article 26 of the Law on Consumers' Rights, a legal entity, having a dominant position on Russian markets and rendering services or providing works, must conclude a contract with a consumer on rendering services or providing works to the consumer.

Intention to Create Legal Relations

The second essential requirement of a valid contract is that an intention to create legal relations must exist. The courts, in an attempt to ascertain what the intentions of the parties are, will apply an objective test. In other words, would an ordinary, reasonable man, looking at the express terms of the contract and the conduct of the parties, be of the view that the parties intended to be legally bound by the agreement?

The simplest possible definition of a contract is a legally binding agreement. However, although all contracts are the outcome of agreements, not all agreements are contracts; that is, not all agreements are legally enforceable. In order to limit the number of cases that might otherwise be brought, the courts will only enforce those agreements which the parties intended to have legal effect. Although expressed in terms of the parties' intentions, the test for the presence of such intention is an objective, rather than a subjective one and will be decided on the basis of particular presumptions made by the courts.

Any express statement by the parties to the effect that the contract between them is not to be binding will be conclusive.

Example

The Lessor sought to enforce the lease agreement. The lease agreement between the Lessor and the Lessee was expiring and the Lessor wanted to prolong the lease agreement for a new term with new payment terms. The court held that such prolongation of the agreement on new terms is not prolongation of the same agreement, but a new agreement, and there was no intention from the party of the Lessee to conclude a new agreement, so therefore no intention from the party of the Lessee to create legal relations existed.

Where an agreement is entered into as part of a commercial arrangement then it is presumed to create legal relations. Therefore, in the absence of an express term to the contrary, an agreement between two businessmen in the course of their business will be presumed to create legal relations.

Privity of Contract

The doctrine of privity of contract essentially provides that a contract cannot be enforced in favour of or against someone who is not a party to that contract.

Examples

A agrees to buy a car from B. A then refuses to pay the purchase price. B cannot bring an action against C (A's sister) seeking payment for the car as C is not privy (a party) to the contract and it cannot therefore be enforced against her.

Dmitry supplied tires to a distributor. Under the agreement, the distributor could not resell the tires at less than the prescribed retail price. In addition, if the distributor resold the tires he was under obligation to ensure that the second buyer would agree also not to resell the tires at a price below the retail price. The distributor sold the tires to Sergey, who in turn, resold the tires at a price below the agreed price level. Dmitry sued Sergey for breach of contract. The court held – Dmitry could not sue Sergey as he was not a party to the contract between the distributor and Dmitry.

There are a number of exceptions to the doctrine of privity of contract and they may be listed as follows:

Trust

In case of trust, according to Chapter 53 of the Civil Code, a contract can create a trust in favour of a third party and if there is a breach of trust, the third party (beneficiary) can sue even though it was not a party to the original contract.

Agency

According to Article 1005 of the Civil Code, if an agent is appointed and given authority by the principal to the contract on his behalf, then any contract made by the agent within the scope of his authority will bind the principal even though the principal is not himself a party to the contract.

Commission

According to Article 990 of the Civil Code, if a commissioner is appointed and given authority by the client to contract on his behalf, then any contract made by the commissioner within the scope of his authority will bind the client even though the client is not himself a party to the contract.

Mandate

According to Article 971 of the Civil Code under the contract of mandate, the mandatary shall undertake to perform certain legal actions on behalf of and for account of the mandator. Rights and obligations under the contract of mandate concluded by the mandatary shall accrue directly for the mandator.

Lease

A lease can create rights and obligations which bind future assignees of the lease. A restrictive covenant (e.g. a covenant by a person who has leased a newsagent not to sell fruit) will bind future possessors of the property.

Insurance

Article 965 of the Civil Code provides that a third party can take the benefit of a contract with an insurance company. This gives a person claiming against an insured motorist certain remedies against the insurance company.

Sale of Goods

According to Article 1096 of the Civil Code and Article 13 of the Law on Consumers' Rights, a party who buys goods from a retailer, which turn out to be faulty, can sue the manufacturer of goods as well as the retailer.

Part V. Formation of Contracts

The Moment and Procedure of Conclusion of a Contract

The Moment of Conclusion of a Contract

A contract is regarded as concluded if the parties have agreed on all its essential terms, in a proper form set for similar kinds of contracts. If the law stipulates that the contract is concluded providing some property is transferred, the contract is regarded as concluded from the moment of transfer of the corresponding property.

Example

A loan agreement is regarded as concluded from the moment the money or loaned items are transferred, while a contract of safe custody is concluded from the moment at which the items are transferred for safe custody.

A contract subject to state registration, is regarded as concluded from the moment of its registration, unless the law stipulates otherwise.

Contracts that shall be certified by a notary in accordance with law regulations or a decision of the parties to the contract are recognised to be concluded after notarial certification.

It is necessary to ascertain when the contract is concluded in order to do the following:

- To determine when rights and obligations of the parties to the contract arise
- To decide what legislation is applicable to the contract, since any contract shall correspond to legal regulations that were effective at the moment of its conclusion.

Procedure of Conclusion of the Contract

A contract may be concluded:

- According to the general procedure established by the Civil Code
- Compulsorily
- By a tender.

Express Terms

The contract determines what the precise scope of the obligations and responsibilities of the parties to the contract are. These rights and duties are said to be the terms of the contract. These terms may be divided into two forms: express terms and implied terms.

Express terms are agreed between the parties either verbally or in writing at the time of making the contract.

Example

A states "B, I accept your offer of 720,000 roubles for my Audi." In this scenario the terms of the contract are that A agrees to sell his Audi to B for 720,000 roubles.

Express terms may be subdivided into two further categories:

- Essential terms (conditions)
- Warranties.

Essential Terms (Conditions)

The following terms are recognised as essential:

- Subject-matter of the contract
- Terms directly defined as essential for a given kind of contract by law or by other legal acts (e.g. according to the Civil Code, an essential term for contracts of retail trading with goods is the price for those goods)
- All terms about which, by the statement of one of the parties, an accord shall be reached.

These are major and fundamental terms, a breach of which entitles the innocent party to terminate the contract and sue for damages.

Note

A provision in a contract stating the necessity of an additional agreement between the parties on the price of goods, subject to delivery in a specified period, means that such a provision is an essential condition. The absence of agreement on such a condition will incur recognition of the sale and purchase contract as not concluded[22].

Examples

Person A agrees to build a house for B and does not put a roof on it. This amounts to a breach of conditions and will entitle B to reject the contract and sue for damages.

An actress agreed to sing in an opera. Due to illness she was unable to appear on the opening night and for a few nights afterwards. They had to employ a substitute who insisted that she must be employed for the whole run. The first actress sued for breach of contract. The court held – her failure to perform on the opening night was a breach of an essential term.

---

[22] Decision of the International Commercial Arbitration Court under the Russian Chamber of Commerce and Industry No.129/2003, dated 9 April 2004.

Warranties

Anything that is not a condition is a warranty and is treated with less importance. Breach of warranty merely entitles the injured party to claim for damages. It does not entitle a party to terminate the contract.

Examples

Person A agrees to build a house for B and paints one of the bedrooms green instead of blue as agreed. This amounts to a breach of warranty and will only entitle B to damages.

An opera singer agreed to perform in a show and attend the rehearsals. The singer missed a number of rehearsals. The court held – the requirement to attend rehearsals was subsidiary to the main part of the contract – to perform, and therefore the failure to attend rehearsals was a breach of a warranty.

Implied Terms

Implied terms are those terms not expressed by the parties. These terms are not agreed verbally or in writing but are implied by law into the contract in order to give effect to the presumed intention of the parties.

Example

Person A agrees to sell his car to B, but does not deliver it for six months. The parties never expressly agreed a delivery date. The court in this situation may imply into the contract that the parties intended the car to be delivered within a reasonable time, i.e. a couple of days. Article 314 of the Civil Code stipulates that if the term is not provided directly, the reasonable term is 7 days from the creditor's claim on execution of the obligation.

A term may therefore be implied as follows:

Custom

A term may be implied into a contract based on customs of business turnover. Such customs of business turnover must be well established and any express term to the contrary will overrule the implied term.

Statute

A term may be implied into a contract as it may be required by legislation. Any such term will be implied regardless of the intention of the parties.

Example

Examples of such terms include those implied into contracts of employment, e.g. where the contract is silent regarding the notice to be given by the employee upon termination of the contract. In this case a statutory minimum notice period of two weeks, stipulated by Article 80 of the Labour Code, will imply into the contract.

Application of Dispositive Norms

Most norms in the Civil Code have dispositive (residuary) character.

In cases when the contract provision has been stipulated by the norm, it will be applied unless the parties to the contract agree otherwise (the dispositive norm), the parties may either:

- Exclude its application or
- Introduce a provision, distinct from that norm.

If the parties do not agree on either of these actions, the contract provision is regulated by the dispositive norm.

Fact

At times, the parties may imply a term into a contract where it is obviously necessary to ensure the proper functioning of the contract.

Example

The owners of a wharf agreed that a boat could be unloaded at their wharf. The boat was damaged when the tide went out. The owners of the boat brought an action for breach of contract. The court held – a term was implied into the contract that the defendants would take reasonable care to see that the wharf was safe, this they had failed to do.

Essential Features of a Contract

The essential features of a contract are as follows:

- The parties to a contract must have the capacity to enter into it. In this context, "capacity" simply means the legal right to take the

proposed action. Therefore, a young person with partial capacity can enter into a contract provided it is within the rights generally acknowledged to apply to young persons
- The subject-matter of the contract must be legal. For example, a contract to sell illegal drugs cannot be binding on the parties unless they are authorised by the State to deal in the relevant sale of goods
- The contract must have an element of bargain to the extent that there must be something offered and accepted by the respective parties. Both offer and acceptance imply some form of action – simple contracts may be concluded by spoken words whilst commercial contracts tend to be executed in writing. The law prescribes a specific form for certain types of contract. For example, contracts involving land transactions and mortgages must be executed in notarial form
- The offer must also lay down unambiguous terms and conditions, or norms, that may or may not be accepted by the recipient.

Part VI. Due Execution of Obligations

Obligations shall be discharged in the proper way in conformity with the terms of the obligations and with the requirements of the law and of other legal acts, and in the absence of such terms and requirements - in conformity with customs of business turnover or with other habitually presented demands.

The unilateral refusal to discharge the obligation and the unilateral amendment of its terms is not admitted, unless otherwise provided by law.

The creditor has the right not to accept a partial discharge of the obligation, unless otherwise is provided for by law, by other legal acts and by the terms of the obligation, and unless otherwise does not follow from customs of business turnover or from the substance of the obligation.

Elements of due execution of obligations include:

- Term of execution
- Place of execution
- Proper person
- Subject-matter of the obligation
- Way of execution
- Currency of the obligation.

Note

A major part of the regulations of the Civil Code, with respect to the discharge of obligations, are dispositive norms, i.e. parties to the contract may agree upon other grounds for recognition of obligations as being not properly discharged.

Term of Execution

If the obligation stipulates, or allows to stipulate the day of its discharge or the period of time, within which it shall be discharged, the obligation shall be subject to discharge on this particular day or, correspondingly, at any moment within this period[23].

In the cases when the obligation does not stipulate the deadline for its discharge and does not contain the terms making it possible to define this deadline, it shall be discharged within a reasonable term after the beginning of the obligation.

An obligation which has not been discharged within a reasonable term, and also an obligation, the term of whose discharge has been defined by the moment of demand, shall be discharged by the debtor within seven days of the creditor's presentation of the claim for its discharge, unless the duty of discharge within a different term follows from law, from other legal acts, from the provisions of the obligation, from customs of business turnover, or from the substance of the obligation.

Example

Article 810 of the Civil Code provides that the borrower shall be obliged to return to the lender the received loan amount in the period and in the order prescribed by the loan agreement. In cases where the term of return of the loan amount is not fixed by or determined by the time of demand, the loan amount shall be returned by the borrower within 30 days from the date of a claim by the lender, unless otherwise stipulated by the contract.

The general rule is that the debtor is empowered to discharge the obligation in advance. However, an advanced discharge of obligations, involved in the performance by its parties of business activity, shall be admitted only in cases when the possibility to discharge the obligation before the fixed date has been stipulated by law, by other legal acts or by the terms of the obligation, or follows from customs of business turnover or from the substance of the obligation.

---

[23] Civil Code, Article 314.

Note

Discharge by the debtor of the obligation in advance under its own initiative shall be distinguished from cases when the debtor under the claim of the creditor has to discharge the obligation in advance, e.g. in case of diminution of the charter capital of an LLC, creditors may claim advance execution of obligations.

Place of Execution

Unless the place of discharge has been defined by law, by other legal acts or by the agreement, or it follows from customs of business turnover or from the substance of the obligation, the discharge shall be effected in the following places:

- The obligation to transfer a land plot, a building, a structure or other immovable property - at the place of location of the property
- The obligation to transfer a commodity or other property, envisaging its shipment - at the place of transferring the property to the first shipper for its being forwarded to the creditor
- Other obligations to transfer a commodity or other property - at the place of manufacture or of the bailment of the property, if this place has been known to the creditor at the moment of beginning of the obligation
- The pecuniary obligation - at the place of residence of the creditor at the moment of beginning of the obligation, and if the creditor is a legal entity - at the place of its location at the moment of beginning of the obligation. If the creditor, by the moment of discharge of the obligation, has changed the place of the creditor's residence and has duly informed the debtor thereabout, the place of execution of the obligation shall be at the new place of the creditor's residence or stay. In this case the creditor bears the expenses, concerning the changing of the place of execution
- All other obligations - at the place of residence of the debtor, and in case the debtor is a legal entity - at the place of its location.

Subject-Matter of the Obligation

The general rule is that the debtor is obliged to return the very property prior agreed with the creditor.

The debtor, who is obliged to transfer to the creditor this or that property, or to perform one of two or of several actions, has the right of choice, unless otherwise follows from law, from other legal acts or from the terms of the obligation[24].

Way of Execution

The contract must be discharged in a way that is consistent with the subject of the contract. It must be performed completely and precisely in keeping with the conditions agreed. Partial performance of the contract by one party does not give rise automatically to discharge, as by definition the contract has not been performed in its entirety, and will therefore not generally result in *pro rata* entitlement to consideration. For example, if an author agrees to write a book for a publisher and completes only half the book, the author may not be entitled to half of the payment due for the completed work.

Discharge of the Obligation by Placing a Debt on a Deposit

The debtor has the right to place money or securities he owes on the notary's deposit or the court's deposit[25], if the obligation cannot be discharged by the debtor due to:

- The absence of the creditor or of the person, whom he has authorised to accept the discharge of the obligation, at the place, where the obligation shall be discharged
- The creditor's legal incapacity and his having no substitute
- An obvious absence of any certainty about who is the creditor to the obligation, in particular, in connection with the dispute on this issue arising between the creditor and other parties
- The creditor's avoidance of accepting the discharge of the obligation or any other delay thereof.

The placing of a sum of money or of securities on the notary's or the court's deposit is regarded as discharge of the obligation. The notary or the court must notify the creditor about this.

[24] Civil Code, Article 320.
[25] Civil Code, Article 327.

The Recourse Discharge of Obligations

The recourse discharge is the discharge of the obligation by one of the parties, which in conformity with the agreement has been conditioned by the discharge of its obligations by the other party[26].

Unless otherwise provided by law or by the contract, in case of the obliged party's failure to discharge the obligations stipulated by the agreement, or in case of the existence of the circumstances obviously testifying to the fact that such discharge will not be effected within the fixed term, the party into which the recourse discharge has been imposed, has the right to suspend the discharge of its obligation or to refuse to discharge this obligation, and to claim the compensation of losses.

If the obligation, stipulated by the agreement, has not been discharged in full volume, the party, into which the recourse discharge has been imposed, has the right to suspend the discharge of its obligation or to refuse to discharge the obligation in part, corresponding to such underdischarge.

If the recourse discharge of the obligation has been effected, despite the fact that the other party has not discharged its obligation, stipulated by the agreement, this party shall be obliged to effect such discharge.

Example

In case the leaseholder has not transferred the premises within the stipulated term, it has a right to claim lease payments only after the actual transfer of those premises.

Currency of the Obligation

Pecuniary obligations must be stipulated in roubles of the RF. The rouble of the RF is the legal means of payment, which must be accepted at its face value throughout the entire territory of the RF.

In a pecuniary obligation it may be stipulated that it is subject to payment in roubles of the RF in the amount equivalent to a definite amount in the foreign currency, or in the agreed monetary units, e.g. ECU, the "special borrowing rights", "artificial unit" – u.e., etc. In this case, the amount subject to payment in roubles of the RF is defined in conformity with the exchange rate of the Bank of Russia for the corresponding currency, or defined in the artificial units by the date of payment, unless

[26] Civil Code, Article 328.

another exchange rate or another date of its determination has been established by law or by the parties' agreement[27].

The use of foreign currency, and also the use of payment documents in that foreign currency under obligations in the territory of the RF is admitted only in cases by order of law, and on the terms defined by that law. Payments between legal entities must be exercised in roubles, unless special permission of the Central Bank of the RF has been obtained.

Note

The infringement of the currency legislation of the RF while executing a sale and purchase agreement does not invalidate such an agreement[28].

Proper Person

The contract obligation is regarded to be discharged by a proper person if that person is:

- The debtor or one of the joint and several debtors
- The third party. The discharge of the obligation may be imposed by the debtor upon the third party, unless the debtor's duty to discharge the obligation in person follows from law, from other legal acts, from the terms of the obligation or from its substance. In this case the creditor is obliged to accept the discharge offered by the third party instead of by the debtor
- The third party, undergoing the threat of losing the right to the property of the debtor (the right of lease, of mortgage, etc.) as a result of the creditor's turning the penalty into this property, may for the third party's own account satisfy the creditor's claim without obtaining the debtor's consent. In this case, the rights of the creditor by the obligation shall pass to the third party[29].

Unless otherwise stipulated by the agreement between the parties, and unless otherwise follows from customs of business turnover or from the substance of the obligation, the debtor has the right, while discharging the obligation, to demand proofs of the fact that the discharge is accepted by the creditor himself or by the person the creditor has authorised for this purpose, and shall take the risk of consequences of his failure to present such a demand.

---

[27] Civil Code, Article 317.

[28] Resolution of the Presidium of the High Arbitrazh Court of the RF No.5225/09, dated 17 November 2009.

[29] Civil Code, Article 313.

Joint and Several Obligations

The joint and several promise or the joint and several demand arises if the joint and several nature of the promise or of the demand have been stipulated by the contract or have been established by law, in particular, in case of the indivisibility of the subject-matter of the obligation.

The Joint and Several Promise

In case of the debtors' joint and several promise, the creditor has the right to claim the discharge both from all the debtors jointly (joint promisors), and also from any one of them taken apart, and both in full and in part of the promise[30].

The creditor, who has not been fully satisfied by one of the joint and several promisors, has the right to claim the rest of the promise from the rest of the joint and several promisors.

The joint and several promisors stay under obligation until the moment at which the promise has been discharged in full.

In case of the joint and several promise, the debtor does not have the right to put forward, against the creditor's claims, any objections which are based on relations of the other debtors with the creditor, in which the said debtor does not have involvement.

The discharge of the joint and several promise in full by one of the debtors shall absolve the rest of the debtors from the discharge of the promise toward the creditor.

Unless otherwise is provided for by the relations between the joint and several promisors:

- The promisor, who has discharged the joint and several promise, shall have the right of the recourse claim to the rest of the debtors in equal shares, excluding the promisor's own share
- The amount which has not been paid by one of the joint and several promisors to the debtor, who has discharged the joint and several promise, bears in equal shares this promisor and the rest of the promisors.

[30] Civil Code, Article 323.

The Joint and Several Demand

In the case of joint and several demands, any of the joint and several creditors have the right to present to the debtor the demand in full volume.

Before the claim has been presented by one of the joint and several creditors, the debtor has the right to discharge the obligation towards any one of them at the debtor's own discretion.

The debtor does not have the right to put forward objections against the claim of one of the creditors, which are based on relations of the debtor with other joint and several creditors, in which the given creditor does not have any involvement.

The discharge of the obligations in full toward one of the creditors absolves the debtor from the discharge toward other creditors[31].

The joint and several creditor who has accepted the discharge from the debtor, will compensate what is due to other creditors in equal shares, unless otherwise arises from the relationships between them.

Transfer of Rights in an Obligation

Chapter 24 of the Civil Code is dedicated to the transfer of rights of a creditor and a debtor in an obligation.

The cession may be both onerous and gratuitous.

The cession shall be impossible without a change of parties in the obligation.

Transfer of the Creditor's Rights to Another Person

The right may be transferred by the creditor to another person by cession of the right, or may pass to another person on grounds directly provided for in legislation[32], such as:

- Legal succession
- Court decision
- Pledge obligations
- Subrogation of insurance obligations.

[31] Civil Code, Article 326.3.

[32] Civil Code, Article 387.

Note

The subject matter of the cession shall be the creditor's right of demand to the obligation in case of the absence of any obligations of the creditor before the other party.

To exercise the transfer to another person no consent of the debtor is required.

If the debtor has not been notified in written form of the effected transfer of the creditor's rights to another person, the new creditor shall bear the risk of unfavourable consequences which may arise for the creditor as a result of this. The fulfilment of the debtor's obligations to the primary creditor will be considered as good as due.

Article 383 of the Civil Code states that the creditor may not transfer to a third party the following rights, inseparably linked with the creditor's personality, such as: alimentary rights, health injury rights, etc.

Unless otherwise stipulated by law or by the contract, the right of the primary creditor passes to the new creditor in the volume and on the terms, which existed at the moment of transfer of the right. In particular, the new creditor acquires the rights guaranteeing the discharge of the obligations, and also other rights involved in the claim, including the right to the unpaid interest.

The debtor has the right to put forward objections against the new creditor's claims, which have already been stated to the primary creditor by the moment of receiving the notification about the transfer of the rights under the obligation to the new creditor.

The transaction on cession of rights must be executed in the form necessary for the deal, the rights to which are transferred.

Note

The cession of rights shall be deemed legitimate even during the executory process.

Invalidity of the main obligation shall incur invalidity of the cession of rights under such obligation.

The recourse demand may not be ceded.

The cession of a demand in a continuing obligation is possible if the demand:

- Is undisputable
- Has arisen prior to the cession of the demand, and
- Is not conditioned to the execution by way of recourse[33].

---

[33] Ruling of the High Arbitrazh Court of the RF No.11079/04, dated 14 December 2004.

Transfer of the Debtor's Rights to Another Person

Article 391 of the Civil Code states that the transfer by the debtor of his duties to another person may be executed only with the creditor's prior consent.

The transfer of duties must be executed in the form necessary for the transaction, the rights of which are transferred.

The new debtor has the right to put forward objections against the creditor's claims, based on the relationships between the creditor and the primary debtor.

Note

Transfer of the debtor's rights only in the subsidiary obligation, e.g. by forfeit, shall be contrary to the law.

Part VII. Obligation Security Means

A breach of contract means that the contract was not fulfilled by one of the parties in the proper way, in conformity with the terms of the contract and with the requirements of law and of other legal acts, and in the absence of such terms and requirements - in conformity with customs of business turnover or with other habitually presented demands.

The most major means by which the debtor is made to execute (discharge) their obligation is the reimbursement of loss. Loss reimbursement is supposed to make the creditor insensible to the breach of contractual terms by the debtor. However, to have the loss reimbursed, the creditor must prove the amount of loss incurred and the causation between the loss and the actions of the debtor. Still, even in case the court holds the decision on reimbursement of loss at the expense of the debtor, the court decision may still remain unexecuted, e.g. by insufficiency of the debtor's funds.

The above-mentioned consequences may be avoided by so called "obligation security means".

Article 329 of the Civil Code stipulates that fulfilment of an obligation may be secured by different means, among which one can enumerate the following remedies for breach of contract:

- Mortgage or pledge
- Surety
- Bank guarantee
- Forfeit (liquidated damages)
- Earnest money or advance
- Retaining, etc.

When these obligation security means are applied, a party to the contract has, besides a major obligation (to transfer goods, to perform work or to render services), an additional obligation. This additional obligation comes into force when the debtor fails to fulfil its major obligation.

Mortgage or Pledge

The Civil Code[34] and the Law on Mortgage stipulate main conditions concerning mortgage and pledge.

Pledge is a means of security for an obligation when the creditor (the pledgee) has the right of priority before other creditors of the person to whom this property belongs (the pledger) in the case of the debtor's non-discharge of this obligation. In banking parlance this is the security, or collateral, for the loan. The debt is to be paid off from the cost of the pledged property. The debt shall be covered from the insurance indemnity of the pledged property notwithstanding who is the beneficiary of the insurance indemnity.

The pledge may arise:

- By force of an agreement
- On the basis of the law, in the case when the circumstances indicated within it occur.

The Parties to the Pledge

The parties to the pledge are:

- The pledgee - the creditor under the secured obligation
- The pledger (either the debtor itself or the third party). The pledger of a given thing may be its owner, or a person having with respect to it the right of economic management.

The parties to a mortgage are the mortgagee (lender) and the mortgagor (borrower). The suffix "-or" in the word mortgagor suggests that the debtor "gives" the mortgage, derived from the literal meaning of mortgage, which is the promise to repay.

Individuals and legal entities may possess other property rights - such as a right to lease or a right to the property pledged. The creditor gains the

---

[34] The Federal Law No.367-FZ "On Amendements to Part One of the Civil Code…", dated 21 December 2013, changed drastically its provisions on pledge, and abolished the Law on Pledge. It is in force from 1 July 2014.

right to the property pledged when a pledge is a form of obligation security.

The Subject Matter of a Pledge

The pledged object may be tangible assets (e.g. goods, goods in business turnover, personal goods in pawnshops, immovable property, securities, etc.) and intangible assets (e.g. rights to intellectual property, rights under contracts, etc.). The following types of assets may not be the object of a pledge[35]:

- Property restricted in business turnover (e.g. weapons, drugs)
- Claims inalienably linked to the pledger's personality (e.g. alimentary obligations, claims for compensation of harm caused to life or health)
- Other rights whose alienation to another person is prohibited (e.g. "the golden share")[36].

The Contract of Pledge

Both the pledge agreement and the mortgage agreement shall be concluded in written form according to Article 339 of the Civil Code.

If the contract from which the obligation secured by pledge arises must be notarised, the pledge contract on the pledge of the movable property or of the rights to this property must be made in notarial form as well. A notarial form may be used by the decision of the parties to the contract.

Note

From 2013 the Notary Public shall carry the Register on pledge of movable property.

The state registration of the pledge agreement may also be required under law. All cases of the mortgaging of immovable property[37] are to be

---

[35] Civil Code, Article 336.

[36] Under Articles 5.1. and 63 of the Law on Mortgage, land plots, the owner of which is the state, may not be the object of mortgage.

[37] Article 130 of the Civil Code provides that the following property shall be referred to as immovable property: land plots; land plots with mineral deposits; set-apart water objects; forests; perennial green plantations; buildings and all kinds of structures; everything else which is closely connected with the land, i.e. such objects that cannot be shifted without causing enormous damage to their purpose;

registered, and qualified written form shall be observed, with a single document required. The mortgage agreement shall be registered in the Unified State Register. According to Article 165 of the Civil Code, in case of violation of the form, the mortgage will be considered void.

The contract shall set out:

- The rights and obligations of the parties
- The nature of the security
- The covenants (promises) entered into by the debtor
- The actions that the creditor can take in the event of default.

Key elements of this are of course the promise to repay the capital, interest and any other monies due and the details of the collateral. The contract is normally effective over a fixed term for a fixed value of capital. The contract may also contain additional covenants, financial or non-financial in nature, at the discretion of the lender.

The mortgage agreement must contain the following information:

- Identification of the property mortgaged
- Evaluation of the property mortgaged
- Full description of the terms and conditions of the obligation secured by mortgage.

Note

A pledge agreement which does not contain an evaluation of the pledged property is void.

Subsequent Mortgage

The property already mortgaged may be subject to a subsequent mortgage unless the contrary is directly provided for in the previous mortgage according to Article 342 of the Civil Code.

Theoretically it is legally possible to create any number of obligations secured by the same collateral including co-morgagees, which have equal shares on the object morgaged.

In case of subsequent mortgages the extent depends on the risk profile of the case before the prospective lender. The provision of the contract on prohibition of subsequent morgages except for the real estate is void.

The first mortgagee is in the strongest position, as the contract is completed before other subsequent mortgages and will be registered first.

---

air-borne vessels; sea-going vessels; inland navigation ships; space objects; everything else that the law may refer to as immovable property.

Further prospective lenders may therefore be deterred by the prospect that the first mortgagee has the right to be repaid ahead of them in the event of default. Therefore, claims of a subsequent mortgage are satisfied from the price of the property mortgaged left after satisfaction of demands of the previous mortgagees.

In case of levy on the object of mortgage by the first morgagee, the subsequent morgagee may claim levy together with the first mortgagee. Hovewer the contract with the subsequent mortgagee may limit such right.

The possibility of further loans is therefore usually dependent on the residual value of the collateral net of any existing borrowings secured on it rather than any legal constraint. The mortgagor must inform every subsequent mortgagee of the previous mortgage existing.

Disposal of Mortgaged Property by the Owner

Unless otherwise directly provided for in the contract of mortgage the mortgagor may use the property mortgaged and derive income thereof.

Unless otherwise directly provided in the contract of mortgage, the mortgaged property stays in the custody of the mortgagor[38].

Unless otherwise directly provided for, the mortgagor may upon the mortgagee's consent sell, lend or otherwise transfer the property mortgaged to the third party. The transfer of the property to another owner does not cease mortgage. That means that the creditor (the mortgagee) has the right to demand to sell the property mortgaged and receive the amount due to him from the sale price.

Security of the Pledged Property

The pledger shall take the risks of accidental loss or accidental damage of the pledged property, unless otherwise stipulated by the contract of pledge.

The pledgee is liable for full or partial loss or damage of the object of pledge, transferred to them, that happened through their fault (intention or negligence), and for loss or damage occurring in the course of entrepreneurial activity - unless that loss or damage is caused by force majeure.

The pledger or the pledgee, depending on in whose custody the pledged property is, is obliged, unless otherwise stipulated by the law or by the contract:

---

[38] Civil Code, Article 338.1.

- To insure for account of the pledger the pledged property
- To take measures, necessary to guarantee the security of the pledged property
- To immediately notify the other party about the arising of a threat of loss or damage of the pledged property.

In case of a gross violation by the pledgee of these obligations that creates a threat of loss or damage of the pledged property, the pledger has the right to demand that the pledge be terminated in advance.

The pledgee and the pledger shall both have the right to check the state of the pledged property, which is in the custody of the other party.

Under the parties' agreement the object of the pledge may be exchanged with other property.

Grounds for Levying Execution on the Pledged Property

The Civil Code provides possibilities to seek recovery on the pledged property both under the court decision and without recourse to court.

When periodical payments are due, the systematic infringement of terms of payment (more than three times within 12 months) will incur levy execution on the pledged property as well. Even if the pledger does not execute their agreed obligations on levy execution on the pledged property there may take place a special execution based on notary endorsement.

The pledgee (the creditor) shall inform the pledger of the initiation of the recovery procedure without recourse to court.

In case of levy execution on pledged property any property rights terminate, e.g. rights under lease contract concluded without permission of the pledgee.

In certain cases, e.g. the selling of securities, an independent appraiser shall be invited.

The execution shall be levied on the object of the pledge only under the court decision, in cases when:

- The subject matter of the pledge is property presenting a considerable historical, artistic or other kind of cultural value for society
- The pledger is absent and it is impossible to identify the place of their stay
- The subject matter of the pledge is living premises, belonging to the natural person under the right of ownership
- The pledged property is an object of several pledges

- In general cases involving the pledge of real estate.

A claim for levying execution on the pledged property may be rejected by the court if the violation committed by the debtor, with respect to the obligation secured against by the pledge, is utterly insignificant (i.e. the sum of the overdue obligation is less than 5% of the valuation of the subject matter of the pledge and the overdue period is less than 3 months), and for this reason, the amount of the pledger's claims is obviously disproportional to the cost of the pledged property.

Sale of the Property Mortgaged

A sale of the pledged property shall be admitted not earlier than 10 days from the moment of the pledger's notification.

A sale of the pledged property is executed through an open auction in the order established by the procedural legislation. The pledger may also retain the property under the agreed value with the pledgee (in case the pledgee executes entrepreneurial activity) or sell to another person under market price.

The pledged property shall be sold to the highest bidder.

If the auction is declared as having failed, the pledgee has the right, by an agreement with the pledger concluded within 10 days from the date of declaring the auction as having failed, to acquire the pledged property under the original price of the auction and to offset the sale price by the amount of his claims, secured against by the pledge. The rules of the sale and purchase contract shall be applied to such an agreement.

At a repeated auction, held within 1 month from the date of the original auction, the initial selling price of the pledged property at which the bidding starts is 15% lower than that of the first auction.

If the repeated auction is declared as having failed, the pledgee has the right to keep the pledged property appraised at a value not less than 10% below its initial selling price from the repeated auction.

If the pledgee has not availed himself of the right to keep the object of pledge to himself within one month from the date of the repeated auction being declared as failed, the contract of pledge shall be terminated.

If the amount realised from the pledged property is insufficient to cover the pledgee's claims, the pledgee has the right (in the absence of any other provisions in the law or in the contract) to demand the shortfall from other property of the debtor, while not enjoying the right of priority, based on pledge.

If the amount realised from the pledged property exceeds the size of the pledgee's claims, secured against by the pledge, the excess must be returned to the pledger within 10 days from the date of due payment by the purchaser.

The debtor and the pledger (if the pledge is provided by a third party), have the right at any time before the sale of the pledged object to terminate the sale by fulfilling the obligation secured by the pledge. An agreement restricting this right is void[39].

The debtor has the right to petition for the delay of the sale for up to one year.

Particularities Related to the Pledging of Real Estate

In case of mortgaged property, the information of an open auction shall be made public via the Internet in the order provided by the Government of the RF in 2013[40]. Participants to the auction shall pay earnest money up to 5% of the value of the property at the auction.

An independent appraiser is required to set the initial selling price of the pledged property while levying execution on:

- The right of lease for the immovable property
- The right of claim of participants in the share construction
- Immovable property with an appraisal value of more than 500,000 roubles.

The initial selling price of the pledged property, from which the bidding starts, is 80% of its market valuation as determined by an independent appraiser, unless otherwise provided for by the pledge agreement.

At the repeated auction, held within 1 month from the date of the original auction, the initial selling price of the pledged property from which the bidding starts is 15% lower than that at the first auction.

In case the repeated auction is declared as having failed, the mortgagee has the right to keep the subject matter of the mortgage and to offset the sale price by the amount of his claims, secured against by the mortgage, appraised at a value not less than 25% below its initial selling price at the first auction.

---

[39] Civil Code, Article 350.7.

[40] Rules on Information for the Open Auction of Real Estate in the Course of the Executory Process or in case of Mortgage…, approved by the Order of the Government of the RF No.66, dated 30 January 2013.

Termination of the Pledge (Mortgage)

The pledge (mortgage) is terminated:

- With the termination of the obligation, secured against by the pledge
- In case of purchase of the pledged property by the person being unaware that the property is the object of a pledge
- In case of perish of the pledged object or of the termination of the pledged right, unless the pledger has availed himself of the right of replacement and restoration of the object of pledge
- In case of sale of the pledged property
- In case of recognition of the pledge agreement becoming invalid
- Under the court decision
- In case of levy on the pledged property as a sanction or as satisfaction of the previous pledgee
- In other cases provided by law or by the agreement of the parties.

Surety

Article 361 of the Civil Code states that under the contract of surety, the surety is obliged to the creditor of the other person to answer for the latter's discharge of his obligation in full or in part.

A contract of surety may also be concluded to provide security for an obligation which will arise in the future.

The contract of surety may be either gratuitous, or provide that the creditor pays out to the surety the reward for the surety.

Note that a contract of surety creates a personal obligation in contrast to a pledge contract, which creates obligation in rem. In case of surety, a personal warranty takes place, explaining why personality and material condition of the surety influence the effectiveness of that surety.

Form of the Contract of Surety

A contract of surety must be concluded in written form. Non-observance of the written form will entail the invalidity of a contract of surety.

Note

The mark made by the creditor on the contract between the debtor and the surety is the evidence of the written form of the surety contract[41].

Responsibility of the Surety

In case of failure to discharge, or of an improper discharge by the debtor of the obligation secured by the surety, the surety and the debtor shall be jointly and severally liable to the creditor, unless the surety's subsidiary liability is stipulated by the law or by the contract of surety.

Note

In case of the joint and several liability of the debtor and the surety, the suit of the creditor must not be only against the surety. The creditor has to bring the suit against both the debtor and the surety or first against the debtor and then against the surety[42].

The surety is liable to the creditor in the same volume as the debtor, unless otherwise provided for by the contract of surety.

Rights of the Surety

The surety who has discharged the obligation shall gain the creditor's rights by this obligation, and also the rights which have belonged to the creditor as the pledgee, to the volume in which the surety has satisfied the creditor's claim. The surety also has the right to claim that the debtor pays the interest on the amount of money paid up to the creditor, and compensates other losses which the surety has borne in connection with the liability for the debtor.

The surety also has a right to put forward, against the creditor's claim, objections which could have been put forward by the debtor, even in case the debtor has renounced them or has recognised the debt.

The debtor who has discharged the obligation secured against by the surety must immediately notify the surety of their having done so. Otherwise the surety, who in his turn has discharged the obligation, shall have the right to exact from the creditor the sum that the creditor has groundlessly obtained, or to file a claim of recourse against the debtor. In

---

41 Information Letter of the High Arbitrazh Court of the RF No.28, dated 20 January 1998.

42 Information Letter of the High Arbitrazh Court of the RF No.28, dated 20 January 1998.

the latter case, the debtor has the right to exact from the creditor only the sum the creditor has groundlessly obtained, without any interest or compensation for losses.

Termination of the Surety

The surety is terminated:

- With the termination of the secured obligation
- In case of amendment of the obligation, leading to increase of the liability, or other unfavourable consequences for the surety without the consent of the surety
- As a result of the transfer to another person of the debt by the obligation, secured by the surety, unless the surety has given his consent to the creditor to be liable for the new debtor
- If the creditor has refused to accept proper discharge offered by the debtor or by the surety
- After the expiry of the term indicated in the contract of surety, for which it has been issued. In case such a term has not been stipulated, the surety shall be terminated if the creditor does not file a claim against the debtor within one year from the date of the expiry of the term fixed for the discharge of the secured obligation. If the term of discharge of the principal obligation has not been stipulated and cannot be defined, or if it has been defined by the moment of demand, the surety shall be terminated unless the creditor files a claim against the surety within two years from the date at which the contract of surety was concluded.

Bank Guarantee

According to a bank guarantee contract, under a bank guarantee the bank or another corresponding entity (another credit institution or insurance company) (the guarantor) shall issue, upon the request of the other person, (the principal) a written obligation to pay to the creditor (the beneficiary), in conformity with the terms of the obligation given by the guarantor, a certain amount of money upon the beneficiary's presentation of a written claim for its payment. So, the principal asks the bank to issue a bank guarantee in favour of the beneficiary, in order to secure the proper discharge by the principal of his obligation to the beneficiary (the principal obligation).

Unlike in a surety contract, the principal in a bank guarantee contract pays out to the guarantor a reward for issue of the bank guarantee.

Article 371 of the Civil Code provides that a bank guarantee is irrevocable unless otherwise is provided for in the guarantee. It normally comes into force from the date of issuance, again unless it provides for otherwise.

It is not obligatory to inform the guarantor of the acceptance of the guarantee by the beneficiary unless otherwise is provided for in the bank guarantee contract[43].

The term of the bank guarantee is the essential condition of the bank guarantee contract. In case the term of the guarantee is not indicated in the bank guarantee contract, the bank guarantee contract is invalid.

Note

Omission of an indication of the beneficiary in the bank guarantee shall not invalidate that bank guarantee[44].

The obligation of the guarantor to the beneficiary in the relationships between them does not depend on the principal obligation according to the bank guarantee contract, even if the guarantee contains a reference to this obligation. So, the beneficiary may claim payment from the bank without a prior claim to the principal.

The beneficiary's claim for payment of the sum of money by the bank guarantee must be presented to the guarantor in written form, together with the documents indicated in the guarantee. The beneficiary shall point out, either in the claim itself or in the enclosed documents, the nature of the principal's violation of the main obligation to secure that which the guarantee has been issued for. The beneficiary's claim must be presented to the guarantor before the expiry of the term defined in the guarantee for which it has been issued.

The guarantor's responsibility to the beneficiary for non-discharge or improper discharge of the obligation in the guarantee is not limited to the sum of money for which the guarantee was issued, unless otherwise is stipulated in the guarantee.

On receipt of the beneficiary's claim, the guarantor without delay must notify the principal.

---

[43] Information Letter of the High Arbitrazh Court of the RF No.27, dated 15 January 1998.

[44] P.8 of the Information Letter of the High Arbitrazh Court of the RF No.27, dated 15 January 1998.

Refusal to Satisfy the Beneficiary's Claim

The guarantor may refuse to satisfy the beneficiary's claim:

- If this claim or the documents enclosed with it do not correspond to the terms of the guarantee
- If they are presented to the guarantor after the expiry of the term fixed in the guarantee.

If the guarantor has learned before the satisfaction of the beneficiary's claim that the principal obligation, secured against by the bank guarantee, has already been discharged in full or in the corresponding part, that it has been terminated on other grounds or has been invalidated, the guarantor shall be obliged to notify the beneficiary and the principal of this immediately. The repeated beneficiary's claim, received by the guarantor after such notification, shall be subject to satisfaction by the guarantor.

Note

In case the main obligation has been discharged by the principal, the court may refuse to satisfy the beneficiary's claim under Article 10 of the Civil Code as an abuse of right.

Termination of the Bank Guarantee

The guarantor's obligation to the beneficiary by the guarantee shall be terminated:

- By payment to the beneficiary of the sum of money, for which the guarantee was issued
- After the expiry of the term fixed in the guarantee, for which it has been issued
- As a result of the beneficiary's renouncement of his rights by the guarantee and his return of the guarantee to the guarantor
- As a result of the beneficiary's renouncement of his rights by the guarantee, presenting a written application on relieving the guarantor of his obligations.

The guarantor has the right to recourse demand from the principal to compensate the sums of money paid to the beneficiary by the bank guarantee according to the bank guarantee contract.

Forfeit (Liquidated Damages)

Article 330 of the Civil Code provides that the forfeit (the fine, the penalty) is the sum of money, defined by law or by the agreement, which the debtor is obliged to pay to the creditor in case of his non-fulfilment or partial fulfilment of the obligation, in particular, in case of delay of the discharge.

The creditor does not have to prove that the losses have actually been inflicted upon him.

Types of Forfeit

Depending on the document that provides for a forfeit, it may be of one of two types:

- Legal forfeit (stipulated by law)
- Contract forfeit.

The following types of forfeit depend on the ratio between the right to exact the forfeit and the right to have the loss reimbursed (established by the law or by the contract):

- Offset forfeit - compensation of losses in the part, not covered by the forfeit
- Penalty forfeit - losses may be exacted in full above the forfeit
- Alternative forfeit - according to the creditor's choice, either the forfeit or the losses may be exacted
- Exclusive forfeit - only the forfeit, but not the losses may be exacted.

Note

The general rule provides for the offset character of the forfeit.

Form of the Contract of Forfeit

The agreement on the forfeit must be concluded in written form, notwithstanding the form of the principal obligation. Non-observance of the written form shall entail the invalidity of the agreement on the forfeit.

The creditor has the right to claim the payment of the forfeit, defined by law (the legal forfeit), irrespective of whether the obligation for its payment has been stipulated by the agreement between the parties. The amount of the legal forfeit may be increased by agreement between the parties, unless such action is prohibited by law.

If the forfeit, subject to payment, is obviously disproportionate compared with the consequences of the violation of the obligation, the court shall have the right to reduce the forfeit.

Note

The state bodies of the RF may not dispense legal entities from the forfeit due to non-execution of obligations, including non-delivery or partial delivery of goods. In case of forfeit it is necessary to refer to the corresponding court of general jurisdiction or the Arbitrazh court.

The court shall not decrease the forfeit under its own initiative.

It is contrary to the legislation of the RF to pay a forfeit in a foreign currency, even under credit agreements where the sum of the credit agreement is stipulated in a foreign currency. The sum of the forfeit shall be stated in roubles.

Penalties and fines shall not be recoverable simultaneously.

Forfeit calculated on the sum of the VAT shall be deemed in contradiction to the law.

Earnest Money

Article 380 of the Civil Code recognises earnest money as the sum of money issued by one of the parties to the contract to offset the payments to the other party due from it, as a proof that the contract has been concluded and that its discharge has been secured against.

The agreement on the earnest money, regardless of the sum of money involved, must be effected in written form.

In case there is any doubt about whether the sum of money paid to offset the payments due from the party to the contract is the earnest money, for example, if the agreement is not made in writing, this sum of money shall be recognised as the advance.

If the obligation is terminated before the start of its discharge by an agreement between the parties or as a result of its discharge being impossible, the earnest money shall be returned.

If the responsibility for non-performance of the contract lies with the party which has given the earnest money, it shall be left with the other party. If the responsibility for non-performance of the contract lies with the party which has received the earnest money, it shall be obliged to pay to the other party double the amount of the earnest money. Herein lies the difference between earnest money and an advance. If the responsibility for non-performance of the contract lies with the party which has received an advance, it shall be obliged to pay back to the other party only the amount of the advance.

In cases of both earnest money or an advance, the party responsible for the non-execution of the contract shall be obliged to compensate the other party for their losses.

Functions of the Earnest Money

Payment function - the sum of money is issued by one of the contracting parties to offset payments to the other party due from the first party.

Security function - the earnest money is accounted for as part of the principal obligation and, in this part, secures its execution.

Ascertaining function - by transfer of the earnest money the debtor executes, in full or in part, the principal obligation and, therefore, ascertains that the obligation exists.

Compensation function - the party liable to non-discharge of the contract is obliged to compensate the loss of another party with the offset of the amount of the earnest money, unless otherwise stipulated by the contract.

Retaining

The creditor, in whose custody is the thing subject to the transfer to the debtor or to the person named by the debtor, has the right, in case the debtor fails to discharge in time the obligation on the payment for this thing or the compensation to the creditor of the expenses and of other losses the creditor has borne in connection with it, to retain the thing until the corresponding obligation is discharged.

According to Article 359 of the Civil Code the creditor may retain the thing in his custody, despite the fact that after this thing has passed into the creditor's possession, the rights to it have been acquired by the third party. The parties by the contract can alter this provision.

The powers of the creditor, who is retaining the thing, are equal to the powers under the claims secured against by the pledge. In this case the retentor retains the property against the will of the proprietor and so the retentor does not have the protection of rights if it temporarily loses the property.

Part VIII. Breach of Contract and Remedies

Breach of a contract occurs where one of the parties to the agreement fails to comply, either completely or satisfactorily, with their obligations to that agreement. A breach of contract may occur in three ways:

- Where a party, prior to the time of performance, states that they will not fulfil their contractual obligation
- Where a party fails to perform their contractual obligation
- Where a party performs their obligation in a defective manner.

Any breach will result in the innocent party being able to sue for damages.

Compulsory measures of responsibility act as measures for the protection of the rights and interests of a party to a contract that incurs damage due to the breach of contractual terms by another party. All these measures aim to secure the execution of obligations under a contract or to redress the property loss incurred by a party to the contract. These measures are supposed to protect a party to a contract and, therefore, are applied by court if the party which incurred the loss initiates court proceedings (files an action).

Violation of the Obligation

Grounds of responsibility for violation of the obligation are the non-discharging or improper discharging of the obligation.

Note

Current postal rules do not provide for the liability of postal divisions for non-delivery of simple postal dispatches.

In a general case, a person bears responsibility if the violation of the obligation was through their fault (an intention or negligence on their part). The absence of fault must be proven by the person who has violated the obligation.

With respect to entrepreneurial activity, responsibility is borne regardless of the fault, unless the debtor proves that the proper discharge has been impossible because of a force majeure.

The actions of the debtor's employees, involved in the discharge of their obligation, are regarded as those of the debtor himself.

The debtor is also responsible for an improper discharge of the obligation by the third parties, on whom the discharge of the obligation has been imposed, unless otherwise stipulated by law[45].

Examples

The court held that the debtor is liable before the creditor for the delay of the debtor's bank in the transfer of money to the creditor[46].

Basic Forms of Responsibility

The debtor is obliged to compensate to the creditor the *losses,* caused to him by non-discharge or by improper discharge of the obligations.

The losses shall be defined in conformity with the following rule: loss is the damage *de facto* plus missed profit (profit loss).

When defining losses, the prices shall be taken into account which existed at the place where the obligation should have been discharged, on the date of the debtor's voluntary satisfaction of the creditor's claims, and if the claim has not been voluntarily satisfied - on the date of its submission. Proceeding from the circumstances, the court may satisfy a claim for the compensation of losses, taking into account prices which exist at the time of holding the court decision.

Subsidiary Liability

Before presenting claims against a person who, in conformity with law, with other legal acts or with the terms of the obligation, bears liability in addition to the liability of the other person, who is the subsidiary debtor (the subsidiary liability), the creditor is obliged to present the claim against the principal debtor.

If the principal debtor has refused to satisfy the claim of the creditor, or if the creditor has not received from him a response to the presented claim within a reasonable term, this claim may be presented against the person bearing the subsidiary liability.

---

[45] Civil Code, Article 403.

[46] Case No.5248/96.

Overdue Performance

The debtor who has failed to execute the obligation on time is liable before the creditor for losses caused by the overdue performance, and for the consequences of the impossibility of the performance of the obligation.

If the execution of the overdue obligation has lost interest for the creditor, the creditor has the right to refuse to accept the execution and to claim for compensation of losses.

The debtor is not overdue when the obligation could not have been executed because of the creditor's overdue performance.

The creditor is overdue if the creditor has refused to accept proper execution from the debtor, or if the creditor has not performed actions, stipulated by law, by other legal acts, by the contract, or entailing from customs of business turnover or from the substance of the obligation, before the performance of which the debtor could not have executed his obligation.

Damages

Article 393 of the Civil Code provides that a party may sue for damages as compensation for the loss caused by the breach, the idea being to restore the party who has suffered loss to the same position he would have been in *had the contract been performed.*

The person whose right has been violated is entitled to demand full recovery of the losses inflicted upon him. According to Article 15 of the Civil Code, the losses are the expenses which the person whose right has been violated accrued or will have to accrue to restore the violated right, the loss or the damage done to his property (the compensatory damage), and also the unyielded profits which this person would have derived under the ordinary conditions of the civil turnover had his right not been violated (the missed profit).

The concept of "measure of damages" concerns the assessment of the compensation to be paid to the plaintiff, it is the quantification of damages. The court must decide how much money to award in respect of the breach and its relevant consequences.

Loss "*De Facto*"

Loss *de facto* includes:

- Expenses which the person whose right has been violated accrued or will have to accrue to restore the violated right

- The loss or the damage done to their property.

Missed Profit

Missed profit is considered to be any profit which this party would have derived under the ordinary conditions of the civil turnover, if their right had not been violated.

If the party who has violated the right of another party has derived profits as a result of this, the party whose right has been violated, shall have the right to claim, alongside the compensation of other losses, also the compensation of the missed profit in the amount not less than such profits.

Forfeit

The forfeit is another form of responsibility. The losses shall be compensated, amounting to the part which has not been covered by the forfeit, except for cases when the law or the contract provides for otherwise.

Measure of Damages

As a general rule, the amount of damages awarded is what is needed to put the plaintiff in the position he would have achieved if the contract had been performed. Damages cannot be recovered for any non-financial loss arising from breach of contract.

In awarding damages the court will take into account inflation where it is necessary to adequately compensate the plaintiff.

Non-Discharge of Monetary Obligations

The interest on the total amount of the monetary means shall be due for use of another person's money involving:

- Its illegal retention
- The avoidance of its return
- Any other kind of delay in payment of money, or
- Non-grounded receipt or saving of money at the expense of another person.

Note

Article 395 of the Civil Code concerning non-discharge of monetary obligations shall not be applied to tax or other relations dedicated to payments to the state budget and non-budgetary funds.

The interest rate shall be defined by the discount rate of the bank's interest (the refinancing rate)[47], existing at the date of the discharge of the monetary obligation or of the corresponding part thereof at the place of the creditor's residence, and if the creditor is a legal entity - at the place of location of the creditor.

If the debt is recovered through the court, the court may satisfy the creditor's claim, proceeding from the discount rate of the bank's interest at the date of filing the claim or at the date of holding the decision.

The interest for the use of another person's monetary means is recovered until the date of payment to the creditor, unless the law, other legal acts or the contract provide for otherwise.

Specific Performance

The remedy of specific performance is a remedy by which a party to a contract can be ordered to perform their obligations under that contract according to Article 396 of the Civil Code. Being a remedy, it is discretionary by nature; it is, however, awarded or refused on well-established principles.

Generally, the rule is that specific performance will be awarded even where damages would be an appropriate remedy, if otherwise is not provided for by law or by the contract.

In case of non-fulfilment of the obligation to transfer a specific thing into the ownership, into the economic or the operative management, or into the gratuitous use of the creditor, the creditor has the right to claim forcible withdrawal of the specific thing from the debtor and its transfer to the creditor on the terms of the obligation.

Payment of the forfeit and the compensation of losses in case of an improper execution of the obligation do not absolve the debtor from the discharge of the obligations in kind, unless otherwise stipulated by law or by the contract.

Compensation of losses in case of non-execution of the obligation and payment of the forfeit for its non-execution absolves the debtor from the discharge of the obligation in kind, unless otherwise stipulated by law or by the contract.

---

[47] As of 14 September 2012 the refinancing rate is 8.25% per annum.

Instead of claiming for the transfer of the specific thing, the creditor has the right to claim for the compensation of his losses.

Examples

A enters into a contract to purchase B's house, which is unique as it has a spectacular view of the beach. B breaches the contract and refuses to honour his obligations. The court may award an order for specific performance as damages will not adequately compensate A for the loss he has suffered as a result of B's breach.

Specific performance of a partnership agreement was refused in circumstances where the plaintiff's complaint was that the defendant had failed to pay an agreed sum: the complaint could be met by an award of damages, and so specific performance was refused.

Part IX. Changes and Termination of Contracts

Article 450 of the Civil Code provides that changes may be introduced into a contract with the mutual consent of the parties to the contract, unless otherwise is stipulated by the Civil Code, by other legal acts or by the contract. The same rule is applied to the termination of a contract.

In case of changes to the contract the parties' obligations shall be preserved in the changed form. In case of termination of the contract, the parties' obligations shall be terminated. Termination is preferred to changes to the contract by the court.

Changes

Changes may be made to a contract with the mutual consent of the parties. In case the parties to the contract do not reach mutual consent, the respective changes may be introduced to the contract by a court decision at one party's initiative in the following cases:

In case of an essential **breach** of the contract by the other party

Only an essential breach of a condition will result in a termination of the contract. As an essential breach of the contract by one of the parties shall be recognised as such a violation of the contract which entails for the other party, losses to a considerable extent, depriving that party of what it could have counted upon with proper conclusion of the contract. A breach of condition may occur where one party fails to perform his obligations under the agreement. If the other party treats the contract as ended, then the contract will be discharged.

If one party to a contract states in advance that he will be unable to perform the contract or has no intention of performing, the other party may treat this as an anticipatory breach and treat the contract as discharged or he may elect to allow the contract to continue until the actual breach occurs.

Examples

The plaintiff was employed as a courier to go on a tour of Europe commencing on June 1st. On May 11th the defendant wrote to the plaintiff informing him that his services were no longer required. The plaintiff commenced legal proceedings on the 22nd of May for breach of contract. The defendant claimed that there was no actionable breach until 1st June. The court held – the plaintiff was entitled to sue as soon as the anticipatory breach occurred on the 11th May.

The defendant had entered into a contract to supply paraffin to the plaintiff. The defendant told the plaintiff that he might not be able to supply paraffin for two months. The plaintiff then refused to take any orders from his customers. He sued the defendant for loss of profits. The defendant argued that the plaintiff should have ordered the oil regardless. The court held – the defendant's statement that he may be unable to supply paraffin was an anticipatory breach entitling the plaintiff to sue.

In case of the **refusal** of a party to the contract to fulfil its obligations under the contract, when such refusal is directly permitted by law

In case of **essential changes** to the circumstances provided for a coincidence of the following conditions:

- At the moment of concluding the contract, the parties have proceeded from the fact that no such change of the circumstances will happen
- The change of circumstances has been called forth by the causes, which the interested party could not overcome after they have arisen, within the scope of care and circumspection which have been expected from it by the nature of the contract and customs of business turnover

- The execution of the contract without amending its provisions would so much upset the balance of property interests of the parties to the contract, and would entail such loss for the interested party that it would have been to a considerable extent deprived of what it could have counted upon when concluding the contract
- Neither customs of business turnover, nor the contract presumes that the risk, involved in the change of the circumstances, shall be borne by the interested party
- Cancellation of the contract contradicts to public interests or entails losses for the parties, considerably exceeding the expenses necessary for the execution of the contract on the terms amended by the court.

Termination

The contract may be dissolved by mutual consent of the parties to the contract. In case the parties to the contract do not reach mutual consent, the contract may be dissolved by the court decision at a party's initiative in the following cases:

In case of an essential **breach** of the contract by the other party (violation of the contract by one of the parties, which entails for the other party, losses to a considerable extent, depriving it of what it could have counted upon with a proper conclusion of the contract)

In case of the **refusal** of a party to the contract to fulfil its obligations under the contract, when such refusal is directly permitted by law

In case of **essential changes to the circumstances** provided for a coincidence of the following conditions:

- At the moment of concluding the contract, the parties have proceeded from the fact that no such change of the circumstances will take place
- The change of circumstances has been called forth by the causes, which the interested party could not overcome after they have arisen, within the scope of care and circumspection, which have been expected from it by the nature of the contract and customs of business turnover

- The execution of the contract without amending its provisions would so much upset the balance of property interests of the parties to the contract, and would entail such loss for the interested party that it would have been to a considerable extent deprived of what it could have counted upon when concluding the contract
- Neither from customs of business turnover, nor from the contract it follows that the risk, involved in the change of the circumstances, shall be borne by the interested party[48]

An obligation may be terminated in the following cases as well:

Agreement

A contract is made by an agreement and equally it can be discharged or ended by an agreement. A contract may be ended by an agreement in the following manner:

- A contract may provide that it will not take legal effect unless a certain condition is satisfied, this is known as a precedent (or suspensive) condition
- A contract may be ended, provided that the other party gives the requisite notice as agreed in the contract, this is known as a subsequent condition
- A contract may be ended by another agreement. In order for such an agreement to have legal effect, it must be supported by consideration. If neither party has performed the contract then the consideration will be the excusing of both parties from their obligations under the agreement. If one party has performed their obligations and the other has not, then the party who has not performed the obligations must provide the other party with a consideration such as the payment of a cancellation fee.
- By an agreement between the parties, the obligation may be terminated by way of paying an indemnity (compensation) instead of the discharge (the payment of money, the transfer of property, etc.). The parties shall establish the amount, the term and the procedure for paying the indemnity[49].

---

[48] Civil Code, Article 451.
[49] Civil Code, Article 409.

Note

The obligation shall be terminated from the moment of giving the compensation and not from the moment of agreement of the parties on compensation[50].

From the moment of giving the compensation all obligations under the contract shall terminate, including the obligation on forfeit[51].

- The obligation may be also terminated if the creditor remits the debt, absolving the debtor from the obligations borne by him, as long as this does not violate the rights of the other parties with respect to the creditor's property[52]. The relationship between the creditor and the debtor on the debt remission shall be qualified as a donation[53]. Donations between commercial legal entities are prohibited by the Civil Code.

Performance

The proper fulfilment terminates the obligation under the contract.

While accepting the fulfilment, the creditor is obliged, upon the debtor's claim, to give him a receipt for accepting the fulfilment in full or in the corresponding part thereof.

If the debtor has issued to the creditor a promissory document to certify the obligation, the creditor, while accepting the fulfilment, shall be obliged to return it, and in case it is impossible to return the mentioned document, he is obliged to indicate this in the receipt he issues. An inscription made on the returned document may replace the receipt. The debtor's custody of the promissory document certifies the termination of the obligation, unless otherwise provided.

If the creditor refuses to issue the receipt, to return to the debtor the promissory document or to indicate in the receipt that it is impossible to return it, the debtor has the right to delay the fulfilment. In these cases the creditor shall be regarded as overdue.

A contract may be discharged or terminated when its purpose has ended.

---

[50] P.1 of the Information Letter of the Presidium of the High Arbitrazh Court of the RF, dated 21 December 2005 No.102 "Review of the Practice of Application by Arbitrazh Courts of Article 409 of the Civil Code of the RF".

[51] P.3 of the Information Letter of the Presidium of the High Arbitrazh Court of the RF, dated 21 December 2005 No.102 "Review of the Practice of Application by Arbitrazh Courts of Article 409 of the Civil Code of the RF".

[52] Civil Code, Article 415.

[53] Information Letter of the Presidium of the High Arbitrazh Court of the RF No.104, dated 21 December 2005.

Examples

A builder agreed to build a house by a certain date. The contract provided that compensation to the builder would be paid after the builder completed the house. The builder left the house incomplete and another builder was required to finish the work. The original builder sued for the work he had done. The court held – he was not entitled to compensation according to Article 711 of the Civil Code as he had not fully performed the contract as agreed.

A plaintiff's husband had been employed on a ship sailing from Jamaica to Liverpool. He was to be paid on completion of the journey. He died three-quarters of the way through the journey and his widow sued for a proportion of his wages based on the work he had done. The court held – his widow was not entitled to the wages as he had not fully performed the contract.

If time is of the essence in a contract, then late performance of such a contract will not discharge the party's obligations. Either party may make time of the essence in a contract, even though it may not necessarily have been so originally.

Example

An original contract required the building of a car chassis to be completed within seven months. The deadline passed and the purchaser agreed to wait longer. Once again, the chassis was not completed on time at which stage the purchaser served a notice requiring completion within a four-week period or he would cancel the order. The four week extension passed without delivery. The chassis was delivered three months later. The court held – the contract had not been performed as time was made of the essence.

There are a number of exceptions to the previous example, where a party may be entitled to compensation, i.e. divisible contracts, where the other party prevents performance, partial performance, etc.

In Case of Novation (Innovation)[54]

The obligation is also terminated by an agreement between the parties on replacing the primary obligation which has existed between them, with another obligation between the same persons, stipulating a different object or a different way of discharge (the novation).

[54] Civil Code, Article 414.

The novation is not admissible with respect to obligations on compensation for harm inflicted to life or health, and also with respect to those receiving alimony.

The novation terminates additional liabilities connected with the primary obligation, unless otherwise stipulated by the agreement between the parties.

Note

All essential conditions of the contract shall be agreed by the parties to terminate the obligation by novation[55].

An obligation on payment of a forfeit may be novated into a loan obligation[56].

In Case of Offset[57]

The obligation is terminated in full or in part by setting off a similar claim for which the deadline has arrived or has not been fixed, or has been defined by the moment of the demand. For the offset, the application from one of the parties shall be sufficient, i.e. the offset is a unilateral transaction.

In the following cases, offset is not permitted:

- If, by the application of the other party, the limitation period shall be applicable to the given claim, and the said term has expired
- For compensation of harm, inflicted to life or health
- On recovery of alimony
- For life maintenance.

Coincidence of the Debtor and the Creditor in One Party[58]

Frustration

Frustration[59], i.e. impossibility of the execution of an obligation, which is caused by circumstances beyond the responsibility of the parties (force majeure).

[55] P.3 of the Information Letter of the Presidium of the High Arbitrazh Court of the RF, dated 21 December 2005 No.103 "Review of the Practice of Application by Arbitrazh Courts of Article 414 of the Civil Code of the RF".

[56] P.5 of the Information Letter of the Presidium of the High Arbitrazh Court of the RF, dated 21 December 2005 No.103 "Review of the Practice of Application by Arbitrazh Courts of Article 414 of the Civil Code of the RF".

[57] Civil Code, Article 410.

[58] Civil Code, Article 413.

A contract may be discharged due to some event outside the control of either party, which occurs after the contract has been entered into and which radically alters the contract entered into by the parties.

Originally, a party could not avoid a contract where some event occurred, through no fault of his own, which rendered performance impossible or futile.

This doctrine was taken to absurd lengths in the following:

Example

In the terms of an insurance policy, it stated that the insured should inform the company of any accident within seven days. The insured died by drowning, and then didn't have the good grace to notify the company! The company was not, it was held, liable to pay out on the policy of insurance, notwithstanding that it was impossible for the deceased to meet his obligation: he should have, it was held, arranged for another person to do so on his behalf in those circumstances.

The law specified such a position. Article 401 of the Civil Code provides that unless otherwise stipulated by the law or by the contract, a person who has failed to discharge or has discharged in an improper way their obligation, while performing their business activity, shall bear responsibility unless he proves that the proper discharge has been impossible because of a force-majeure, i.e. because of extraordinary circumstances which were impossible to avert under the given conditions.

Example

A music hall was destroyed by fire. The organiser of a concert sued the hall owner for not providing him with a music venue as agreed. The court held – the contract was impossible to perform due to the destruction of the subject-matter (the hall) and was therefore discharged. The plaintiff did not succeed in his action.

Where performance of a contract will be in breach of the law, the contract will be discharged due to frustration.

Example

This case involved a contract between companies in two different countries. With the outbreak of war, any dealings between the companies were deemed illegal, as such dealings would then have been considered consorting with the enemy. The contract was frustrated.

---

[59] Civil Code, Article 416.

A contract will be frustrated due to the non-occurrence of a fundamental event to the contract.

Example

The defendant paid a deposit to hire a room from which he could view the coronation procession of Edward VII. The procession was called off due to the illness of the King and the defendant was sued for the balance. The court held – the room was hired for the sole purpose of viewing the coronation. The non-occurrence of that event led to the contract being frustrated.

It should be noted that a frustrating event terminates the contract *de futuro* (from the date of the frustrating event). Therefore, while the plaintiff in the previous example was entitled to retain the deposit (as it was paid initially as part of a valid contract), he was not entitled to sue for the remainder as the contract had been terminated.

Example

A steamboat was hired to view the coronation (above) and also the naval review, arranged as part of the proceedings. The coronation was cancelled and the hirers refused to fulfil the contract claiming that it had been frustrated. The court held – the contract had not been frustrated. While the coronation had been cancelled, this was not the sole reason the steamboat had been hired. The hirers could still view the naval review and use the boat for pleasure.

A contract will not be discharged by frustration where:

- An alternative mode of performance is still possible
- Performance simply becomes more expensive
- One party has accepted the risk that he may be unable to perform his obligations under the contract
- The counter-agents of the debtor under the contract have violated their obligations
- The commodities, indispensable for the discharge of the contract are absent on the market
- The necessary monetary means at the debtor's disposal are absent.

An act of the state body makes the performance of the obligation impossible in full or in part[60] (e.g. a cancellation of a resolution of a governor of a region on a permission (license) to conduct research and development and technological works for construction purposes)

Death of the creditor or the debtor, if the obligation is connected with the personality of the creditor or the debtor[61]

Liquidation of the legal entity[62].

Note

Death of the head of a legal entity does not incur termination of rights of the legal entity under the credit agreement, because the borrower under such transaction is not an individual, but the legal entity.

Article 452 of the Civil Code states that the agreement on changes to, or termination of a contract shall be done in the same form as such contract, unless otherwise provided for in the contract, laws or customs of business turnover.

The parties may not claim the executed under the contract prior to implementation of changes or termination of the contract.

Part X. Obligations in Tort

Chapter 59 of the Civil Code is dedicated to obligations in tort. Tort, or civil wrong, is an undue action or behaviour of an individual or a legal entity, which is within the scope of civil legislation. The word "tort" derives from the French term "avoir tort" – to be wrong. These undue actions include negligence, trespass, slander, libel and deception.

According to the general rule, an obligation in tort arises and the damages are to be reimbursed if the following requirements are met:

- Undue (unlawful) actions or deeds. The damage must have arisen from the unlawful conduct of the person alleged to have caused it. The conduct may involve taking actions that should not have been taken, or alternatively omitting to take actions that would have prevented the damage. Note that the term is "unlawful" and not

[60] Civil Code, Article 417.

[61] Civil Code, Article 418.

[62] Civil Code, Article 419.

"illegal". It is not necessary for a criminal act to have occurred for the harm to be established and this test to be fulfilled.

- Fault committed or presumed. There is fault, either through intent or negligence (carelessness or oversight) on the part of the person inflicting the damage. This does not necessarily require proof of intent to cause damage: it may arise from pure carelessness or oversight.
- Real damages present. This damage may be monetary or in kind, such as the loss of stock caused by a fire which in turn was caused by carelessness on the part of an individual. The damage may be moral or non-pecuniary in nature. It may also be physical damage to a person.
- The damages are the direct consequences of an above-mentioned deed. There must be a causal link between the damage and the conduct of the person. In practice, this must be both reasonably proximate and foreseeable. For example, the failure to drive a car with due care may cause an accident and may result in a claim for compensation, but if the injured person failed to check in for a flight as a result of the accident and that resulted in the loss of a contract to his business, the claimant may not necessarily succeed in a claim for loss of business arising from the missed flight as this may not be regarded as sufficiently foreseeable or proximate.

Losses arising from non-contractual obligations may also be compensated on the basis of *de facto* losses and missed profits.

Under the general rule, losses shall be compensated by the person who has caused those losses. However, cases arise where the losses may be payable by others. For example, if a driver crashes a car belonging to his company, there is a potential liability for the driver and the company, as ownership of the car is material to the claim. If an employee caused damage in the normal course of his or her duties, the company may be vicariously liable for his or her actions.

Therefore, a legal entity bears full responsibility for losses and damages caused by its employee to any third party, if such losses and damages were caused while exercising by the employee his labour or contractual obligations and functions.

If damages or losses were caused by a group of persons, the person who suffered losses may sue all or any of these persons at the choice of the injured for the full amount of losses and damages (joint and several liability).

The member of the group who has reimbursed the full amount of damages and losses may in his turn sue the others for reimbursement in the respective proportion.

Moral Damage

Article 1099 of the Civil Code provides that "moral damage" (emotional distress) is moral and physical suffering caused to an individual by undue actions or deeds violating his non-material rights. Moral damage caused by undue actions or deeds violating material rights is subject to reimbursement only in cases directly provided for in legislation.

Moral damage shall be reimbursed regardless of the fault of the inflictor of damages in the following cases where:

- The injury has been inflicted to life or the health of an individual by an activity with increased hazard to people around (especially dangerous objects), such as a motor vehicle
- Damages have been caused to an individual as a result of his illegal conviction, illegal proceedings against him, illegal application of remand in custody as a measure of suppression or of a written understanding not to leave his place of residence, illegal imposition of the administrative penalty in the form of arrest or correctional labour
- Damages have been inflicted by the spread of information denigrating a person's honour, dignity and business reputation.

Moral damage shall be reimbursed in monetary form.

Note

Moral damage may be inflicted only to an individual and not a legal entity.

Activity with Increased Hazard to People around (Especially Dangerous Objects)

Legal entities and individuals conducting activity associated with increased hazard to people around (use of transport vehicles, mechanisms, high voltage electric power, atomic power, explosives, building and other related activity, etc.) are obliged to redress any injury inflicted by a source of increased hazard to people around, unless they can prove that the injury has been inflicted as a consequence of force majeure or by the intent of the injured person.

An owner of a source of increased hazard to people around is not liable for the injury inflicted by this source, if he proves that the source was out of his possession as a result of the illegal actions of other people.

Owners of sources of increased hazard to people around bear joint and several liability for the injury inflicted as a result of the interaction of these sources (the collision of transport vehicles, etc.) to the third parties.

Compensation of Damages

Damages shall be compensated by the person who committed the damage.

The amount of compensation for moral damage is determined by the court, depending on the nature of physical and moral suffering caused to the injured, and also on the degree of fault of the inflictor of the damage.

The nature of physical and moral sufferings must be estimated by the court with due account of the actual circumstances under which moral damage was inflicted and of the individual features of the injured.

Damages in the course of justifiable defense and those arising in the state of absolute necessity are not subject to compensation.

The injury inflicted on an individual or a legal entity as a result of unlawful actions (inaction) of state and local self-government bodies or of their officials, including as a result of issuance of an act of a state or self-government body inconsistent with the Russian law or any other legal act, are subject to redress. The injury is redressed from the state treasury of the RF, the respective Subject of the RF or the respective municipal body, as the case may be.

Note

Damages caused during administrative court proceedings in other cases (namely, when a dispute is not settled on its merits) as a result of the unlawful actions (or inaction) of a court (a judge), including cases of violation of reasonable terms of court proceedings (if the guilt of a judge is established not by a court sentence but by some other appropriate court decision), are subject to compensation as well[63].

In case of damages caused to an individual or a legal entity by the state and by local self-government bodies or by their officials, the following is subject to compensation:

- Salary
- Pension

[63] Ruling of the Constitutional Court of the RF No.1-P, dated 25 January 2001.

- Confiscated property
- Penalty on execution of the court decision
- Fees for legal consultancy[64].

The defendant in such cases of compensation of damages shall be the MinFin of the RF[65].

Damage Caused to the Health or Life of Individuals

In case of injury to the health of an individual, the following is subject to compensation:

- The earnings (income) which have been lost by the injured person, which he had or could definitely have had
- The expenses incurred by the injury to his health, including the expenses of medical treatment, additional nutrition, acquisition of medicines, care by other people
- The sanatoria and spa treatment
- The acquisition of special transport vehicles
- The retraining, if the injured person needs such aid and care and has no right to receive such aid and care free of charge.

The amount of the earnings lost by the injured and subject to compensation, is determined in percentage of the average monthly earnings (income) before the injury, and in the absence of professional ability to work – of the degree of loss of the general capacity for work.

The average monthly earnings of the injured person are reckoned by dividing by 12 the total sum of his earnings for the 12 months of work that preceded the injury.

In case the injured does not work, the amount of his earnings before the dismissal or the usual amount of labour remuneration for the employee of his qualification in the given locality (but not less than the cost of living in the given locality) is taken into consideration according to the will of the injured.

---

[64] Decree of the Presidium of the Supreme Council of the USSR, dated 18 May 1981.

[65] Letter of the Supreme Court of the RF "On Certain Questions of the Court Practice on Civil Cases Concerning Suits to the State"; Letter published in "The Bulletin of the Supreme Court of the RF", No.10, 1997.

In case of the injury of a minor under 14 years of age, the person responsible for the inflicted injury is obliged to reimburse the expenses incurred by the impairment of his health.

In the event of injury to a minor from 14 to 18 years of age, the person who inflicted the injury is obliged to redress the injury caused by the loss of capacity for work in addition to the reimbursement of the expenses incurred by the injured on the basis of the rate of the cost of living of an employable person in the RF.

Compensation in the Event of the Death of the Breadwinner

In the event of the death of the breadwinner, the right to the redress of injury shall belong to:

- The persons incapable of work, who were dependants of the deceased person or who had by the time of their death the right to receive maintenance from that person
- The child of the deceased person which was born after their death
- One of the parents, the spouse or any other family member, regardless of his or her ability to work, who does not work or take care of the children of the deceased, grandchildren, brothers and sisters under 14 years of age or needs care by other people because of poor health under the decision of medical bodies
- The persons who were dependants of the deceased person and who have become disabled withing five years of their death.

One of the parents, the spouse or any other family member who does not work and takes care of the children, grandchildren, brothers and sisters of the deceased person and who has become disabled during the period of care, retains the right to the injury after the end of taking care of these persons.

In the event of the death of the breadwinner the injury must be redressed to the following persons:

- Minors until they reach 18 years of age
- Students over 18 years of age until graduation from their full-time educational institutions, and at least until they reach 23 years of age
- Women over 55 years of age and men over 60 years of age
- Disabled persons - for the time of disability
- One of the parents, the spouse or another family member who takes care of his dependent children, grandchildren, brothers and sisters until they reach 14 years of age, or there are changes in the state of their health.

Amounts to be paid to individuals for compensation of harm caused to life or health of the injured are subject to indexing, in the event of an increase in the cost of living, taking into account the level of inflation in the procedure and cases stipulated by law.

The redress of the injury is effected by monthly payments.

In case of reorganisation of the legal entity, the obligation to make appropriate payments shall be borne by its legal successor. Claims for the redress of injury shall be addressed to the successor of the legal entity.

Vicarious Liability

If the liability of an individual or a legal entity is *insured*, such an individual or legal entity is liable when insurance compensation is not sufficient to redress the inflicted injury.

The legal entity shall compensate for the damage caused by its employees.

Parents, adopters or trustees are liable for the injury inflicted by minors under 14 years of age, unless they prove that the injury has been inflicted not through their fault.

Minors aged from 14 to 18 years bear liability for inflicted injury on general grounds.

The court may impose liability on the parent, for an injury inflicted by a minor, within three years after the parent has been deprived of parental rights, if the child's behaviour that entailed the infliction of injury was deemed to be the result of the improper exercise of parental duties.

Article 1096 of the Civil Code and Articles 18 & 29 of the Law on Consumers' Rights stipulate that an injury inflicted owing to defects in goods is subject to redress under the option of the injured by the seller or the manufacturer of the goods.

Damage caused by the defects of works or services shall be reimbursed by the contractor who performed the works or rendered the service.

Damage caused by the defects of goods or services shall be reimbursed within the guarantee period. In case the guarantee period is not stated, damage shall be reimbursed within 10 years from the date of production of the goods (rendering of services)[66].

---

[66] Civil Code, Article 1097.

Chapter Roundup

1. The following types of transactions may be distinguished:

- Unilateral, bilateral and multilateral
- Real and consensual
- Onerous and gratuitous
- Under condition and abstract transactions

2. Forms of contracts are the following:

- Oral
- Written Form
  - Simple
  - Qualified
    - Notarisation
    - State Registration

3. Essential elements of a binding contract are:

- Offer
- Acceptance

4. A contract shall be recognised as concluded from the moment of:

- Reaching the agreement – a consensual contract
- Transfer of property – a real contract

5. The following terms are recognised to be essential:

- Subject matter of the contract
- Terms directly defined as essential for the given kind of contracts by law or by other legal acts
- All terms, about which, by the statement of one of the parties, an accord shall be reached

6. The essential features of the contract are as follows:

- Capacity of the parties
- Subject matter of the contract must be legal
- Specific form
- Contract must have an element of bargain
- Offer must contain unambiguous terms and conditions

7. Elements of due execution of obligations include:

- Term of execution
- Place of execution
- Proper person
- Subject matter of the obligation
- Way of execution
- Currency of the obligation

8. Fulfilment of an obligation may be secured by different means, such as the following remedies for beach of contract:

- Mortgage or pledge
- Surety
- Bank guarantee
- Forfeit (liquidated damages)
- Earnest money or advance
- Retaining

9. The following remedies for violation of an obligation shall be recoverable:

- Real damages
- Missed profit
- Forfeit

10. The main cases of termination of a contract are the following:

- Agreement / Novation
- Performance
- Offset
- Frustration/Force Majeure
- Act of State Body
- Death or Liquidation

11. An obligation in tort arises and the damages are to be reimbursed if the following requirements are met:

- Undue Action or Deed
- Fault Committed or Presumed
- Real Damages Present
- The Damages are the Direct Consequences of the Deed

12. Vicarious liability rules shall be applied in the following cases:

- Employer for employee
- Parents for children up to 14 years of age
- Insurance company for a person who inflicted damage
- Manufacturer for seller in case of defects in goods

Questions

1. Which of the following transactions is the unilateral transaction?

- Obligation on insurance
- Obligation on surety
- Obligation on custody
- Refusal of inheritance

2. Transactions between a legal entity and an individual shall be done in which of the following forms?

- Orally
- In simple written form
- By keeping silence
- In any form

3. Transactions between individuals of a sum exceeding 10,000 roubles shall be concluded in which of the following forms?

- In simple written form
- In notarised form
- Orally
- In any form

4. Non-observance of the simple written form deprives the parties of the right, in confirmation of the transaction, to refer to what?

- Written evidence
- Witness evidence
- Expertise
- Exhibits

5. A transaction is deemed to be invalid from the moment of what?

- Unilateral restitution
- Bilateral restitution
- Recognition as invalid by the court decision
- Its conclusion

6. In relation to contract law:

(a) Describe what is meant by "freedom to contract" and explain the limitations that exist under the Russian law in respect of this freedom.

(b) Explain the ways in which a contract may be terminated.

7. A commercial bank gave credit to a company limited by shares (J-SC) under the pledge of goods, at the warehouse of the company limited by shares. Under the agreement the goods must have been transported to the bank's warehouse within three days from the moment of signing the agreement. However, as there was no place at the bank's warehouse the transportation did not take place. In five days from the conclusion of the agreement, the warehouse of the company limited by shares was robbed and the goods were stolen to the value of 100,000 roubles. The goods were also damaged. The pledged goods were damaged and stolen, valuing 20,000 roubles.

The company limited by shares filed the suit on reimbursement of losses to the bank thinking that it was the bank's fault. While trying the case the following circumstances were discovered: the signalling was not in order when the goods were stolen and the pledged goods were not insured.

Required:

Give reasonable explanations as to whether the company limited by shares or the bank shall bear any liability.

Further Readings

1. A.Shashkova, Financial & Legal Aspects of Doing Business in Russia, M. – 2011.
2. A.Shashkova, Russian Corporate Law, M. – 2009
3. The Arbitrazh Procedural Code of the Russian Federation No.95-FZ, dated 24 July 2002
4. The Civil Procedural Code of the Russian Federation No.138-FZ, dated 14 November 2002
5. The Civil Code of the RF, Part III No.146-FZ, dated 26 November 2001, Part IV No.230-FZ, dated 24 November 2006
6. Stepanov, Dmitry, Articles of Association as a Form of Transaction (November 17, 2009). Civil Law Review, Vol. 9, pp. 4-62, 2009. http://ssrn.com/abstract=1507850
7. SINO-RUSSIAN BUSINESS: FIVE TIPS ON RUSSIAN CONTRACT LAW. http://www.cmslegal.cn/Hubbard.FileSystem/files/Publication/c1caf231-d4bf-4450-885b-92fc3ed0649f/Presentation/PublicationAttachment/efd3b0c0-ec3c-4c91-80cd-937a486e2902/Five%20tips%20on%20Russian%20contract%20law.pdf
8. Contract law in Russia and USA. http://prezi.com/nhftwydd6oh5/contract-law-in-russia-and-usa/
9. Russian Civil Law Reform: Recent and Upcoming Amendments. http://www.morganlewis.com/pubs/RussianLawUpdate_Summer2013_Newsletter.pdf
10. Modern Russian Law of Contracts: A Functional Analysis. http://digitalcommons.lmu.edu/cgi/viewcontent.cgi?article=1510&context=ilr
11. A. Shashkova. PLEDGE – RECENT CHANGES IN RUSSIAN LEGISLATION. http://www.accaglobal.com/gb/en/student/acca-qual-student-journey/qual-resource/acca-qualification/f4/technical-articles/changes-russian-legislation.html
12. Jack Beatson and Daniel Friedman. Good Faith and Fault in Contract Law. Published to Oxford Scholarship Online: March 2012
13. Damages for breach of contract: a Russian and English law comparison. http://uk.practicallaw.com/6-504-1460
14. 10 key facts about English contract law. http://www.seqlegal.com/blog/10-key-facts-about-english-contract-law
15. *Fisher v Bell* [1961]. http://www.e-lawresources.co.uk/Fisher-v-Bell.php
16. *Balfour v Balfour* [1919]. http://www.e-lawresources.co.uk/Balfour-v-Balfour.php

17. *Bettini v Gye* [1876]. http://www.e-lawresources.co.uk/Bettini-v-Gye.php
18. *Olley v Marlborough Court* [1949]. http://www.e-lawresources.co.uk/Olley-v-Marlborough-Court.php
19. KEY ASPECTS OF THE LAW OF CONTRACT AND THE TORT OF NEGLIGENCE. http://www.accaglobal.com/gb/en/student/acca-qual-student-journey/qual-resource/acca-qualification/f4/technical-articles/key-aspects-of-the-law-of-contract-and-the-tort-of-negligence.html
20. DAMAGES. http://www.accaglobal.com/gb/en/student/acca-qual-student-journey/qual-resource/acca-qualification/f4/technical-articles/damages.html
21. THE TORT OF NEGLIGENCE. http://www.accaglobal.com/gb/en/student/acca-qual-student-journey/qual-resource/acca-qualification/f4/technical-articles/tort-negligence.html
22. ICC INTRODUCES NEW INTERNATIONAL COMMERCIAL TERMS. http://www.accaglobal.com/gb/en/student/acca-qual-student-journey/qual-resource/acca-qualification/f4/technical-articles/icc-introduces-new-international-commercial-terms.html
23. Ralph H. Folsom, Michael W. Gordon. International Business Transactions: A Problem-Oriented Coursebook. 2012.
24. INCOTERMS 2010: ICC OFFICIAL RULES FOR THE INTERPRETATION OF TRADE TERMS. http://www.searates.com/reference/incoterms/fca/
25. INCOTERMS 2013. http://www2.miq.com/cms/INCOTERMS2013/
26. Incoterms Definitions. http://www.universalcargo.com/blog/bid/94731/Incoterms-Definitions-Part-3-DAT-DAP-DDP
27. UN Convention on Carriage of Goods by Sea (Hamburg, 1978)
28. UN Convention on Contracts for International Sale of Goods (1980)
29. UNCITRAL Model Law for ICC (1985)
30. UN Conventions on International Bills of Exchange & International Promissory Notes (NY, 1988)
31. UNCITRAL Model Law on International Credit Transfers (1992)
32. UN Convention on Independent Guarantees & Stand-by Letters of Credit (NY, 1995)
33. UNCITRAL Model Law on Electronic Commerce (1996)
34. UNCITRAL Model Law on Cross-Border Insolvency (1997)

CHAPTER THREE

THE FORMATION AND CONSTITUTION OF BUSINESS ORGANISATIONS

Part I. Overview

Since the dissolution of the USSR, various types of companies, in particular the J-SC, LLC and the commandite (limited) partnerships, have replaced state enterprises and associations of state enterprises as the principal organisational forms in the Russian economy. The enactment of the Civil Code and the J-SC Law, and the conversion of large state enterprises into J-SCs in the process of privatisation have facilitated the development of investment and business activities in Russia.

The Civil Code recognises various forms of business organisations, including general and commandite partnerships, LLCs, open and closed J-SCs, and state and municipal unitary enterprises[1]. Russian legislation does not contemplate a joint venture as a separate business entity. Instead, foreign investors may act as founders, participants or shareholders of any entity, organised in a form, recognised by the Civil Code.

Classification of legal entities is provided in the Civil Code four times: in Article 48, Article 50, Article 65 and in Article 66.3. All classifications are very important, because the assignment of a legal entity to a particular group determines its special legislative regime.

Classification Based on the Rights of the Legal Entity and its Participants

The First Model

The essence of the first model lies in the fact that founders (participants) of the legal entity completely lose their rights of estate to their property when transferring that property to the business entity.

---

[1] Civil Code, Articles 69-115.

Similarly, they do not have these rights to the acquired property. Accordingly, property transferred by founders (participants) and acquired by the legal entity itself is deemed to be owned by the legal entity. Losing its rights of estate, a founder (a participant) acquires corporate rights instead. Corporate rights mean that founders have a right to participate in such legal entities and form its highest management body. Legal entities built by the first model include partnerships, companies, production and consumer cooperatives.

The Second Model

The peculiarity of the second model is that the founder, transferring corresponding property to the legal entity in the possession and disposal, remains the owner of that property. Also, the founder is deemed to be the owner of all property acquired by the business entity during its operation. Therefore, the rights of estate for one and the same property are possessed both by the founder (owner) and by the legal entity. The legal entity owns the property under the right of economic management or operative management, derivative from the property right. The given model is applied to the state and municipal unitary enterprises, and organisations, financed by the owners (institutions). In particular, these are organisations whose owner is the RF, a Subject of the RF or a municipal entity (a ministry, a department, a school, an institute or a hospital, etc.).

The Third Model

Finally, according to the third model, the legal entity becomes the owner of all the property in its possession. Unlike the first and the second models, founders (participants) of the legal entity do not possess any property rights for the legal entity, neither rights of obligation, nor rights of estate. Such legal entities include public and religious organisations (unions), charities and other funds, associations and unions of legal entities.

The difference between the above-mentioned three models is most apparently revealed when a business entity is being liquidated. Participants of a legal entity that is built according to the first model have the right to demand the property left in part corresponding to their share (half, quarter, etc.). Founders of a business entity formed according to the second model receive everything that is left after settlements with creditors. According to the third model, founders (participants) do not acquire any rights for the property left, after the liquidation of an entity.

Classification Based on the Rights of Participation in the Legal Entity

In corporate legal entities participants have a right to participate in the legal entities and form its highest management body. Such legal entities include partnerships, companies, production and consumer cooperatives.

Corporate rights include the following:

- To get information and be acknowledged with the booking balance of the legal entity
- To appeal decisisons of the management bodies of the corporation
- To claim compensation of damages on behalf of the corporation
- To appeal transactions of the corporation.

In unitary legal entities, participants do not get a right to participate in the legal entities. Such legal entities include funds, institutions, autonomous non-commercial organisations, etc.

Classification Based on Publicly Placed Shares

J-SC is public in case of public/open quotation of its shares. In case it is not directly named that the legal entity is public it is dedemed public in case open subscription for shares of such company is admitted. A collective executive board of at least 5 persons shall be formed in a public J-SC. A collective supervisory board of at least 5 persons shall be formed in a public J-SC.

Note

LLCs and Closed J-SCs are non-public legal entities.

Classification Based on the Activity's Objective: Commercial and Non-Commercial Legal Entities

The second classification holds a binomial characteristic. Article 50 of the Civil Code of the RF divides all business entities into commercial and non-commercial organisations, proceeding from the objective of the activity performed by the organisation. Business entities may be either organisations which view the deriving of profits as the chief goal of their activity (commercial legal entities), or those organisations which do not view a deriving of profits as such a goal, and which do not distribute the derived profit among their participants (non-commercial legal entities).

Commercial legal entities include partnerships and companies, production cooperatives, state and municipal unitary enterprises, while non-commercial legal entities include consumer cooperatives, public and religious organisations (unions) financed by their owners, charities and other funds, and other legal entities stipulated in law that possess the above-mentioned characteristics.

Non-commercial organisations have the right to carry out entrepreneurial activity, provided that they meet two conditions simultaneously: first, such entrepreneurial activity is to serve for the achievement of goals set before the organisation, and second, this activity is to be performed in a way appropriate for achieving these goals. The gained profit may not be distributed among participants of non-commercial organisations.

Part II. Non-Commercial Legal Entities

A non-commercial legal entity is a company which does not have profit as the main purpose of its business and does not distribute the profit gained among its members. A non-commercial legal entity executes its activities on the basis of the Law on Non-Commercial Organisations. The law distinguishes the following types of non-commercial legal entities:

- Consumer cooperatives
- Public organisations, including political parties
- Associations and unions, including non-commercial partnerships, self-regulated organisations, unions of employers, Notary and Lawyers' Chambers
- Property real estate partnerships
- The Cossack societies
- Societies of Indigenous people of the RF
- Funds
- Institutions
- Autonomous non-commercial organisations
- Religious organisations
- Public law companies.

Notes

The Law on Non-Commercial Organisations does not require state registration of non-commercial organisations of certain types. In case such organisations do not have state registration they may perform their functions, but may not conflict with the interests of third parties. Contracts concluded by such organisations are void.

The law states that non-commercial organisations shall be liquidated in case of the systematic execution of activities contradictory to their charter goals.

Business Activity of Non-Commercial Organisations

According to Article 50 of the Civil Code, non-commercial legal entities may engage in business activity only in case:

- It helps them to achieve those goals for which they have been established, and
- Business activity is of the kind that corresponds to those goals.

Thus non-commercial legal entities have special (not general) contractual capacity. Notwithstanding the special contractual capacity of non-commercial legal entities, Chapter 25 Profit Tax of the Tax Code, defines taxpayers without paying attention to the commercial or non-commercial categorisation of a legal entity.

There are also certain limitations on the business activity of non-commercial legal entities.

Examples

Article 121 of the Civil Code stipulates that if the participants of the association (the union) decide that the association will perform business activities, such association shall be transformed into a commercial legal entity.

Article 12.4 of the Law on Charity Organisations prohibits charity organisations to participate in commercial legal entities together with other individuals or legal entities.

Article 825 of the Civil Code provides that only commercial legal entities may act as agents in a contract of factoring.

Under Article 1015.1 of the Civil Code the trust administrator in the contract of trust of property may be only a commercial legal entity or an individual entrepreneur.

Part III. Commercial Legal Entities. Partnerships

Commercial legal entities are the following:

- Commercial partnerships and companies
- Production cooperatives
- State and municipal unitary enterprises.

Commercial Partnerships and Companies

Types of commercial partnerships and companies are the following:

- The general (unlimited) partnership
- The commandite (limited) partnership
- The economic partnership[2]
- The J-SC
- The LLC.

The Commercial Partnership

Special Features

Commercial partnerships and companies have the following characteristics:

- They are commercial organisations with authorised (joint) capital, divided into shares (investments) of founders (participants)
- Property, formed for account of the founders' (the participants') contributions and the property produced and acquired by the commercial partnership or by the company in the process of its activity, belong to the commercial partnership or company under the right of ownership
- The charter capital and the property gained at the process of business activity of the commercial partnership or the company belongs to the commercial partnership or to the company under the right of ownership.

The General (Unlimited) Partnership

The formation and operation of general partnerships is governed by Articles 69-81 of the Civil Code. A general partnership is established by the agreement between two or more individual entrepreneurs or legal entities. A person may participate in only one general partnership. Each partner bears unlimited joint and several liability for obligations of the partnership with their entire property.

The trade name of the partnership contains either the names of all its partners and the words "unlimited partnership", or the name of one or of

---

[2] Since 1 July 2012. The Federal Law No.380-FZ "On Ecomonic Partnerships", dated 3 December 2011.

several of its partners, with the words “and Co.” and “unlimited partnership” to be added.

The constituent document of the partnership is the constituent agreement (partnership agreement), which may provide for joint conduct of partnership operations, or alternatively each partner has the right to operate in the name of the partnership. A general partnership must enter into contracts in the name of one of its partners. The profits and losses of a general partnership are distributed among the partners in proportion to their share in the stated joint capital, unless the constituent agreement provides for otherwise. Partners in a general partnership may transfer their shares in the partnership with the consent of other partners. A partner in a general partnership may not engage in transactions similar to those set forth in the partnership’s constituent agreement on its own behalf or in the interest of the third parties without the consent of other partners.

All management decisions are taken with the unanimous consent of the partners, although the constituent agreement may provide for majority voting in the event of failure to reach a unanimous decision, or on certain other issues. Each partner has one vote unless the constituent agreement provides for otherwise.

Characteristics

The general partnership has the following characteristics:

- Participants (general partners) of the general partnership bear responsibility of the general partnership by its obligations with all property in their possession, including personal property
- A person has the right to be a participant of only one general partnership
- Every partner must take part in the management (general meeting of participants (hereinafter – GM)). Special management bodies are not constituted in the general partnership.

Rights of Participants

Every partner has an absolute right, which may not be altered by an agreement, to leave the partnership at any time, provided that he gives notice of no less than six months to other partners. If the withdrawal of a partner leaves the partnership with only one partner, the partnership must be liquidated or reorganised into an LLC.

The cost of the share of the partnership's property is paid out, corresponding to this participant's share in the joint capital, to the participant who has withdrawn from the general partnership.

In case one of the participants has withdrawn from the partnership, the shares of the remaining participants in the partnership's joint capital correspondingly increase.

The participant of the general partnership has the right, with the consent of the rest of its participants, to transfer its share in the joint capital, or a part thereof, to another participant of the partnership or to a third party.

Liability of Participants

Participants bear joint and several liability for obligations of the general partnership. A participant who has withdrawn from the general partnership is liable for obligations of the partnership that have arisen before the moment of their withdrawal, on par with the rest of the participants, within two years from the date of the approval of the accounting report on the activity of the partnership for the year the participant withdrew from the general partnership. An agreement of the general partnership participants on the restriction or elimination of such liability of participants is void.

Levies on the Participant's Share in the Joint Capital

The seizure of the participant's share in the joint capital of the partnership by the participant's own debts is admissible only if its own property proves to be insufficient to cover its debts. Creditors of such a participant have the right to demand from the general partnership that it separates the part of the partnership's property that would correspond to the debtor's share in the joint capital, so that the penalty may be subjected to this property. The part of the partnership's property subject to being singled out, or the cost thereof, shall be defined by the balance sheet as compiled at the moment when creditors file the claim for it to be separated.

The Commandite (Limited) Partnership

Limited partnerships are governed by Articles 82-86 of the Civil Code and also by provisions of the Civil Code which apply to general partnerships, to the extent that such provisions do not contradict Articles

82-86 of the Civil Code. A limited partnership is an independent legal entity formed by an agreement between two or more individual entrepreneurs or legal entities to engage in joint economic activity. The difference between a general partnership and a limited partnership is that in a limited partnership, there are two types of participants: general participants and limited participants. Such "limited partners" are generally liable up to the amount of their respective capital contributions, subject to the limitations in Articles 53.3, 56.3 and 105 of the Civil Code. The maximum number of limited partners in a commandite partnership is 20.

The limited (commandite) partnership is a partnership in which, alongside the partners who are engaged in the performance of the business activity on behalf of the partnership and are responsible for the obligations of the partnership with their property (the general partners), there is (are) also one or several participant investors (commanditaires), who bear the risk of the losses in connection with the partnership's activity within the amount of their investments and who do not take part in the performance of the partnership's business activity.

The participant of the general partnership shall not be the general partner in the commandite partnership.

The trade name of the commandite partnership shall contain either the names of all its partners and the words "limited partnership" or "commandite partnership", or the name of at least one of its general partners and the words "and Co.", and also the words "limited partnership" or "commandite partnership".

If into the trade name of the partnership is included the name of the investor, this investor shall become the general partner.

Characteristics

A limited partnership has the following characteristics:

- General partners form the main part of the limited partnership
- Limited partners only bring contributions to the limited partnership
- Limited partners do not answer with their property under obligations of the limited partnership. Limited partners may lose only their contributions to the limited partnership.

The advantages of the commandite partnership are:

- Simplicity
- Control.

The disadvantages are:

- The unlimited liability of general partners
- The limited ability to raise capital.

The commandite partnership shall terminate or fundamentally change with the withdrawal or death of a partner.

Rights and Obligations of Partners

Partners may freely transfer their share in the partnership subject to the priority right of other partners to acquire such shares. They are entitled to withdraw from the partnership at the end of the fiscal year and receive their contribution to the partnership in accordance with the constituent agreement. A general partner in a limited or general partnership may be a partner with full liability in only one partnership at any given time.

A limited partnership operates on the basis of a constituent agreement which contains:

- General information
- The amount and composition of the partnership's contributed capital
- The procedures for making capital contributions
- The procedures for changing the amount and composition of the general partners' participatory shares.

The general partners in a limited partnership conduct the management of the partnership in the same manner as in a general partnership. Limited partners do not have the right to participate in the management of the limited partnership (i.e. do not vote). However, they do have the right to receive a share of the profits of the partnership proportionate to their contribution as provided in the constituent agreement.

Article 73.2 of the Civil Code (which appears to apply to limited partnerships pursuant to Article 82.5 thereof) provides that a general partner must contribute 50% of its capital share at the time of the partnership's registration[3], and must contribute the remaining portion within the period established by the constituent agreement. If such contributions are not made on time, the general partner must pay a penalty

[3] This provision of the Civil Code concerning limited partnerships differs with the provisions of the Civil Code concerning LLCs. In the case of an LLC, any or all of the participants may contribute 50% of the charter capital of the LLC prior to the state registration of the LLC.

of 10% annual interest on the uncontributed portion and compensate the partnership for any resulting losses, unless the constituent agreement provides for otherwise.

A general partner in a limited partnership may transfer part or all of its partnership interest to a third party with the consent of other general partners. A limited partner may transfer its share to the third party subject to the priority right of other limited partners to purchase such shares.

The limited partners of a limited partnership have the following rights:

- To receive part of the partnership's profit, due for their share in the joint capital, in conformity with the procedure stipulated by the constituent agreement of the limited partnership
- To be instructed of the partnership's annual reports and balances
- At the expiry of the fiscal year, to withdraw from the partnership and to withdraw their investment in conformity with the procedure laid down by the constituent agreement of the limited partnership
- To transfer their share in the joint capital or a part thereof to another limited partner or to a third party.

Liquidation

The limited partnership must be liquidated if all limited partners have withdrawn from it. However, general partners have the right, instead of liquidating the limited partnership, to transform it into a general partnership.

In case of liquidation of the limited partnership, limited partners have the priority right before general partners to get back their investments from the property of the partnership left after creditors' claims have been satisfied.

The property of the partnership left after this, shall be distributed among general partners and limited partners proportionately to their shares in the partnership's joint capital.

The Economic Partnership

On 1 July 2012 a new type of commercial legal entity came to life. The economic partnership is a mix between a company and a partnership, that makes it quite a flexible vehicle of the economic activity: high control of the partnership is combined with limited liability of the company. It is a Russian version of a European limited partnership.

The economic partnership shall not be formed by way of reorganising an existing legal entity. Though the economic partnership can be reorganised only through its transformation into a J-SC.

The economic partnership shall not be a founder of other legal entities but associations and unions of legal entities.

Note

The law provides no norm for the term of formation of the statutory capital as well as no minimum statutory capital. Such a term shall be agreed by the participants in the Agreement on Management of the partnership. The volume of the statutory capital is not public information, only shares of participants in the statutory capital shall be disclosed. Persons who are parties to the Agreement on Management of the partnership, but not participants of the economic partnership shall not be included into the register. This may result in a legal entity without any real property, and persons dominating the partnership being without any liability before creditors.

Statutory capital contributions shall not include securities, excluding those securities satisfying certain requirements, e.g. securities under bank guarantee.

The economic partnership shall not issue any securities, including bonds. It cannot advertise its activity. Still, the economic partnership is presumed to have general legal capacity.

Participants of the Economic Partnership

Participants of the economic partnership are at least 2 persons:

- Natural persons
- Individual entrepreneurs
- Legal entities.

The maximum number of participants is 50 persons. In case the number of participants becomes more than 50, the economic partnership shall be reorganised into a J-SC within 1 year. In case of non-reorganisation, the economic partnership shall be liquidated.

New participants shall be admitted to the economic partnership only under the unanimous vote of the existing partners. Rights and obligations of a participant will be transferred to the new participant according to the special agreement between a new participant and the rest of the participants, which becomes an integral part of the Agreement on Management of the partnership.

In case of the sale of shares, other participants have the priority right to buy those shares. The term to exercise such rights is within 30 days from the date of receipt by the partnership of the offer to sell the share.

A participant shall not pledge their share, unless otherwise provided by the Agreement on Management of the partnership.

The economic partnership may buy and transfer its shares without any limitations.

Participants may withdraw from the economic partnership in case it is provided by the Agreement on Management of the partnership with three months prior notice. In case of contribution to the statutory capital of the right to use property, such a right shall stay at the disposal of the partnership, unless otherwise provided by the Agreement on Management of the partnership. Withdrawal of the last participant is prohibited.

A participant may be excluded from the partnership under a court decision. This provision is similar to the provision on LLCs. In case of the unanimous vote of the rest of the participants of the economic partnership, or in case of non-contribution in due time of their part of the statutory capital, a participant may be excluded from the partnership without recourse to the court.

Statutory Documents

The law provides for the Charter of the partnership and the Agreement on Management of the partnership.

The Agreement on Management of the partnership and any changes thereto shall be subject to the notary's endorsement, but shall not be subject to state registration. Thus the Charter of the economic partnership is the only statutory document of the partnership.

In case of amendments to the Agreement on Management of the partnership, each participant shall have one vote, regardless of the volume of their contribution to the statutory capital. This document shall not be taken into consideration while concluding agreements with third parties.

The Agreement on Management of the partnership may provide disproportional rights of participants to the volume of their contributions to the statutory capital or restrictions in share transfers.

Note

Such important information as disproportional rights of participants shall be set not in the Charter of the economic partnership, available for creditors and other third parties, but in the Agreement on Management of the partnership, which is an internal document.

Liability

Liability of the economic partnership is separate – the economic partnership is liable to its obligations with the entire property in its possession; participants are not liable to obligations of the partnership and bear the risk of losses in the amount of their contributions to the statutory capital.

The main distinctions between the liability of an economic partnership and the liability of an LLC are the following:

- In case creditors of the economic partnership put execution on the exclusive rights on the results of the intellectual activity of the partnership, any or all participants of the economic partnership may execute obligations before the creditors on behalf of the partnership[4]
- There is a possibility of provision in the agreement with the creditors of the partnership of the partial or complete termination of obligations of the economic partnership before the creditors in case of occurrence of the events indicated in the agreement.

Management Bodies

Management in the economic partnership shall be effected by a CEO (e.g., a general director), who shall be elected from the economic partnership's participants. Such a management body shall be elected for the term stipulated in the Charter of the economic partnership, or according to the unanimous decision of the economic partnership's participants, for the whole term of the partnership's activity.

The CEO shall carry the Register of participants.

The Particular (Simple) Partnership Agreement

Particular partnership is the simplest business form that involves more than one person. It relies on a formal agreement between the partners in the business and anything not covered in the partnership agreement relies on a high degree of trust between the business principals. No special legal entity is created.

Under the contract of particular partnership (the contract for joint activity) two or several persons (the partners) undertake to pool their

[4] Article 3.4 of the Partnerships Law.

contributions and to act jointly without forming a business entity for the deriving of profit or for the achieving other goals consistent with law[5].

Parties to the particular partnership contract, dedicated to execution of entrepreneurial activity, shall be only business entities or individual entrepreneurs.

Definition of a Partnership

A partnership is a relationship which exists between persons carrying out business in common with a view to making profit.

Business Carried on in Common

This requirement essentially means that in order for a business to constitute a partnership, each partner must effectively be the agent of the other partner for the purpose of business.

Making Profit

A relationship will only constitute a partnership where it is carried on with the intention of making profit if possible.

It is not essential that the business actually turns a profit. It is sufficient if that what the parties intended.

An agreement between two or more persons to share returns or profits is *prima facie* evidence of a partnership. However, such an agreement does not itself constitute evidence of a partnership.

Liability

If a contract of particular partnership is not associated with the business activity of its participants, each partner shall be liable for the common contractual obligations within all their property in proportion to the value of his contribution to the common business.

The partners shall be liable jointly for common obligations not arising from the contract.

Termination

A partnership is terminated:

---

[5] Civil Code, Article 1041.

- By agreement
- On dissolution of the contract of particular partnership by notice of one of the partners
- On repudiation of either partner to participate in the particular partnership contract of unlimited duration
- If either of the partners lacks active legal capacity, is recognised as restrictedly capable or missed for an unknown reason
- In case of death, reorganisation, liquidation or insolvency of either partner if the contract of particular partnership does not provide for maintenance of the contract herewith or for a substitute
- On expiry of the term of the partnership
- On alienation of the partner's share under the claim of the creditor
- By the state bodies in case the business of the partnership is for an illegal or improper purpose.

The Investment Partnership[6]

A particular form of a simple partnership – an investment partnership – has been provided for by Russian legislation since 1 January 2012. Some similarities between an investment partnership and a limited partnership are obvious. It is a form in between a simple partnership and organisational forms of partnership.

The particularity is the form of the contract – such a contract is subject to notarisation. No notary's certification is required in case of amendments to the contract under the initiative of one of the parties under the court decision[7].

The investment partnership contract shall be concluded for a fixed-term period of not more than 15 years.

Parties to the contract may be both commercial legal entities, individual entrepreneurs and non-commercial legal entities in case of execution of entrepreneurial activity. Foreign legal entities and other associations shall also be admitted.

The number of parties allowed is from 2 to 50. No limitations on participation in several investment partnerships are stated.

There are two types of parties to the contract: managing and non-managing partners. Joint activity of the investment partnership shall be executed by the managing partner or managing partners of the investment

---

[6] The Federal Law No.335-FZ "On the Investment Partnership", dated 28 November 2011.

[7] Article 450.2 of the Civil Code, Article 17.2 of the Investment Partnerships' Law.

partnership. Such a managing partner shall be a legal entity. Joint matters shall be adopted by the joint agreement of the partners.

Only a managing partner may contribute non-monetary means to the common activity of the investment partnership.

Liability of managing and non-managing partners differs. Liability of non-managing partners is limited by their contribution to the joint property of the partnership. Managing partners are jointly liable before any third parties – subjects of entrepreneurial activity.

Note

In contrast to the particular partnership contract, the investment partnership contract shall not be terminated in case of a change of the parties to the contract.

Distinctions between Commercial Partnerships and Companies

A Partnership - General	A Company
Association of persons	Association of capital
Participants must directly (personally) take part in business activity of a partnership	It is sufficient for participants to take part in business activity of a company by capital participation
Based on the constituent (partnership) agreement	Based on the Charter
Participants are only legal entities and individual entrepreneurs	Participants can be any subjects of civil law of the RF
Cannot be founded by one person	Can be founded by one individual or legal entity only
The activities are only the activities of a partnership itself. Partners manage the partnership themselves	Rights and obligations of a company are accrued by the activities of the management bodies of a company. Special management bodies are created for management of the company
Full partner may be only in one partnership	Participation in multiple companies is possible
There is no minimum requirement for the Charter capital	Minimum amount of Charter capital is established by law (proper capitalisation)
Business name includes the name of at least one of its participants	No similar requirement

Full property subsidiary liability	No property liability. Participants bear only the risk of losses in the amount of the contributions to the company
Should terminate or fundamentally change with the withdrawal or death of a partner	Has perpetual succession
No statutory requirement	Requires strict compliance with formalised statutory obligations (e.g. record keeping, reporting, shareholder communications)

Commercial partnerships and companies of one type may be transformed into commercial partnerships and companies of another type or into production cooperatives, under the decision of the GM.

In case a partnership is transformed into a company, each general partner, who has become a participant (a shareholder) of the company, shall bear subsidiary responsibility within 2 years with his entire property under the obligations, which have passed to the company from the partnership.

Part IV. Legal Personality

The business entity is deemed to be an organisation, which has in its ownership, economic management or operative management of set-apart property, and which is answerable by its obligations with this property and may on its own behalf acquire and exercise property and personal non-property rights, discharge duties and appear as a plaintiff or as a defendant in the court.

A company is a commercial or non-commercial legal entity that is formed and registered in the relevant state bodies of the RF. Both commercial and non-commercial legal entities must be registered in the local departments of the Tax Service of the RF.

A business entity exists in law entirely separate from its owners, also called participants or shareholders, and directors, who manage the company. The company is therefore a legal person having a separate legal identity; this feature is also referred to as corporate personality. Legal entities have an independent balance or an estimate.

Main Features of a Business Entity – Separate Legal Personality

The main features of a business entity are the following:

- **Unity of the organisational structure of a company**

That means that a company has its internal structure and its interdependent elements, which together form an organic whole (management bodies). Such unity of the organisational structure is expressed in the constituent documents of a business entity. The form of the organisational unity is the organisation's constituent document (the Constituent Agreement (Memorandum of Association), the Charter), in individual cases, provisions adopted on the basis of general provisions concerning organisations of that type. It means that a legal entity possesses a corresponding stable structure.

The acting of a business entity as a whole is guaranteed by the fact that a corresponding entity is headed by a body (or bodies) with the defined powers. Such a body (or bodies) executes interior management of the business entity and acts in external relations on behalf of the business entity. Those who are situated inside of the legal entity (managers and employees) must know what the given entity is, what are its current and future activities, who manages it and how, what its property is, etc. The same is equally important for those who are planning to enter, or have already entered legal relations with that entity.

- **Separate estate of a company**

The content (implementation) of this characteristic is the legal provision required from founders in order to form the entity's aggregate (for economic companies) or charter (for other legal entities) capital. No business entity may be set up without aggregate or charter capital, since its absence would mean the impossibility to meet creditors' claims or a lack of any commercial risk for founders.

Separate estate of a legal entity also means that the estate of a company is separated from the estate of all other subjects of civil relationships: the property of a legal entity shall be separated from the property of its founders (participants). The volume of separate estate differs: the highest volume of the separate estate is personal property (ownership) of a company. There must be an accounting aspect of a separate property: the balance (when a company has personal property or property under its economic management) or the estimate (when a company has property under its operative management). Disposal of set-apart property by other rights (such as for example, the right of lease) is not allowed.

A company has its own bank account. A business entity has its own name as well.

- **Independent property responsibility**

The business entity also bears independent property responsibility for the entirety of the property in its possession.

Note

Such provision of the Civil Code shall be interpreted in the way that a business entity shall answer not only with the property in its ownership, but as well with advance payments on its bank accounts, loans and other funds which the business entity does not possess under the right of ownership.

Unless otherwise stipulated by law or by the constituent documents, neither administrators nor participants of the business entity are responsible for debts, and subsequently, the business entity is not responsible for debts of its founders (participants).

Participants of a general partnership bear joint and several liability for the obligations of the general partnership.

In case the insolvency (bankruptcy) of the legal entity has been caused by the participants, by the owner of the legal entity's property or by other persons who have the right to issue obligatory instructions for the legal entity or may determine its actions in any other way, if the legal entity's property proves to be insufficient, the subsidiary liability of the legal entity's obligations may be imposed upon such persons.

- The ability to act in civil turnover on its own behalf (conclusion of contracts, acting as a claimant or a defendant in court, etc.)

A business entity's ability to act on its own behalf is implemented by the fact that each entity has its own official name, which is stipulated in its Charter or other constituent documents as of the moment of state registration. The official name of the entity specifies its type of activity and the legal-organisational form, and thereby specifies the entity and singles it out as a subject of civil turnover.

The ability to act in civil turnover on its own behalf means that branches or representative offices of a company can act only on behalf of the company that formed them. A company is liable under its obligations with all of its property.

These four characteristics of a legal entity comprise its "separate personality", which can be summarised to the following:

- The business entity has separate property either under the right of ownership or under the right of economic or operative management
- 'Property' has broad meaning: things, rights on those things and obligations considering those things
- Property shall be separated from property of the founders or participants/shareholders of the legal entity
- The concrete form of separate property is either a legal entity's own financial balance (for commercial organisations) or its own budget (for non-commercial organisations).

Only when demonstrating all four characteristics may a legal entity participate in civil turnover as such. Inclusion of a legal entity into the Unified State Register for Legal Entities is a prerequisite, sufficient and at the same time indisputable proof of the fact that the given entity is deemed to be a legal entity according to the established procedure. Collective establishments that are not business entities do not have the right to act in civil turnover on their own behalf.

If wrongful actions by the management of the company or its shareholders has been proven, the corporate veil shall be lifted.

Consequences of State Registration

- Separate corporate personality of the company. Any business assets are owned by the company itself and not by shareholders. This is normally a major advantage in that the company's assets are not subject to claims based on the ownership rights of its members. The company has a contractual capacity in its own right and can sue and be sued in its own name. Contracts are entered into in the company's name and the company is liable for any such contracts
- Limited liability of members for the indebtedness of the company. As stated, limited liability is a statutory development and not a necessary consequence of the recognition of corporate personality
- Transferability of interests means that the shares can be transferred between individuals and the company remains unaffected
- Perpetual succession – a company continues to exist until it is wound up or otherwise dissolved, regardless of any change of shareholders, directors etc. As the corporation exists in its own right, changes in its membership have no effect on its status or existence. Members may die, be declared bankrupt or insane, or

transfer their shares without any effect on the company. As an abstract legal person the company cannot die, although its existence can be brought to an end through the winding up procedure

- Floating charges – state registration enables a legal entity to use charges over assets as security for borrowings. A floating charge is an equitable charge which hovers over assets which match a description, e.g. stock-in-trade. The company can continue to deal with those assets until the charge crystallises and becomes fixed on the assets remaining in that category. A fixed charge attaches to specific identifiable property and the company is restricted in its dealing with that asset
- Large membership – membership of an LLC or a closed joint-stock company is limited, but a company can involve large numbers of people
- Taxation – there are different, and at times beneficial tax regimes for companies, e.g. small business entities
- Legal actions – a company can file a law suit and be sued
- Statutory obligations – a company is subject to statutory obligations of registration.

Legal Capacity of a Legal Entity

A business entity enjoys civil rights that correspond to the goals of its activity stipulated in its constituent documents, and discharges duties relating to this activity.

The legal capacity of a company begins from the moment of the registration of that company, and is determined by law and the constituent documents of the company. The legal capacity of a legal entity shall terminate from the moment of the recorded exclusion of that legal entity from the Unified State Register of Legal Entities. The legal capacity of a company can be limited by law, it is dependent on the purposes of activity of a company, which are listed in the constituent documents of that company.

A company is liable for its delicts. That means that a company is liable for its own actions and for the actions of representatives who are acting on behalf of the company.

Types of Legal Capacity of a Business entity

There are different types of legal capacity:

- **General legal capacity**

Possessing general contractual capacity, a business entity may carry out all kinds of activities not prohibited by legislation. As a rule, all commercial legal entities possess general contractual capacity, except for state and municipal unitary enterprises and some other types of legal entities stipulated by law (e.g. insurance organisations may not perform production, banking or trading activity).

This type of legal capacity is usual for most commercial legal entities, excluding, for example, insurance and banking organisations, which are acting under the corresponding license and thus possessing special legal capacity.

Notes

A commercial organisation, including an LLC or a J-SC, which does not contain a closed list of goals in its Charter may not be rejected in obtaining the license on the grounds that the licensed type of activity is not provided by the constituent documents of the legal entity.

Expiration of a license after the conclusion of a contract does not create grounds for finding the contract invalid[8].

- **Special legal capacity**

Special contractual capacity implies that a legal entity may only perform certain activities. Non-commercial legal entities and special commercial legal entities (e.g. unitary enterprises, banks or insurance organisations) possess special contractual capacity.

The law allows for the restricting of the contractual capacity of any commercial legal entity even in cases when such restriction is not required by law. In this case founders of the legal entity shall draw up necessary clauses in the legal entity's constituent documents. The fact that a commercial business entity has a restricted contractual capacity has important legal implications. Any transaction effected by the commercial legal entity in contradiction with the goals set in that legal entity's constituent documents may be regarded as null and void by the court decision.

Non-commercial legal entities have only those rights and obligations which correspond to the aims of the activity of the business entity

---

[8] Ruling of the Presidium of the High Arbitrazh Court of the RF No.3386/07, dated 17 July 2007.

stipulated in the constituent documents. Those legal entities which conduct their activities under license have special legal capacity.

Subject matters of the legal capacity of a company are the following:

- Types of activities of a company, which a company conducts at its own discretion
- Licensed types of activities of a company. To conduct such types of activities a company must obtain special permission, i.e. a license.

Limitation of the Legal Capacity of a Legal Entity

Legal capacity of a company can be limited by the following:

- By law
- By the necessity of a special license for certain types of activities of a company
- By constituent documents of a company. In this case a business entity itself limits its activities by stipulating special aims in its constituent documents.

Note

Finding the constituent agreement null and void does not presume the lack of legal capacity of a legal entity to perform a disputable transaction.

Part V. Creation of Business Organisations

One or more Russian or foreign business entities and individuals may establish a Russian legal entity, except that an entity 100% owned by another person or entity may not be the sole founder of a J-SC or an LLC.

The formation of a business entity in Russia, including J-SCs and LLCs, generally does not require prior approval by any governmental entity (other than, under certain circumstances, the Anti-Monopoly Service).

Each type of Russian business entity is formed upon the adoption by its founders of a Charter and/or constituent agreement, and the registration of such documents, so a legal entity is subject to state registration.

Issuance of shares by a J-SC must be registered with the Central Bank[9]. The notification and approval procedures must be followed with respect to the acquisition of a J-SC's stock.

---

[9] Financial Markets' Service transferred its powers to the Bank of Russia under the Federal Law No.251-FZ, dated 23 July 2013.

The registration of a legal entity is conducted in accordance with the Law on Registration of Legal Entities.

The state registration of business entities is deemed to be conducted and the legal entity recognised as created at the moment of entry to the Unified State Register of Legal Entities.

The state body which conducts the state registration of a business entity is the local department of the Tax Service. The local department of the Tax Service makes the decision on creation, reorganisation and liquidation of a legal entity, as well as amendments and modifications to the Charter of a legal entity.

Registration of an entity may be denied only if the filing or procedures followed by its founders were improper. The local department of the Tax Service, denying registration, is obliged to give written notice of a decision to refuse to register an entity within 5 working days from the date of the submission of documents. If the registration is improperly denied, the denial may be appealed in court and the responsible local department of the Tax Service found liable for losses to the business entity.

Certain types of legal entities are registered according to special procedures. Banking and other credit institutions must obtain a license from the Central Bank[10]. Activities in industries such as mass communications[11], brokerage[12], insurance[13], oil and gas[14] and other natural resources require special licensing or permissions from relevant authorities.

Trade registration shall be carried out in the RF for business entities, effecting trading activity.

The Constituent Documents of a Legal Entity

The legal entity operates on the basis of the Charter, or of the constituent agreement and the Charter, or only of the constituent agreement. In law-stipulated cases, a business entity, which is a non-commercial legal entity, may operate on the basis of the general provisions made for that type of legal entity.

---

[10] Law on Banks and Banking Activity, Article 1.

[11] Law on Mass Communications No.2124-1, dated 27 December 1991, Article 15.

[12] Securities Market Law, Article 39.

[13] Law on Insurance, Article 6.

[14] Law on Subsoil Resources, Article 11.

The Constituent Documents of Legal Entities

Legal entities, except commercial partberships, base their activity on the Charter.

Partnerships base their activity on the Constituent agreement[15].

The Agreement of Formation

Both the J-SC Law and the LLC law provide that the founders shall sign an agreement of formation of the company[16]. The court practice confirms that the agreement of formation is not a constituent document of the company.

The Charter

The Charter is the fundamental law of the company. The Charter is the condition upon which the company is granted incorporation, and the company is therefore bound by its content. The company is allowed to exist on the basis that its activities are within the parameters of what it says it will do in the Charter. This enables persons outside the company who invest in or deal with the company to ascertain what its name is, what its objectives are, what its liability is and what the charter capital is.

A legal entity created by a sole founder, operates on the grounds of the Charter approved by this founder, and the decision of the founder to create such a legal entity.

The charter capital of a Russian entity is a fixed amount, representing:

- The officially stated amount contributed to the company by its founders/shareholders
- The minimum amount of net capital that should be maintained by the company at all times for the purpose of ensuring creditor protection, and
- For a J-SC, the sum of the nominal values of all issued (floated) shares.

The required charter capital amounts are calculated as of the date of a company's registration.

---

[15] Civil Code, Article 52.

[16] In the case of an LLC, a similar document is called the agreement of *establishing* the company.

Contributions to the charter capital include money, securities, other property and property titles, intellectual property in the form of the right of use of that intellectual property, or other rights with a monetary evaluation. The minimum statutory capital shall be paid by a corporation only in money.

If a participant who has contributed a right to use his property for a specified period of time is expelled (or withdraws), this property remains at the company's disposal until that period of time expires.

Functions of the charter capital are the following:

- The property contributed to the charter capital is the material ground for the company, especially at the moment of starting business
- The stake of a participant or shareholder shall be determined on the basis of the volume of contribution by the participant to the charter capital of the company
- The volume of the charter capital represents the minimum property amount to guarantee interests of the company's creditors.

Amendments

Every company has the right to amend the Charter. The amendments made in the constituent documents, come into force for third parties from the moment of their state registration.

The Name and the Place of Location of a Legal Entity

The legal entity has its own name, which contains an indication of its organisational form. The names of non-commercial legal entities, and in cases specified by law, the names of commercial legal entities shall contain an indication of the nature of the business entity's activity. Non-compliance of the name of the legal entity with the legislation of the RF may be grounds for refusal of the state registration of the legal entity[17].

The place of location of a business entity is determined by the place of its state registration indicated in the Unified State Register for Legal Entities. The state registration of a legal entity is carried out at the location of an executive management body thereof. In case of the absence of the executive management body, the registration of a legal entity is carried out by another body or person empowered to act on behalf of the legal entity.

---

[17] Federal Law No.88-FZ, dated 19 May 2010.

Legally meaningful messages shall be delivered to the address stipulated in the Unified State Register for Legal Entities. The legal entity shall bear the risk of absence at this address, as in such case legally meaningful messages shall be considered to have been delivered properly.

The legal entity which is a commercial organisation, has a trade name. The legal entity has the exclusive rights to the use of its trade name.

The Branches (Subsidiaries) and the Representative Offices

There may be two types of structural subdivisions of a business entity:

- Set-apart subdivisions of a legal entity, such as branches and representative offices
- Subdivisions of a legal entity, situated at the place of location of a legal entity, such as divisions, services, departments, etc.

The representative office is a set-apart subdivision of the business entity, situated outside of the place of location of the legal entity, which represents and protects the legal entity's interests.

The branch is the business entity's set-apart subdivision, situated outside of the place of location of the legal entity and performing all its functions or a part thereof, including the functions of representation.

Representative offices and branches of a legal entity shall be indicated in the Unified State Register of Legal Entities.

Do Branches and Representative Offices Have the Status of Legal Entities?

Under Article 105 of the Civil Code neither representative offices nor branches have the status of a legal entity. They are given the property of the legal entity and operate it in conformity with the provisions approved by the business entity.

Notes

A transaction under which a branch secures an obligation of a business entity, whose structural subdivision such a branch is, shall be deemed not to be concluded.

A transaction concluded by a branch on its own behalf and without necessary powers, is void under Article 168 of the Civil Code.

To create a representative office or a branch of a foreign business entity, such a legal entity has to first get accreditation for the representative office or the branch in the State Registration Chamber of the

RF[18] within 12 months from the date of the decision on the formation of a branch, and then register it in the local department of the Tax Service. If permission is necessary, it is granted by the appropriate federal ministry, depending on the type of activity of the foreign business entity. Accreditation may take up to 25 working days.

The branches and the representative offices incur tax liability themselves according to Article 19 of the Tax Code.

The branches and the representative offices may open current and settlement accounts in banks.

The heads of the representative offices and the branches are appointed by the legal entity and act on the basis of the power of attorney, provided by the legal entity.

The representative offices and the branches must be provided for in the constituent documents of the business entity.

The relationships between the representative offices and the branches of the legal entity and the business entity are based on:

- The decision on the creation of the branch or the representative office
- The constituent documents of the legal entity
- Articles on the branch or on the representative office
- A power of attorney, given to the head of the branch or of the representative office.

[18] From 1 January 2015 accreditation of foreign branches and representative offices will take place in the Federal Tax Service.

Basic Forms of Business Entities Representing Foreign Interests in the RF

Provision	Representative Office	Branch	LLC
Status	Structural set-apart subdivision of a foreign legal entity	Structural set-apart subdivision of a foreign legal entity	Legal entity
Functions	Represents and protects a foreign legal entity's interests	Performs all functions of a foreign legal entity or a part thereof	Any type of business activity under Russian law provided by the charter of the LLC
Activity	Only such types of representative functions which may be accounted by the chief accountant to be representative	All functions of a foreign legal entity or a part thereof as provided in the statutory documents of the foreign legal entity and the articles on the branch	Any activities not contrary to Russian law
Types of business activity prohibited	Any	That which is not provided in articles on the branch	• That which is not provided in the charter • Licensed types of activity without such a license • Any directly prohibited by law of the Russian Federation
Liability	Very limited	Very limited	• Liable for its own activity • Not liable for the obligations of its participants

Liability of the principal (parent) legal entity	The foreign legal entity and not the representative office bears liability for obligations of the representative office as the representative office is a subdivision of the foreign legal entity	The foreign legal entity and not the branch bears liability for obligations of the branch as the branch is a subdivision of the foreign legal entity	Two types of liability of the principal company under the obligations of the daughter company: Joint and several liability under the transactions, concluded by the daughter company when the principal company has used the right to give obligatory instructions to the subsidiary company Subsidiary liability in case of bankruptcy, which has occurred under the fault of the principal company. The insolvency (bankruptcy) of a subsidiary company shall be considered to have occurred through the fault of the principal company only when the principal company has used the right to give obligatory instructions to the subsidiary company, being aware that as a consequence of actions of the subsidiary company thereof, the insolvency (bankruptcy) of the subsidiary company shall follow. In other cases no liability

Documents for registration	• Written application for opening a representative office signed by the head of the foreign legal entity • Registration certificate or extract from the trade register • Charter of the foreign legal entity • Decision of the foreign legal entity on establishment of a representative office in Russia • Recommendation letter from the bank of the foreign legal entity • Power of attorney for the head of the representative office in Russia • Power of attorney for a person effecting registration and accreditation of the representative office • Articles on the representative office • Document certifying a business address in Russia	• Written application for accreditation and inclusion of a branch into the state register signed by the head of the foreign legal entity • Registration certificate or extract from the trade register • Charter of the foreign legal entity • Decision of the foreign legal entity on establishment of a branch in Russia • Bank letter on solvency of the foreign legal entity • Power of attorney for the head of the branch in Russia • Power of attorney for a person effecting accreditation of the branch • Articles on the branch • Document certifying business address in Russia • Recommendation letters from Russian partners of the foreign legal entity • Card with the information on accreditation	• Written application signed by the head of the LLC • Copies of founder's statutory documents and an extract from the trade register • Signed resolution of the management body of the founder, authorising the establishment of the Russian LLC • Charter and constituent agreement of the LLC • Minutes of meeting of founders approving the constituent documents of the LLC • Bank letter on solvency of the foreign legal entity • Reference from the bank on notification of the local department of the Tax Service on opening of the settlement account • Reference from the bank on payment of 50 per cent of the charter capital • Minutes on appointment of the director • Document certifying business address Foreign documents shall be legalised or apostilled, translated into Russian, translation notarised Majority of documents refer to LLC

	• Recommendation letters from Russian partners of the foreign legal entity • Card with the information on the representative office • Reference from the revenue service of the country of the registration of the foreign legal entity Foreign documents shall be legalised or apostilled, translated into Russian, translation notarised Majority of documents refer to the foreign legal entity	• Document on the coordination with administrations of the subjects of the Russian Federation • Expert examinations in cases provided by Russian law • Reference from the revenue service of the country of the registration of the foreign legal entity Foreign documents shall be legalised or apostilled, translated into Russian, translation notarised Documents will be looked through by Russian authorities more thoroughly than in case of a representative office or an LLC Majority of documents refer to the foreign legal entity	

Registration procedure and term	• Accreditation at the Federal Tax Service (at least 1 month, extra fee – 1 week) • Seal of approval (1-3 days) • Registration at the Tax Service (at least 5 business days) • Statistics registration (1-3 days) • Funds (social insurance, medical, pension) (1-3 days)	• Accreditation at the Federal Tax Service (at least 1 month, extra fee – 1 week) • Seal of approval (1-3 days) • Registration at the Tax Service (at least 5 business days) • Statistics registration (1-3 days) • Funds (social insurance, medical, pension) (1-3 days)	• Registration at the Federal Tax Service (at least 5 business days) • Statistics registration (1-3 days) • Funds (social insurance, medical, pension) (1-3 days)
Minimum registration expenses	• Accreditation. Fee for 1 year - RUR 35,000 (approximately – 1,060 USD); for 2 years – RUR 65,000 (approximately – 1,970 USD); for 3 years – RUR 80,000 (approximately – 2,420 USD) OR • Accreditation in the Chamber of Commerce and Industry. Fee for 1 year – USD 1,500; for 2 years – USD 2,500; for 3 years –	• Accreditation. State duty for branch - RUR 60,000 (approximately – 1,800 USD) • Accreditation fee for 1 year - USD 500; for 2 years – USD 1,000; for 3 years – USD 1,500; for 5 years – USD 2,000 • Registration fee	• Minimum charter capital – RUR 10,000 (approximately 300 USD) • Registration fee – RUR 2,000 (approximately USD 60)

	USD 3,500 • Registration fee		
Double taxation	Applicable in case bilateral double taxation treaty is signed between the countries	Applicable in case bilateral double taxation treaty is signed between the countries	Not applicable
Personnel hiring	Russian citizens and citizens of the country of origin of a foreign legal entity without permission, others with permission of the Ministry of Internal Affairs of the Russian Federation	Russian citizens and citizens of the country of origin of a foreign legal entity without permission, others with permission of the Ministry of Internal Affairs of the Russian Federation	Russian citizens without permission, others with permission of the Ministry of Internal Affairs of the Russian Federation
Contractual capacity	On behalf of the foreign legal entity within the representative and protective functions	On behalf of the foreign legal entity in the fields authorised by articles on the branch	On its own behalf, any contracts not prohibited by law
Funds in the settlement account	• Received only from the foreign legal entity • Spent only on representative functions, which may be accounted by the chief accountant to be representative	• Received from the foreign legal entity or from its own business activity • No limitations on spending	• Received from its own business activity • No limitations on spending

Powers of the chief executive officer (CEO) stipulated	• In the articles on the representative office • In the power of attorney May not act *ultra vires*	• In the articles on the branch • In the power of attorney May not act *ultra vires*	• In the Charter • Acts without power of attorney Shall not be deemed to act *ultra vires* in case actions are further approved by the authorised bodies
Liability of the CEO	Full financial liability for the direct damage to the representative office and the foreign legal entity	Full financial liability for the direct damage to the branch and the foreign legal entity	Full financial liability for the direct damage to the LLC
Dismissal of the CEO	Power of attorney may be revoked at any time	Power of attorney may be revoked at any time	At any time by the general participants' meeting

Liability of a Legal Entity

A legal entity is liable under its obligations with all its property.

A participant of the legal entity or an owner of its property is not liable under the legal entity's obligations. The legal entity is not liable under the obligations of the participant or of the owner of its property.

In case the insolvency (bankruptcy) of the business entity has been caused by the participants, by the owner of the business entity's property or by other persons who have the right to issue obligatory instructions for the business entity or may determine its actions in any other way, if the business entity's property proves to be insufficient, the subsidiary liability of the business entity's obligations may be imposed upon such persons.

Part VI. Legal Status of Foreign Persons in the Russian Federation

The law, applicable to civil legal relations involving participation of foreign individuals or foreign legal entities or civil legal relations complicated by another foreign factor, in particular, in cases when an object of civil rights is located abroad, is determined on the basis of international treaties of the Russian Federation, the Civil Code and other laws and customs recognised in the Russian Federation.

Note

The Ruling of the Supreme Court of the Russian Federation No.9-G02-16, dated 7 July 2002, states that the Russian courts are obliged to consider cases with participation of foreign persons notwithstanding presence or absence of an international treaty of the Russian Federation with the country of citizenship of the foreign person or persons.

If an international treaty of the Russian Federation contains provisions governing a relevant relation, norms of law of conflict are prohibited to apply.

Foreign law shall be applicable in the Russian Federation, irrespective of the applicability of Russian law to similar relations in the relevant foreign state, except for cases when the application of such foreign law on a reciprocal basis is required by law.

Where the application of foreign law depends on reciprocity, such reciprocity shall be deemed to exist unless the contrary is proven.

Imperative Norms

Article 1192 of the Civil Code states that imperative norms of Russian law must be applied irrespective of the law that is subject to application.

Relevant Laws and Regulations

The basic law governing foreign investment is the Foreign Investments Law. The law provides for greater protection of foreign investors than existed before, and regulates foreign entrepreneurial activity in Russian territory. It also offers tax benefits to foreign investors investing more than 1 billion roubles in a project and protects such investors from some future tax increases. The law is generally clear and consistent with other legislation, and therefore provides a stable framework within which foreign investors may operate. Investments in the banking and insurance sectors are regulated by separate respective laws.

The Foreign Investments Law must be read in conjunction with the Civil Code, the J-SC Law, the LLC Law, the Privatisation Law, the Securities Market Law and accompanying regulations, as well as banking, foreign currency, tax, customs and other legislation which affects foreign investment.

The Russian Federation is also a party to international conventions, multilateral treaties and bilateral treaties which could affect specific foreign investments. The Russian Federation has accepted the international obligations of the former Soviet Union, including all treaties that have not been replaced with the treaties signed by Russia.

With respect to conditions for admitting foreign capital to the national economy of the Russian Federation, the current international economic inter-state cooperation most commonly operates with two notions:

- The regime of "national treatment", and
- The regime of "most favourable treatment" ("most favourable nation treatment").

The National Treatment Regime

Definition of a Foreign Investor

A foreign investor may be any individual or legal entity, who/which is a citizen of a foreign state or is registered in a foreign state, and is authorised to conduct investments under the law of that foreign state.

International organisations and foreign states also fall under the "foreign investor" definition[1].

According to the Foreign Investments Law, foreign investors enjoy the same treatment regarding investment activities, referred to as a "national treatment regime", which means that they are subject to the same benefits and restrictions as Russian investors[2]. Any additional restrictions imposed upon foreign investors may be introduced by federal laws only.

Under the Foreign Investments Law, legal treatment of foreign investors' activity and their use of profit from investments may not be less favourable than those set for Russian investors, with the following exceptions:

- Stimulating exceptions (benefits) may be established only in the interests of development of the Russian Federation (forms and procedures of granting benefits are stipulated by Russian legislation)
- Restrictive exceptions may be stipulated by federal laws only for protecting the foundations of the constitutional order, morality, health, rights and lawful interests of other persons and to ensure the country's defense and state security.

The national treatment regime does not mean that a foreign investor turns into a national subject of law or, in other words, legally changes their citizenship. The investor does not change their legal status either, from that which was established by the legislation when the investor was set up (registered).

Types of Foreign Investment

Legal regulation of foreign investment depends on the type and forms of the foreign investment. There are two types of foreign investment:

- Public investment, and
- Private investment.

Public investment is, as a rule, effected in the form of international agreements on loans, credits, etc. to the socio-economic infrastructure of the host country.

Private investment has the following forms:

---

[1] Foreign Investments Law, Article 2.

[2] Constitution, Article 62; Civil Code, Article 2.

- Real or direct investment, e.g. buying enterprises, presenting credit lines
- Portfolio investment, e.g. investment into securities, participation in partnerships and companies.

Foreign investment is an investment of foreign capital into objects of business activity in the territory of the Russian Federation. Foreign investment shall be deemed any of the following:

- The obtaining by a foreign investor of 10% or more of the charter capital of a commercial partnership or company
- The investment of capital into capital funds of a branch of a foreign legal entity, registered in the Russian Federation
- The leasing by a foreign investor of capital assets with the customs value of not less than 1 billion roubles.

Activities Open to Foreign Investment

The Foreign Investments Law provides that foreign investments may be made in all sectors of the economy except those prohibited by law (there are currently very few prohibitions). In certain industries, such as oil and gas and insurance, restrictions exist on the percentage of shares which may be held by foreigners. Further restrictions may be found in Charters of individual companies, but as the Foreign Investments Law provides that additional restrictions on foreign investors may only be made by federal laws, such provisions (if contested in court) are unlikely to be effective.

Certain transactions, under which more than 25% of direct or indirect control over a Russian business entity is acquired, are subject to preliminary approval under Articles 9-12 of the Federal Law No.57-FZ "On the Order of Foreign Investment into Russian Business Entities of Strategical Importance to the National Defence and the Security of the State", dated 29 April 2008.

Registration of Business Entities with Foreign Investment

Foreign investment regulations in Russia do not establish a single registration or licensing authority for foreign investments. Registration of business entities with foreign investment or acquisitions of interests by foreigners must be completed according to the same procedures as business entities with no foreign investment.

Forms of Investment

Russian legislation permits the establishment of a wholly foreign-owned company or a joint venture company in any legal form recognised by the Civil Code, the most common of which are J-SCs and LLCs. The size of the investment is not limited, except that Russian business entities must have the minimum charter capital required by the applicable legislation. Higher requirements may be imposed for entities conducting activities in certain fields, such as banking or financial services.

In addition, Russian law permits the acquisition of all or part of an existing entity or other property or property rights.

Capital Contributions by Foreign Investors

Contributions to the capital of a Russian entity may be made in cash or in-kind. Cash contributions by foreign investors may be made in foreign currency or in roubles obtained from an authorised bank or received as revenues from activities in the Russian Federation.

In-kind contributions generally may be valued by the agreement between the parties (although certain requirements for independent appraisals do exist), but the value should be in line with market prices or there is a risk that it will be challenged during the registration process or by other authorities in the future.

Protection of Investments

The Foreign Investments Law grants foreign investors certain protections with respect to their investment activity in Russia, including the following:

- Foreign investors may enjoy all forms of legal protection of their interests and rights as provided for by the Civil Code, other laws of the Russian Federation, and international treaties
- Foreign investments can be made in any form which is not prohibited by laws of the Russian Federation
- All rights and property of foreign investors are assignable in accordance with the Russian legislation, and
- A foreign investment (which would include loans) may not be expropriated or nationalised except in accordance with applicable

legislation, in which case the foreign investor must be compensated for losses[3].

Guarantees

In accordance with the legislation of the Russian Federation, foreign investors are guaranteed to have the following rights:

- To freely use income and profit for reinvestment and to transfer it outside Russia in relation to investments made earlier, including:

    (i) Profit, dividends, interest on investments
    (ii) Money paid to honour obligations under contracts and other transactions
    (iii) Money received from liquidation of a commercial legal entity with foreign investments or a branch of a foreign legal entity, and due to alienation of invested property, rights of estate, etc.
    (iv) Compensation due for requisition or nationalisation of property.

- To freely take out of Russia property and information initially imported as foreign investment
- To be secured against enforced seizure of property, including requisition and nationalisation (except for cases and grounds stipulated by a federal law or an international treaty). If the property is requisitioned, its value must be paid. If the circumstances relating to requisition cease to prevail, the investor may demand, applying to court, that the requisitioned property be returned, provided the compensation amount is repaid, accounting for losses from the decreased value of property. If the property is nationalised, its value and other losses must be compensated. The compensation will be equal to the value of the asset expropriated at the time of expropriation. If the asset is nationalised, the compensation should also include other related damages, including loss of profit
- To acquire shares and other securities of Russian commercial legal entities and government securities, according to the Russian legislation on securities
- To acquire land plots, other natural resources, immovable property, according to the legislation of the Russian Federation and the

[3] Foreign Investments Law, Article 8.

subjects of the Russian Federation[4]. Commercial legal entities with foreign investments may acquire the right to lease a land plot at an auction, unless otherwise provided for by the legislation of the Russian Federation

- To transfer rights and obligations. Under Russian legislation, a foreign investor is able to transfer their rights and obligations to another legal entity if it is provided for by law or under a court decision
- To receive indemnification for damages caused by unlawful action (inaction) of state bodies, local self-government bodies or their officials
- To participate in the privatisation of facilities in state and municipal ownership, on terms and under procedures stipulated by the legislation on privatisation.

Additional Guarantees to Foreign Investors (Grandfather's Clause)

'Grandfathering' is a concept that is widely applied in international business relations. Its aim is to promote and maintain the confidence of those who choose to do business across international frontiers. One of the many risks faced by such persons and businesses is that future political and economic change may compromise the position of the foreign investor. For example, a future government may enact legislation that is prejudicial to the interests of foreign participants in the economy who might then be unable to recover their investments.

The Russian legislation envisages additional guarantees to foreign investors against unfavourable changes in legislation, but only in case a foreign investor executes, in Russia, a so-called "priority" investment project, i.e. a project where:

- Total foreign investments amount to at least 1 billion roubles (such projects may be implemented both with foreign investor's participation in a Russian commercial legal entity or without it)
- The share of foreign investors in the charter capital of a Russian commercial legal entity is at least 100 million roubles (such projects may be implemented only with foreign participation in the Russian legal entity).

---

[4] Article 15 of the Land Code states that foreign citizens, foreign legal entities or Russian legal entities where the participation of foreign capital is 50% or more, may not have land at the state border of the Russian Federation at the right of ownership.

Note

The Foreign Investments Law and supplemental legislation provide some incentives for foreign investors: property which is to be contributed to the charter capital of a Russian entity is not subject to customs duties[5].

Priority investment projects are to be included in the list approved by the Government of the Russian Federation.

If newly issued federal laws and other normative acts of the Russian Federation which make the status of such an investor, who has already invested in a Russian project, less favourable:

- Resulting in increase of an aggregate tax burden on activity of foreign investors and commercial legal entities with foreign investments
- Setting a regime of prohibitions and restrictions relating to foreign investors,

such acts do not apply to foreign investors and commercial legal entities implementing priority investment projects during the payback period, not reaching more than seven years. Different payback periods are set by the Government of the Russian Federation according to the types of investment projects[6].

An aggregate tax burden is determined as the total amount due to the budget and to non-budgetary funds. An aggregate tax burden does not include:

- Customs duties introduced for the protection of state interests of the Russian Federation
- The value added tax (VAT) and the excise tax on goods manufactured in the Russian Federation
- Charges to the Pension Fund as a portion of the unified social tax[7].

Changes in an aggregate tax burden due to changes in legislation are calculated proceeding from the burden, effective as of the date when the financing of the priority investment project starts.

---

[5] Decision of the Government of the Russian Federation No.883 "On Exemptions from Import Customs Duty and VAT for Commodities Imported by Foreign Investors as a Contribution to the Registered (Shared) Capital with Foreign Investments", dated 23 July 1996.

[6] Foreign Investments Law, Article 9.

[7] Foreign Investments Law, Article 9.

Goods imported to Russia under the investment project that enjoys the guarantee from unfavourable changes in legislation are to be used exclusively for implementing such a project.

According to the international practice, this regime is secured by international treaties.

Examples

The Treaty between the Government of the Russian Federation and the Norwegian Government "On Trade and Economic Cooperation", dated 26 March 1996, stipulates the establishing of the national treatment regime with respect to the access of individuals and business entities to the court and administrative bodies.

The Treaty between the Russian Federation and the USA "On Stimulating and Mutual Protection of Investments", dated 17 June 1992, stipulates the establishing of the national treatment regime with respect to foreign investment.

A Most Favourable Treatment Regime

A foreign investor enjoying a most favourable treatment regime gets rights and obligations equal to the rights and obligations of investors from other countries – participants to similar treaties.

Examples

The Treaty between the Government of the USSR and the Government of the United Kingdom of Great Britain and Northern Ireland "On Stimulating and Mutual Protection of Investments", dated 6 April 1989, stipulates the establishing of a most favourable treatment regime with respect to foreign investments and compensation of damages, concerning investments.

The Treaty between the Government of the Russian Federation and the Cabinet of Ministers of Ukraine "On Stimulating and Mutual Protection of Investments", dated 27 November 1998, stipulates the establishing of the national treatment regime and a most favourable treatment regime with respect to foreign investments.

Regime of Granting Preferences

Another term applied in the international practice is the regime of granting preferences. Strictly speaking, it is not a separate regime, since it grants preferences only to individual categories of investors or to an individual investor (usually those from neighbour states) and such a regime is not applied to other, third countries. Generally, the possibility to grant preferences is considered by the parties to the treaty.

Examples

Article 3.3 of the Treaty between the Government of the USSR and the Government of the Republic of Finland "On Stimulating and Mutual Protection of Investments", dated 8 February 1989, establishes that "the regime envisaged by the treaty does not cover privileges and preferences that one of the parties to the treaty grants with respect to investments and income of investors from third states on the basis of agreements on economic union, customs union or free trade zones, on developing international economic cooperation or on avoiding double taxation".

Article 3.3 of the Treaty between the Government of the Russian Federation and the Cabinet of Ministers of Ukraine "On Stimulating and Mutual Protection of Investments", dated 27 November 1998, establishes that "the regime envisaged by the treaty does not cover privileges and preferences that one of the parties to the treaty grants with respect to investments and income of investors from third states on the basis of agreements on economic union, customs union or free trade zones, on developing international economic cooperation or on avoiding double taxation".

Restrictive Exceptions

Restrictive exceptions from the national treatment regime are established only by federal laws.

Examples of restrictive exceptions are the following:

- Establishing the quota of foreign capital in the banking system of Russia
- Prohibition of the activity of intermediaries in the area of insurance that implies conclusion of insurance contracts on behalf of foreign insurance companies.

Restrictive exceptions from the national treatment regime in individual cases are established by bilateral agreements on protection of investments.

Examples

Under the Treaty signed between the USSR and the USA "On Stimulating and Mutual Protection of Investments", dated 17 June 1992, each party to the treaty assumes an obligation to admit, on its territory, investments of citizens and business entities of another party under conditions of a specific

- "mixed"- treatment regime. Thus, the USSR and the USA kept the right to preserve or establish in future restrictions for investors of another party, but only with respect to the stipulated list of activities. The USA included 18, and the USSR 17 activities. The list of the USSR included insurance, banking, state grants, land ownership, subsoil use and use of other natural resources, immovable property ownership and activities related to that ownership, acquisition of state and municipal property in the course of privatisation, state loans (credits), activities in the sphere of mass media, etc.

Later on the parties to the above treaty to a certain extent implemented the restrictions: thus, on 4 August 2001 the State Duma of the Russian Federation introduced into Article 19.1 of the Law on Mass Media the amendment prohibiting foreign business entities and Russian business entities with more than 50% foreign participation from being founders of television and video programmes.

Disputes among foreign investors and the state or foreign investors and Russian business entities are to be heard by Russian courts, unless otherwise provided by law or, if so agreed by the parties, by domestic or foreign arbitration. Settlement by an international dispute resolution body is permissible if provided for by an international treaty.

Liquidation of Foreign Investment Business Entities

The Foreign Investments Law provides only that liquidation shall be carried out according to the Civil Code and other relevant legislation, including the Bankruptcy Law.

Legal Immunity of a Foreign State

Immunity of the state means that no state may execute its power on another state.

Types of immunity of the state in international law are the following:

- Immunity from the legislation of the foreign state
- Jurisdiction immunities: court immunity, immunity from the preliminary security of the suit, immunity from the execution of the decision
- Immunity of the state property

Immunity of the state may be recognised as:

- **Absolute**

In this case the state acting in the international economic relations acts as a sovereign and therefore shall enjoy absolute immunity in those transactions.

- **Limited**

When the state acts in civil or civil international transactions as a usual subject of civil law the immunity of the state is limited to the proportions which permit the state to fulfil its obligations and bear liability for the obligations (e.g. the immunity does not cover commercial activity of an international organisation not provided by international agreements, the charter and the agreement on headquarters).

A foreign state enjoys legal immunity in Russia with respect to:

- A claim presented to it in the Arbitrazh court of the Russian Federation
- Its involvement in proceedings in the capacity of a third party
- Arrest of property belonging to the foreign state and located in the territory of the Russian Federation
- The court measures against the foreign state to secure the suit and property interests.

Levy into this property shall be admissible only with the consent of the competent bodies of the corresponding state, unless otherwise provided for by an international treaty of the Russian Federation or by a federal law.

The legal immunity of international organisations shall be determined by an international treaty of the Russian Federation and by a federal law.

Part VII. Reorganisation and Liquidation of Business Organisations

In Russia, a legal entity may be terminated in the following ways:

- By reorganisation
- By voluntary or compulsory liquidation
- By bankruptcy
- By dropping the company (not a legal way to terminate the company).

The business entity may be terminated according to the decision of participants or by a court decision.

Grounds for Termination of Business Entities

Grounds for Termination of a Business Entity according to the Decision of Participants	Grounds for Termination of a Business Entity by a Court Decision
• Expiration of the term of formation of a business entity • Achievement of goals of formation of a business entity • Multiplication or reduction of the number of participants of a legal entity, which have come to contradict the Charter or the law of the RF • Court decision on invalid registration of a legal entity due to irremovable violations of legal acts • Insolvency (bankruptcy) • Under other circumstances	• Business activity without a special permission (license) • Business activity prohibited by law • Multiple and gross violations of law and other normative acts • Systematic activity of a public or religious organisation, charity or other fund, not provided by the Charter of such a business entity • Insolvency (bankruptcy) • Other cases, provided by law

Reorganisation of a Business Organisation

Within 3 working days of the decision on reorganisation of a legal entity, the legal entity must inform (in writing) the Federal Tax Service indicating the type of reorganisation that will occur. An LLC, after the inscription in the Unified State Register of Legal Entities of the reorganisation commencement data, shall publish twice, once a month, in "The Vestnik of the State Registration" information on the reorganisation.

The creditors have the right to demand immediate fulfilment of obligations and reimbursement of damages caused to them. This demand shall be presented to the company in writing within 30 days of the final publication on reorganisation in "The Vestnik of the State Registration". Publications shall take place twice, once a month.

Joint and several liability shall be borne by the legal entities formed as a result of the reorganisation, and by persons being able to manage actions of the reorganised legal entities in case the legal entity cannot fulfil anticipatory claims of the creditor and no obligation security means are provided to the creditor.

Reorganisation may be recognised invalid in court no later than 3 months after the inscription, in the Unified State Register of Legal Entities, of the reorganisation commencement data.

Modes of Reorganisation for a Business entity

Modes of reorganisation for a business entity are the following:

- Voluntary reorganisation, under the decision of the GM of a legal entity
- Authorised reorganisation, under the consent of state bodies, if it is directly provided by law (e.g. a federal government entity)
- Compulsory reorganisation, under the decision of the authorised state bodies or the court, if it is directly provided by law.

Forms of Reorganisation of a Legal Entity

Reorganisation of a legal entity may be held in one of the following forms:

- **Merger**

A merger is the establishment of a new company with the transfer to it of all rights and duties of two separate companies, the dissolution of the latter shall be recognised as the merger of companies.

The decision to exercise the merger of companies must be taken by the GM of each of the companies.

The GM of each of the companies also approves the contract of merger as well as a draft of the Charter of the newly created company and the transfer act.

The contract of a merger must be subsequently signed by all participants of the newly created company, and will form together with the Charter, the constituent documents of the newly created company.

In case of the merger of companies, all rights and obligations of each company pass to the company that is set up as a result of the merger in conformity with the transfer act.

- **Take-Over (Acquisition)**

Take-over is the dissolution of one or several companies with the transfer of all their rights and obligations to another company.

The BD of each company submits for decision at the GM participating in the take-over, issues concerning reorganisation in the form of a take-over and concerning approval of the take-over agreement.

The BD of the annexing company additionally submits for decision at the GM, the issue of the approval of the transfer act.

The joint GM of the companies taking part in the take-over, adopts a resolution, concerning the introduction of amendments and modifications to the Charter and, if necessary, concerning other matters. The take-over agreement determines the voting procedure for the joint GM.

In a take-over, the rights and obligations of the former legal entity pass to the latter legal entity in conformity with the transfer act.

- **Division**

Division is the dissolution of a company with the transfer of all rights and obligations to newly created legal entities.

The BD of the company being reorganised in the form of division submits for the agenda of the GM, issues concerning:

- Reorganisation of the company in the form of division
- Procedure, terms and conditions of the division
- Formation of new companies
- Procedure for converting the shares of the company being reorganised into the shares and/or other securities of the companies being created[8]
- Approval of the divisional balance.

The GM of a legal entity makes a decision on reorganisation.

In a division of the legal entity, its rights and obligations pass to the newly created legal entities in conformity with the divisional balance.

In accordance with Article 57.2 of the Civil Code in the cases provided for by law, division of a business entity shall be performed under the decision of its authorised body or by a court decision.

Therefore, under the Competition Law, in case business entities have performed breaches of the anti-monopoly legislation, the Anti-Monopoly Service may file a claim to court on the division of such business entities.

---

[8] J-SC Law, Article 18.

- **Separation (Spin-Off, De-Merger)**

Separation is the creation of one or several companies with the transfer to it or to them of a part of rights and obligations of the company being reorganised without dissolution.

Separation is the only form of reorganisation of business entities where the reorganised legal entities do not terminate.

The BD of a company being reorganised in the form of separation, puts the following issues on the agenda of the GM:

- Reorganisation of the company in the form of separation
- Separation procedure and terms
- Formation of a new company (companies)
- Conversion of the shares of the company undergoing reorganisation, into shares of the newly created company (distribution of the shares of the newly created company among the shareholders of the company undergoing reorganisation, the acquisition of the shares of the newly created company by the company undergoing reorganisation)[9]
- Procedure for conversion (distribution, acquisition)
- Approval of the divisional balance.

The GM of a company being reorganised in the form of separation adopts a decision on reorganisation in the form of separation.

The GM of participants (shareholders) of each of the newly created companies adopts decisions on approval of the Charter and formation of management bodies.

In the separation of one or several business entities, rights and obligations of the legal entity pass to every one of these entities in conformity with the divisional balance.

- **Transformation (Reformation)**

A company may be transformed into another type of company, e.g. an LLC may be transformed into a company limited by shares or a cooperative (a change of the organisational (corporate) form of the company)[10].

---

[9] J-SC Law, Article 19.

[10] A J-SC may be transformed into a commercial company or into a commercial partnership. Order of the FSFM No.08-32/pz-n, dated 12 August 2008.

The BD of the transforming legal entity submits for approval at the GM, the decision on transformation of the legal entity. The GM of the company being reorganised in the form of a transformation shall make a decision on such a reorganisation, on the procedure and the conditions of the transformation, the procedure of the exchange of the unit of each participant for the shares of the company limited by shares or for the unit (units) of the members of the production cooperative, on the approval of the Charter of the company being set up as a result of its transformation, and also on the approval of the transfer act.

By a unanimous decision of all shareholders of the J-SC, a J-SC may transform itself into a non-commercial partnership.

Note

Transformation of a joint-stock company of one type into a joint-stock company of another type is not deemed to be reorganisation of the business entity, because its legal form is not changed. Therefore, the state requirements of Article 58.5 of the Civil Code and of Articles 15.5, 20, 75 of the J-SC Law concerning the transfer act, notification of creditors and the right of shareholders to claim the redemption of shares, etc. shall not be observed[11].

The GM of the transforming company adopts a resolution concerning:

- Transformation of the company
- Procedure, terms and conditions of carrying out the transformation
- Procedure for the exchange of the shares of the company for the contributions of the participants of the LLC, or shares of the members of the production cooperative[12].

Participants of the newly created business entity adopt at their joint meeting a decision concerning approval of its constituent documents and formation of the management bodies.

In case of the transformation of a legal entity of one type into a legal entity of a different type (a change of its organisational form), the rights and duties of the reorganised legal entity pass to the newly created legal entity in conformity with the transfer act.

In a merger, take-over, division or transformation, one or several legal entities terminate.

[11] Ruling of the High Arbitrazh Court No.10, dated 18 November 2003; Ruling of the High Arbitrazh Court No.5178/07, dated 16 October 2007.

[12] J-SC Law, Article 20.

Forms of Reorganisation of Legal Entities

Forms of Reorganisation	Legal Succession Passes:	Document of Legal Succession	In Cases Provided for by the Legislation Reorganisation is Carried out by:
Merger – emergence of a new company by handing over to it all rights and duties of two or more companies, with the termination of the latter	To a newly created entity	Transfer act	Approval of the authorised state bodies
Take-Over – termination of one or several companies with all their rights and duties handed over to another company	To an acquiring entity	Transfer act	Approval of the authorised state bodies
Division – termination of the company with all its rights and duties handed over to newly created companies	To newly created entities	Divisional balance	Approval of the authorised state bodies or by a court decision
Separation – establishing one or several companies with partial rights and duties of the reformed company handed over to them without its termination	Partially to newly created entities	Divisional balance	Approval of the authorised state bodies or by a court decision
Transformation – a company limited by shares may be transformed into an LLC or a production cooperative; an LLC may be transformed into a company limited by shares, a production cooperative	To a newly created entity	Transfer act	Approval of the authorised state bodies

Before the empowered body takes a decision on reorganisation it is advisable that the following documents are provided and considered:

- Draft agreement on merger (take-over) or draft resolution on division (separation)
- Draft constituent documents of the legal entities to be established as a result of merger, division, separation or transformation or constituent documents of the entity to which the company is acceding
- Annual reports and balance sheets of all entities participating in the reorganisation for the last fiscal year
- Quarterly reports prepared not later than six months before the date of the meeting at which the issue of reorganisation is to be considered, if more than six months have passed since the end of the last fiscal year
- The draft transfer act and divisional balance
- The rationale (logic) for the reorganisation.

Grounds for Legal Succession

The grounds for legal succession of a business entity are the following:

- Under the transfer act or divisional balance
- Under law.

The transfer act and the divisional balance must contain provisions on the legal succession of all obligations of the reorganised legal entity with respect to all its creditors and debtors, including those obligations disputed by the parties.

The transfer act and the divisional balance must be approved by the participants of the legal entity or by the management body of the company which has adopted the decision on the reorganisation of the legal entities, and must be presented, together with the constituent documents of the company, for the state registration of the newly created legal entities, or for the introduction of amendments into the constituent documents of the existing legal entities.

The failure to present, together with the constituent documents, the transfer act or the divisional balance, and the absence in these of provisions on the legal succession of the obligations of the reorganised business entity, entails the refusal to effect the state registration of the newly created business entities.

Legal succession plays a central role in the reorganisation of a legal entity. A legal successor of a reorganised legal entity shall execute obligations of the reorganised legal entity to pay taxes and all penalties of the reorganised legal entity herewith on the obligations which were ceded to the legal successor[13]. Any absence of knowledge of facts or circumstances of non-execution of obligations of the reorganised business entity shall not be taken into consideration.

Liquidation of a Business Entity

Notes

Execution by a business entity of business activity subject to licensing, after cancellation of the license, shall be grounds for the liquidation of the business entity.

In case of gross violations while creating a non-commercial legal entity, the absence of a court decision does not affect the liquidation of such a non-commercial legal entity.

The liquidation of a J-SC results in its termination, with no transfer by succession of its rights and obligations to other persons.

Note

Tax evasion shall not be grounds for the liquidation of a legal entity.

In case a business entity, during the preceding 12 months of the date of the decision of the registering body, has not presented accounting documentation provided by Russian legislation on taxes and levies, and has not operated at least one banking account, that business entity shall be deemed to have terminated its activity and may be struck off from the Unified State Register of Business Entities. The decision on its striking off from the Register shall be published in the printed mass media where the information concerning that legal entity is published, within 3 days of the date of the decision. In case the legal entity presents notice within the established period, but not later than 3 months from the date of the publication, the decision on their striking off from the Unified State Register of Legal Entities shall not be adopted and the legal entity shall be subject to liquidation in the order provided for by the civil legislation of the RF.

Note

Russian court practice views this form of being struck off the Register as a specific form of the termination of the company and not as its involuntary liquidation.

---

[13] Ruling of the Presidium of the High Arbitrazh Court of the RF No.11489/03, dated 17 February 2004.

Special Grounds for Liquidation of a J-SC

A J-SC may be liquidated on the following grounds:

- General grounds (expiration of the term of formation of a legal entity; achievement of goals of formation of a business entity; multiplication or reduction of the number of participants of a legal entity that contradicts the Charter of the legal entity or the Russian law; court decision on an invalid registration of a legal entity due to irremovable violations of legal acts; insolvency (bankruptcy); business activity without special permission (license); business activity prohibited by law; multiple and gross violations of law and/or other normative acts; systematic activity of a public or religious organisation, charity or other fund, not provided by the Charter of that legal entity; other circumstances), provided by law for all types of business entities
- Non-payment of the charter capital within the first year of creation of the J-SC
- When the charter capital becomes less than the minimum amount of charter capital allowed – 1,000 multiples of the minimum monthly pay fixed by the federal law for an open J-SC, and 100 multiples of the minimum monthly pay fixed by the federal law for a closed J-SC
- The number of shareholders of the closed J-SC becomes more than 50, if the closed J-SC was not reorganised into an open J-SC
- If upon the expiry of the second and of each of the next fiscal years the value of the company's net assets proves to be less than its charter capital, the company shall be obliged to declare and to register the reduction of its charter capital. If the cost of the company's assets falls below the minimum size of the charter capital provided by law, the company is subject to liquidation.

Types of Liquidation

The types of liquidation are as follows:

- **Voluntary liquidation**

This is where either the members (the company must be solvent) or the creditors of the company resolve to end the life of the company.

- **Official liquidation/ Compulsory liquidation / Involuntary liquidation**

Such liquidation is done by the decision of the court under the claim of the state or municipal body, or under the claim of the founder of the legal entity. The court may order liquidation on insolvency grounds or on just and equitable grounds where the company may be solvent, e.g. where a company is a vehicle for a partnership, and the partners no longer get on. Non-execution of the court decision on liquidation shall be grounds on which to appoint an arbitrazh manager. If there are not enough funds available to finance the liquidation procedure, such expenses shall be borne by the founders of the legal entity.

Note

Liquidation of a non-commercial business entity which does not have the deriving of profit as the main goal of its activity is not subject to the jurisdiction of the Arbitrazh court.

The liquidation of a company is the point at which it is decided that the affairs of the company will be brought to an end. Liquidation can be instigated by the company itself, the creditors or the courts. In turn, voluntary liquidation may be instigated by the founders of the company or an external body. In practice, the latter may arise either from pressure from external creditors or from a decision of the courts relating to some defect in the company's registration or some unlawful act.

A company is deemed in law to have perpetual succession, but this obviously does not have to be the case. Some companies are established for a specific period of time or for a specific purpose. For example, the founders of a company may establish the company to carry out a specific task or a set of tasks that have a beginning and an end. It therefore follows that once the purposes of the company have been achieved, or the prescribed period of the operation of the company has expired, it is appropriate to liquidate the company.

Stages of Liquidation

The stages of liquidation of a legal entity are as follows:

1. Decision on liquidation

Voluntary liquidation. Voluntary liquidation may arise when the directors decide, with the support of a GM, that the company is no longer financially viable or will not be viable in the future. In such instances, the law enables the company to be liquidated. This must of course involve not only the shareholders of the company but also the creditors.

The process of voluntary liquidation involves the directors, shareholders and creditors of the company. The process is usually invoked by the directors who take an executive decision to put the matter to the GM. The matter can be put formally to the regular GM or to a meeting specially convened for the purpose.

Any decision on voluntary liquidation must be taken by the shareholders, who are the owners of the business. Once a recommendation on voluntary liquidation is sanctioned by the shareholders, the decision must be communicated to the registration authorities. The shareholders then agree on a liquidation commission to oversee the process.

2. Formation of liquidation commission

The BD shall submit for decision at the GM, the issue on liquidation of the company and on formation of the liquidation commission. The GM shall adopt the decision on liquidation of the company and on formation of the liquidation commission. The participants of a legal entity, or the body which has adopted the decision on liquidation of the business entity, are obliged to immediately notify the authorised state body, in written form, about the liquidation of the company. The state body shall then enter the information regarding the given business entity being in the process of liquidation to the Unified State Register of Legal Entities.

In case the RF, a Subject of the RF or a municipal authority is a participant/shareholder of the company, the liquidation commission must include representatives of:

- The federal body on state property control or the agency that deals with the sale of federal property (participant/shareholder – the RF)
- The body with control over property of the Subjects of the RF or the agency that deals with the sale of property of the Subjects of the RF (participant/shareholder – the Subject of RF)
- A local self-government body (participant/shareholder – a municipal authority).

The shareholders of a legal entity or the management body of the company, who have adopted the decision on liquidation of the legal entity, shall appoint a liquidation commission (the liquidator), and shall establish the procedure and the period of liquidation.

As of the appointment of the liquidation commission, the liquidation commission acquires all powers relating to the management of the activity of the company. The liquidation commission acts in court on behalf of the company subject to liquidation. The liquidation commission shall be authorised to represent the legal entity by the power of attorney.

The liquidation commission shall publish notice of the liquidation of the company. Should the monetary funds existing in the company under liquidation prove to be insufficient to meet the creditors' claims, the liquidation commission shall sell other property of the company by public sale according to the procedure established for the execution of court decisions.

3. Entry of the liquidation commencement data to the Unified State Register of Legal Entities

4. Publication regarding the liquidation, on the procedure and the period of liquidation

Creditors' claims shall be submitted within 2 months of the date of the final publication on liquidation in "The Vestnik of State Registration".

5. The finding of the creditors, and the exaction of their debit indebtedness

6. Compilation of an intermediary (preliminary) liquidation balance

The liquidation commission draws up a liquidation balance. This is presented and affirmed by the shareholders and shows whether the company is solvent or not, and where the company is solvent, whether it is liquid or not.

In some cases the company may have sufficient liquid or near-liquid resources to discharge its obligations in full. If this is not the case, the commission must liquidate assets in order to meet the obligations.

An intermediary liquidation balance shall be compiled upon termination of the term of presenting the claims of the creditors. It shall include the information on the assets of the liquidating legal entity, the presented claims of the creditors and the decisions on the consideration of claims.

7. Approval of an intermediary liquidation balance

The intermediary liquidation balance must be approved by the participants of a business entity or by the management body of the company which has adopted the decision on the business entity's liquidation. In cases established by law the intermediary liquidation balance must be approved by the authorised state body.

Note

In case the value of the property of a legal entity, according to the intermediary liquidation balance, is not enough to satisfy the creditors' claims, the liquidation of the business entity shall take place according to bankruptcy legislation.

8. Creditor settlement

The company is now ready to make settlements with creditors. Once this has been done, a further statement is presented to the shareholders, after which surplus assets (if any) may be distributed according to the priorities determined by law. After this distribution, a notice is registered in the Unified State Register of Legal Entities.

Note

The following property is not subject to sale to cover the indebtedness:

- Property under pledge (mortgage)
- Leased property or property under safe custody
- Personal property of employees.

Creditor settlement shall be conducted in accordance with the intermediary liquidation balance. In case of liquidation of a legal entity without sufficient funds to satisfy all creditors, creditors' claims shall be satisfied in the following order of priority (after the satisfaction of creditors' current claims):

- In the first turn, the claims of individuals to whom the liquidated business entity bears responsibility for causing harm to life or health shall be satisfied – under executive documents
- In the second turn, settlements shall be effected that are involved in the payment of retirement allowances and in the remuneration of labour to persons who have been employed under labour agreements, including by contracts for hiring work and labour, and also those involved in the payment of fees by author's contracts – under executive documents

- In the third turn shall be repaid those debts created by obligatory payments into the budget and into extra-budgetary funds and labour remuneration – under payment documents
- In the fourth turn settlements shall be effected with other creditors – under executive documents
- In the fifth turn settlements shall be effected with other creditors – under payment documents.

Claims of each of these groups shall be satisfied after fully satisfying the claims of previous groups.

Satisfaction of claims of creditors by obligations secured against by the property of the liquidated legal entity shall take priority before creditors of other turns.

In case property of the liquidated business entity proves to be insufficient, it shall be distributed among creditors of the corresponding group proportionately to the amounts of claims liable to satisfaction, if otherwise is not provided for by law.

Creditors' claims, lodged after the expiry of the term fixed by the liquidation commission for their submission, shall be satisfied from any property of the liquidated legal entity which has been left after the duly lodged creditors' claims have been satisfied.

Creditors' claims left unsatisfied because of insufficiency of property of the liquidated legal entity shall be regarded as settled, the same as claims of creditors, which have not been recognised by the liquidation commission, if the creditor did not file a claim with the court, and also those claims which have been rejected by the court's decision.

9. Compilation of the final liquidation balance

The final liquidation balance shall be compiled after the creditor settlement.

10. Approval of the final liquidation balance

The GM, on agreement with the local department of the Tax Service shall approve the final liquidation balance.

11. Distribution of the remaining property

The property which remains after the creditors' settlement is distributed between participants (shareholders).

12. Entry into the Unified State Register of Legal Entities.

Priority in the Distribution of the Property of a Liquidated LLC

The assets of an LLC being liquidated that remain after the completion of settlements with creditors shall be distributed by the liquidation commission among the company's participants in the following order:

- In the first place the distributed but unpaid part of the profit shall be paid to the company's participants
- Secondarily, the LLC shall distribute the property of the company being liquidated among the company's participants in proportion to their stakes in the company's charter capital.

Priority in Distribution of the Property of a Liquidated J-SC

The property of the company subject to liquidation remaining after the completion of the settlement of accounts with creditors shall be distributed by the liquidation commission among the shareholders in the following order:

- In the first turn – payments relating to shares which are subject to redemption at the demand of shareholders
- In the second turn – payments for the dividends credited but not paid with regard to preference shares, and to the liquidation value of the preference shares determined by the Charter of the company
- In the third turn – the distribution of assets of the company under liquidation among holders of ordinary shares and all types of preference shares.

The distribution of property at each level of priority is done after the full distribution of property to the preceding priority level. Payment by the company of the liquidation value of preference shares determined by the Charter of the company is done after payment in full of the liquidation value of preference shares of the preceding priority determined by the Charter of the company.

If the value of property existing in the company is insufficient for payment of the dividends credited but not paid, and also the liquidation value determined by the Charter of the company is insufficient for the payment of all the holders of preference stock of one type, then the property shall be distributed among the holders of such preference stocks in proportion to the quantity of shares owned by them.

The liquidation of a company is considered to be complete, and the company is considered to have terminated its existence from the date of entry of the corresponding information to the Unified State Register of Legal Entities.

Chapter Roundup

1. The main forms of legal entities are the following:

- Commercial
  - Partnerships
    - General
    - Limited
  - Companies
- Limited liability companies
- Companies limited by shares
- Non-commercial

2. Distinctions between companies and partnerships are the following:

Partnership	Company
• Association of Persons • Participants Directly Take Part in Business Activity • Participants – LE and Individual Entrepreneurs • Activities – Only Activities of Partnership • No Norm for Charter Capital • Full Property Subsidiary Liability	• Association of Capital • Participants Take Part in Business Activities by Capital Participation • Participants – Any Subjects of Civil Law of the RF • Rights and Obligations Accrued by Activities of Management Bodies • Minimum Amount of Charter Capital Established by Law • No Property Liability. Participants Bear Risk of Losses in Amount of Contributions

3. Separate legal personality notions are the following:

- Unity of the organisational structure
- Separate estate
- Independent property responsibility
- Ability to act in civil relations on its own behalf

4. Consequences of the creation of a company are the following:

- Corporate personality

- Limited liability of members
- Transferability of interests
- Perpetual succession
- Large membership
- Legal actions
- Statutory obligations

5. Statutory (constituent) documents are the following:
- Partnerships – Partnership (constituent) agreement
- Companies – Charter

6. Contributions to the charter capital shall be made:
- In money
- By property
- By securities
- By property rights
- By other rights, having monetary evaluation

7. Functions of the charter capital are the following:
- Material ground
- Determination of the stake of the participant
- Creditors' guarantee

8. Types of reorganisation of legal entities are as follows:
- Merger
- Take Over (Acquisition)
- Division
- Separation (Spin-Off, De-Merger)
- Transformation

9. The following stages of liquidation may be distinguished:
- Decision on liquidation
- Formation of liquidation commission
- Entry to the Unified State Register of Legal Entities of the liquidation commencement data
- Publication on the liquidation
- Finding of the creditors and the exaction of the accounts receivable
- Intermediary liquidation balance
- Creditor settlement

- Final liquidation balance
- Entry into the Unified State Register of the Legal Entities on Liquidation

10. Priority of satisfaction of creditors' claims:

- Individuals, to whom harm to life or health was caused – under executive documents
- Payment of retirement allowances and in remuneration of labour – under executive documents
- Debts by obligatory payments into budget + labour remuneration – under payment documents
- Other creditors – under executive documents
- Other creditors – under payment documents

Questions

1. The legal capacity of a legal entity arises from which moment?

- The decision on its formation
- The opening of a bank account
- The starting of its activity
- Its formation

2. Which of the following is the moment of creation of a legal entity?

- The acquisition of separate estate
- The opening of a bank account
- Its acting as respondent under the transactions concluded
- Its state registration

3. A legal entity is deemed to be reorganised, except in the form of takeover, from the moment of what?

- The composition of the divisional balance
- The appointment of the manager of the legal entity by the court
- The state registration of newly created legal entities
- The decision of the authorised state bodies on the division of the legal entity

4. The term to present creditors' claims may not be more than how long after the moment of publication of the liquidation of a legal entity?

- 10 days
- 1 month

- 2 months
- 3 months

5. While liquidating a legal entity, which of the following creditors' claims are satisfied in the first turn?

- Claims on discharge of the debts by the obligatory payments into the budget and into the extra-budgetary funds
- Claims of creditors by the obligations, secured against by the property of the liquidated legal entity
- Settlements involved in the payment of retirement allowances and in the remuneration of labour to the persons who have been employed under labour agreements, including by contracts for hiring work and labour, and also those involved in the payment of fees by the author's contracts
- Claims of the individuals to whom the liquidated legal entity bears responsibility for causing harm to life or health, by way of capitalisation of the corresponding regular payments

6. In relation to limited liability companies:

(a) State and explain the essential features of a limited liability company.

(b) Describe the matters that must be included in the constitutional documents of a limited liability company.

7. Vladimir is the only participant of OOO "Ust" (a Limited Liability Company) and is the General Director of this company. On October 3rd, 2011 Vladimir, acting as General Director of the company, issued a power of attorney in the name of the company in favour of Yaroslav. This power of attorney contained the following text:

"Moscow, RF, October 3rd, 2011.

Hereby OOO "Ust" (all requisites duly indicated) represented by its General Director Vladimir (all requisites duly indicated) empowers Yaroslav (all requisites duly indicated) to represent the above mentioned company in relations with all individuals and legal entities for the purposes of receiving goods and production due to OOO "Ust" according to the contracts concluded.

(Signature and seal duly done)"

Yaroslav was also verbally instructed by Vladimir to receive goods and production due to OOO "Ust" according to the contracts concluded between OOO "Ust" and respective individuals and legal entities, and also to do his best to establish relations and conclude contracts with other producers of the same type of goods.

During the period from November 2011 until April 2012 Yaroslav was representing OOO "Ust" according to the power of Attorney. On April 25th, 2012 he concluded a contract of sale of goods in the name of OOO "Ust" with OOO "Renessanse" according to which the obligation of OOO "Ust" was to execute pre-payment for the goods.

On May 14th, 2012 Vladimir sold 100% of his part in the share capital of OOO "Ust" to Mr Ivanov.

Required:

(a) Advise whether Yaroslav had the right to conclude the contract with OOO "Renessanse" and who bears responsibility in case of non-execution of the pre-payment.

(b) Explain whether the fact that Vladimir sold 100% of his part in the share capital of OOO "Ust" to Mr Ivanov directly ceases:
(i) Vladimir's powers as General Director;
(ii) The validity of power of attorney issued in favour of Yaroslav.

(c) State whether, in case a new General Director of OOO "Ust" is appointed, the validity of power of attorney issued in favour of Yaroslav will directly cease.

Further Readings

1. Aleskerov F. Power Distribution in Russian Parliament Working Papers of the HSE WP13/2008/06. — M.: ГУ ВШЭ.
2. Amedeo Argentiero, Michele Bagella, Francesco Busato. Springer Science + Business Media. 26/2008.
3. Лаптев В.В. Предпринимательское право: понятие и субъекты. М., 1997.
4. Лейст О.Э. Санкции в советском праве. М., 1962.
5. Малеин Н.С. Юридическая ответственность и справедливость. М., 1992.
6. Матвеев Г.К. Основания имущественной ответственности частных предпринимателей // Государство и право. 1993. № 9.

7. Андрианов В.А. Торговые товарищества: возникновение и развитие. «Журнал российского права», N 10, октябрь 2001 г.
8. Арзамасцев А.Н. Охрана социалистической собственности по советскому гражданскому праву. Л., 1956.
9. Аушев И. Уменьшение уставного капитала общества с ограниченной ответственностью. «Российская юстиция», N 1, январь 2001 г.
10. Венедиктов А.В. Гражданско-правовая охрана социалистической собственности в СССР. М.; Л., 1954.
11. Венедиктов А.В. Государственная социалистическая собственность. М.-Л., 1948. С. 47-309; гл. IX § 82 С. 563-586.
12. Генкин Д.М. Право собственности в СССР. М., 1961.
13. Гуккаев В.Б. Формирование уставного капитала организации. «Консультант бухгалтера», N 1, январь 2005 г.
14. Егоров Н.Д. Гражданско-правовое регулирование общественных отношений. Л., 1988; гл. 2 – Право собственности и право оперативного регулирования имуществом. С. 41-79.
15. Козлова Н.В. Гражданско-правовая природа отношений между юридическим лицом и его уч-редителями. «Законодательство», N 7, 8, июль, август 2004 г.
16. Коновалов А.В. Владение и владельческая защита в гражданском праве. СПб., 2001.
17. Маттеи У., Суханов Е.А. Основные положения права собственности. М., 1999.
18. Невзгодина Е.А. Представительство по советскому гражданскому праву. Томск, 1976.
19. Пайпс Р. Собственность и свобода. М., 2000.
20. Райхер В.К. Абсолютные и относительные права // Известия экономического факультета Ленинградского политехнического института. Вып. 1. Л., 1928.
21. Рубанов А.А. Проблемы совершенствования теоретической модели права собственности // Развитие советского гражданского права на современном этапе / Отв. ред. В.П. Мозолин. М., 1986;
22. Русская философия собственности XVIII-XX. Авторы-составители К. Исупов, И. Савкин. СПб., 1993.
23. Рясенцев В.А. Основания представительства в советском гражданском праве // Ученые записки ВЮЗИ, М., 1948. Вып. 1.
24. Слепцова Е. Н. Ведение дел полного товарищества и товарищества на ве-ре.//Практический журнал для руководителей и менеджеров «Законодательст-во», 1998, N 4.
25. Скловский К.И. Собственность в гражданском праве. М., 1999.

26. Сонькин Н. Б., Матвеев С. П. Развитие корпоративного права в России. – М.: ВИ МВД России, 2000.
27. Степанов П.В.Корпорации в российском гражданском праве. «Законодательст-во», N 4, апрель 1999 г.
28. Тихомиров М. Ю. Юридические лица: правовое положение, порядок создания, учредительные и внутренние документы. – М.: Издание г-на Тихомирова М. Ю., 2000.
29. Тихомиров М.Ю. Учредительные договоры хозяйственных товариществ. М. - 2003.
30. Толстой Ю.К.: Понятие права собственности // В кн. Проблемы гражданского и административного права / Под ред. Б.Б. Черепахина, О.С. Иоффе, Ю.К. Толстого. Л., 1962.
31. Черепахин Б.Б. Органы и представители юридического лица // Ученые записки ВНИИСЗ, М., 1968. Вып.14.
32. Шинкаренко Е.В. Торговые товарищества в праве современной Германии. «Журнал российского права», N 12, декабрь 2001 г.
33. Шкредов В.П. Экономика и право. Опыт экономико-юридического исследования общественного производства. 2-е изд. М., 1990.
34. Щенникова Л.В. Вещное право. Учебное пособие. Пермь, 2001.

CHAPTER FOUR

LEGAL IMPLICATIONS RELATING TO COMPANIES IN DIFFICULTY OR IN CRISIS

Part I. Overview

Articles 25 and 65 of the Civil Code provide that an individual entrepreneur or a legal entity which is a commercial organisation, with the exception of a state-run enterprise or a business entity operating in the form of a consumer cooperative, or of a charity or another kind of fund, may be recognised by a court decision as insolvent (bankrupt), if it is incapable of satisfying creditors' claims.

The recognition of the business entity to be bankrupt shall entail its liquidation.

An individual entrepreneur incapable of satisfying the claims of his creditors related to his performance of business activities may be recognised as insolvent (bankrupt) by the Arbitrazh court's decision. From the date of such a decision, his registration in the capacity of an individual entrepreneur shall be deemed no longer valid. The procedure for the recognition of a person as bankrupt is stipulated in the Bankruptcy Law.

Insolvency (bankruptcy) is defined in the Bankruptcy Law as a debtor's inability, as recognised by the Arbitrazh court, to fully meet creditors' claims on monetary obligations and obligatory payments (taxes, charges, etc.)[1].

The Bankruptcy Law is somewhat inconsistent with other federal laws, including the Civil Code, the Arbitrazh Procedural Code and the federal laws concerning privatisation[2].

The UNCITRAL Model Law on Cross-Border Insolvency of 1997, as well as other UNCITRAL acts on insolvency not applied in Russia as provisions of the Law were not incorporated into national law.

---

[1] Bankruptcy Law, Article 2.

[2] Ruling of the Plenum of the High Arbitrazh Court No.4, dated 8 April 2003, gives practical recommendations on the application of the Bankruptcy Law.

A business entity which is a commercial organisation, and also a business entity operating in the form of a consumer cooperative or of a charity or another kind of fund, may with creditors, jointly adopt the decision on declaring itself to be bankrupt and on its voluntary liquidation.

Articles 61-65 of the Civil Code provide a general foundation for liquidation and the bankruptcy procedures of business entities. Grounds for the court recognising a business entity to be bankrupt or for its declaring itself bankrupt, and the procedure for liquidation of such a business entity is stipulated in the Bankruptcy Law.

The Bankruptcy Law also stipulates the procedure of appointment and activity of the arbitrazh managers, measures for preventing bankruptcy, pre-trial sanation, procedure for hearing bankruptcy cases in the Arbitrazh court, monitoring, financial sanation, procedure for establishment of trusteeship, receivership, amicable settlement and other matters.

Signs of Bankruptcy

According to Article 3 of the Bankruptcy Law, a business entity shall be deemed incapable of meeting claims of creditors related to monetary obligations and/or to execute the duty of making mandatory payments, if the person does not discharge the obligations and/or duties within three months after their due date[3].

The Tax Service acts as a creditor in the bankruptcy procedures, representing the interests of the RF on payments to the federal budget and non-budgetary funds.

The Determination of the Amount of Monetary Obligations

The amount of monetary obligations and mandatory payments shall be determined as of the date of filing an application with the Arbitrazh court for declaring a debtor bankrupt.

The following shall be taken into account to determine the availability of evidence of the bankruptcy of a debtor:

- The amount of monetary obligations, in particular the amount of debt for delivered goods, completed works and provided services, loan amounts with the interest the debtor has to pay, the amount of debt occurring as a result of non-grounded (unjust) enrichment

[3] Bankruptcy Law, Article 3.

(conversion), and the amount of debt occurring as a result of damaging property of creditors, except:
  - Obligations to the individuals to whom the debtor is liable for inflicted harm to life or health
  - Obligations to pay out benefits and wages/salaries to persons working under labour contracts
  - Obligations to pay out royalties to owners of the results of intellectual activities
  - Obligations to debtor's founders (participants) proceeding from such participation
  - Obligations to pay a penalty, fine, interest
- A mandatory payment amount without taking into consideration of fines (penalties) and other financial sanctions established by the legislation of the RF.

The following shall not be taken into consideration in the assessment of the availability of evidence of the bankruptcy of a debtor, as subject to application for a default in or improper performance of an obligation:

- Forfeit money (fines, penalties)
- Interest for payment deferment
- Losses subject to compensation for a default in an obligation
- Other property and/or financial sanctions, in particular, for a breach of the duty to make mandatory payments.

Notes

Monetary obligations which have arisen after the Arbitrazh court has accepted the application on finding the debtor bankrupt (notwithstanding the maturity of the term of their execution prior or during the trusteeship) shall be deemed current for the purposes of the trusteeship. As current payment demands shall not be included into the register of creditors' claims, such demands shall be resolved in accordance with the procedural legislation outside of the bankruptcy case[4].

After introduction of the next bankruptcy procedure, payments under obligation of the debtor which have arisen before the introduction of bankruptcy and that are due before introduction of the next bankruptcy procedure, shall not be deemed current. Payments on the obligations which have arisen after acceptance of the application on bankruptcy, shall be deemed current notwithstanding change in bankruptcy procedures[5].

---

[4] Ruling of the Presidium of the High Arbitrazh Court of the RF No.5754/04, dated 24 August 2004.

[5] P.3 of the Ruling of the Presidium of the High Arbitrazh Court of the RF No.29, dated 15 December 2004.

A creditor's claim on transfer to them of the property in kind by the debtor, who is under bankruptcy procedures, may be filed outside of the bankruptcy case[6].

Therefore, a business entity or an individual entrepreneur is recognised bankrupt under the following conditions:

- When they cannot meet creditors' claims
- Three months have passed after creditors filed their claims
- The sum total of their obligations exceeds the value of the property owned by the business entity or individual entrepreneur
- The Arbitrazh court has decided upon recognising the business entity or individual entrepreneur bankrupt.

Voluntary Liquidation on an Insolvent Company

The debtor's CEO may declare the debtor's bankruptcy and liquidation:

- If the bankruptcy symptoms are evident, in case written consent of all creditors has been received
- By decision of the owner of the unitary enterprise or of the body authorised by the debtor's constituent documents to decide on liquidation.

Declaration of the debtor's bankruptcy and liquidation is published in the Court Bulletin, indicating the deadline for creditors to file claims and objections (at least two months from the date of the publication).

Publication on bankruptcy shall take place weekly in printed mass media (with at least 30,000 copies) within 10 days from the moment of submission of information to the printed mass media by the arbitrazh manager[7].

If there is at least one creditor's written objection against the liquidation of the debtor sent to the debtor's CEO or to the Arbitrazh court, the debtor's CEO shall file a claim on bankruptcy of the debtor with the Arbitrazh court.

Any creditor may file a claim on bankruptcy of the debtor with the Arbitrazh court before liquidation is completed.

---

[6] Ruling of the Presidium of the High Arbitrazh Court of the RF No.4562/04, dated 13 July 2004.

[7] The price of 1 square centimetre of publication is fixed by the Order of the MERT No.293, dated 12 July 2010.

Note

The Arbitrazh court will not consider the bankruptcy case if there is no evidence that there is sufficient debtor's property to cover bankruptcy expences[8].

The Arbitrazh Manager

The crucial point about any liquidation is the appointment of arbitrazh managers. If it is a members' voluntary liquidation, then the members will appoint an arbitrazh manager more sympathetic to their interests. The same is true for a creditors' voluntary liquidation.

The regulating state body exercising the control over the activity of the self-regulated organisations[9] of arbitrazh managers, is the Ministry of Justice of the RF.

The arbitrazh manager is approved by the Arbitrazh court to guide the bankruptcy procedures and to carry out other duties imposed by law. The arbitrazh manager must be a Russian citizen. Candidates of monitors are nominated by the self-regulated organisation of arbitrazh managers under the creditor-claimant's application on bankruptcy, stipulating the name of the prospective arbitrazh manager or the name of the self-regulated organisation of arbitrazh managers. In case the arbitrazh manager is not nominated within a 6 month period from the date the arbitrazh manager is to be nominated under law, the Arbitrazh court terminates the case.

Requirements of an Arbitrazh Manager

Requirements for an arbitrazh manager are the following:

- A professional higher education
- At least a year's work experience in leading positions and at least six months experience in a position of the arbitrazh manager's assistant[10]
- To have successfully passed theoretical examinations for arbitrazh managers
- No convictions for economic crimes and other gross offences, no disqualification for administrative violations

---

[8] Ruling of the Plenum of the High Arbitrazh Court of the RF No.91, dated 17 December 2009.

[9] Federal Law No.315-FZ "On Self-Regulated Organisations", dated 1 December 2007.

[10] The arbitrazh manager does not have to obtain continuous work experience. The required term as an aggregate is enough.

- Participation in one of the self-regulated organisations of arbitrazh managers
- To have insured liability for at least 3 million roubles per year.

The arbitrazh manager may conduct entrepreneurial activity in case there is no conflict of interest with bankruptcy procedures he rules.

If an arbitrazh manager rules a case improperly, any interested person to the case may appeal to the Arbitrazh court for the discharge of the Arbitrazh manager.

The arbitrazh manager must have a neutral position during the bankruptcy procedures. Thus, the arbitrazh manager shall not have any interest in the bankruptcy procedures. Therefore persons who have an interest in the debtor or the creditors shall not be appointed as arbitrazh managers.

The remuneration of the arbitrazh manager shall comprise of a fixed sum and interests. The fixed sum shall be the following:

- For the interim manager – 30,000 roubles per month
- For the administrative manager – 15,000 roubles per month
- For the external manager – 45,000 roubles per month
- For the receiver – 30,000 roubles per month.

The Bankruptcy Law also stipulates the amount of interest accrued, which is calculated on a regressive scale, e.g. the amount of interests of the monitor starts at 4% of the balance assets of the debtor with balance assets valued up to 250,000 roubles.

The Bankruptcy Law provides for the possibility of increasing the remuneration of the arbitrazh manager under the decision of the creditors' meeting. Additional remuneration of the arbitrazh manager may also be provided at the expense of the creditors.

The Self-Regulated Organisation of Arbitrazh Managers

The self-regulated organisation of arbitrazh managers is a non-commercial organisation executing regulation and control over activities of its participants (arbitrazh managers). The Ministry of Justice of the RF executes control over self-regulated organisations of arbitrazh managers and conducts the Register for self-regulated organisations of arbitrazh managers.

Requirements for the state registration of a self-regulated organisation of arbitrazh managers:

- Membership of at least 100 arbitrazh managers

- Participation of the members in at least 100 (aggregate) bankruptcy procedures
- Formation of a compensation fund to the amount of at least 50,000 roubles per member.

The Names of the Arbitrazh Managers

The arbitrazh managers have the following names depending on the stage of the bankruptcy procedures:

- The monitor (the interim manager) in monitoring (observation)
- The administrative manager in financial sanation
- The trustee (the outside manager, external manager) in trusteeship (outside management, external management)
- The receiver (liquidator) in receivership (competitive proceedings, liquidation).

Application to the Arbitrazh Court

Bankruptcy cases are considered in the Arbitrazh court.

A bankruptcy case may be initiated in the Arbitrazh court if claims addressed to a debtor being a business entity, in their aggregate, make up at least 100,000 roubles, and if addressed to a debtor being an individual – at least 10,000 roubles, unless otherwise provided for by the legislation of the RF.

The following persons have the right to file a suit for declaring a debtor bankrupt:

- The debtor
- The arbitrazh manager
- The bankruptcy creditors, and
- The authorised state bodies

Article 7 of the Bankruptcy Law states that the suit on declaring a debtor bankrupt shall be filed with the Arbitrazh court not less than 30 days after the applicant has submitted the writ of execution to the court bailiff.

The applicant shall bear the expenses concerning the bankruptcy procedures. In case the applicant is the debtor, who is insolvent, the founder shall incur the expenses.

The head of the debtor's legal entity or the individual entrepreneur must file an application of the debtor with the Arbitrazh court to find the debtor bankrupt, in case:

- The meeting of claims of one creditor or several creditors makes it impossible for the debtor to discharge monetary obligations, to execute the duty of making mandatory payments and/or other payments in full to other creditors
- The debtor's management body, authorised under the debtor's constituent documents to make the decision to liquidate the debtor, has adopted a decision to file a debtor's application to find the debtor bankrupt with the Arbitrazh court
- The body authorised by the owner of property of the debtor being a unitary enterprise has decided to file a debtor's application to find the debtor bankrupt with the Arbitrazh court
- A levy of execution is going to significantly aggravate or make impossible the pursuit of the debtor's economic activity
- In other cases specified by law[11].

The debtor must file a debtor's application to find the debtor bankrupt with the Arbitrazh court if at the winding up of the legal entity it was established that creditors' claims could not be met in full.

The debtor's application shall be forwarded to the Arbitrazh court within one month from the date of the above-named circumstances.

In the event of insolvency it is a criminal offence for the General Director of the company to:

- Destroy information about the assets of the company, their value and location, or the transfer of the company's assets to another person
- Falsify accounting records
- Satisfy the claims of some creditors when the company is aware of its insolvency, to the detriment of the remaining unpaid creditors (fraudulent preference)
- Deliberately create insolvency, or deliberately make the insolvency worse
- Enter into fictitious bankruptcy.

The application by the debtor to have itself declared insolvent is submitted to the Arbitrazh court in writing. The application should specify:

- The name of the Arbitrazh court to which the application is submitted

[11] Bankruptcy Law, Article 9.

- The amount of the claims of creditors (which are not challenged by the debtor)
- The amount of indebtedness for compensation to citizens to whom the company bears the responsibility for the causing of harm to life or health
- The amount of indebtedness for unpaid royalties
- An explanation of why the debtor is unable to satisfy the claims of the creditors in full
- Information about the assets of the debtor, including its cash and receivables
- Details of its bank accounts
- The name of the arbitrazh manager or the name of the self-regulated organisation from which the interim manager should be appointed.

The debtor must send copies of the application to the Arbitrazh court to:

- Its bankruptcy creditors
- The authorised state bodies
- The BD of the company.

Note

The initiation by the Arbitrazh court of bankruptcy procedures should suspend the execution of the executory process until the case on the bankruptcy procedures is decided by the Arbitrazh court on its merits.

The first hearing on the bankruptcy case shall take place no later than 7 months from the date of receipt of the application to recognise the debtor as bankrupt.

Note

The norm of Article 51 of the Bankruptcy Law contradicts Article 134 of the Arbitrazh Procedural Code, which states that the term of pre-trial preparation of the case to the Arbitrazh hearing shall be not more than 2 months. The specific law – the Bankruptcy Law – shall prevail in this case.

The following persons participate in the Arbitazh process in a bankruptcy case:

- The representative of the employees of the debtor
- The representative of the owner of property of the debtor – the unitary enterprise
- The representative of the founders (participants) of the debtor

- The representative of the creditors' meeting or creditors' committee
- The representative of the federal executive body in the area of security in case the execution of powers of the arbitrazh manager is connected to the accessing of information constituting a state secret
- The persons empowered to represent interests of the Subjects of the RF or of the municipalities of the RF
- Other persons under the Arbitrazh Procedural Code or the Bankruptcy Law.

The Creditors' Meeting and Committee

Types of Creditors

Types of creditors are the following:

- Bankruptcy creditors (i.e. the creditors on monetary obligations. Only such creditors may participate in the bankruptcy procedures, have a right to file a claim to the Arbitrazh court on finding the debtor bankrupt and have a right to vote at the creditor's meeting. Bankruptcy creditors may be Russian or foreign individuals or legal entities, the RF, the Subjects of the RF, municipal formations) and other creditors
- Major and petty creditors
- Creditors-claimants and other creditors
- Ordinary and extraordinary creditors, due to the priority of satisfaction of the creditors' claims. Extraordinary creditors are both top priority creditors (e.g. the arbitrazh manager) and creditors whose claims shall be satisfied after the satisfaction of claims of ordinary creditors (e.g. the founders).

All actions concerning the debtor are taken on behalf of the creditors by the creditors' meeting and the creditors' committee. The quantity of votes of each of the creditors is *pro rata* the monetary claims of the creditor under the register of claims on the date of holding the creditors' meeting.

The Creditors' Meeting

The following persons/bodies may convene the creditors' meeting:

- The Arbitrazh Insolvency Monitor (the monitor)
- The creditors' committee
- Creditors whose claims amount to at least 10% of the total amount of claims.

The first creditors' meeting is convened by the monitor not later than ten days before the end of monitoring[12].

The creditors' meeting may make decisions on the following:

- On introduction of financial sanation, outside management or on recognition of the debtor's bankruptcy, and initiating receivership (on resorting to the Arbitrazh court with an appropriate application)
- On approval of the financial sanation and outside management plan and schedule for debt repayment (during financial sanation and outside management accordingly)
- On concluding an amicable settlement (at any stage of the bankruptcy procedures)
- On election of the members of the creditor's committee
- On additional requirements to the candidates to the administrative manager, external manager and receiver
- On determination of the self-regulated organisation of the arbitrazh managers, which shall provide the Arbitrazh court with the candidate of the arbitrazh manager
- On election of the holder of the register from those accredited by the self-regulated organisation of the arbitrazh managers
- Other decisions in connection with bankruptcy procedures[13].

The Creditors' Committee

A creditors' committee may be formed if the total number of creditors amounts to at least 50. Members of the creditors' committee are elected at the first creditors' meeting. The number of creditors may not be below three or over eleven. The creditor's committee elects a single representative for litigation. The creditor's committee consists of individuals; legal entities are not admitted to be members of the creditor's committee.

The creditors' committee:

- Represents the creditors' interests
- Keeps control over the monitor's actions
- Carries out other duties assigned by the creditors' committee[14].

---

[12] Bankruptcy Law, Article 72.1.

[13] Bankruptcy Law, Article 12.

[14] Bankruptcy Law, Article 17.

The Register of Creditors' Claims

The register of creditors' claims includes information about creditors, amounts of creditors' claims and priority for claims repayment. Claims may only be included into the register of claims if the Arbitrazh court primarily ruled on them and they had not been executed by the debtor within three months after maturity. A corresponding court decision must determine the amount and composition of the claim. The register of claims is held by the monitor or a registrar, and they are personally liable for non-performance or improper performance of their duties in connection thereof[15]. Claims may be included into the register of claims at any stage of the bankruptcy procedure.

Part II. Stages of Bankruptcy

Prevention of Bankruptcy - Sanation[16]

Founders of legal entities and government authorities are obliged to take all necessary preventative measures to ensure that entities do not become bankrupt. One such step is financial rehabilitation ("sanation") of a debtor by way of a capital injection. This measure should be applied before any formal bankruptcy procedures have commenced against the debtor.

Founders of the debtor, its creditors, federal executive bodies of the the RF, executive bodies of the Subjects of the RF, local self-government bodies as well as third parties are allowed to inject necessary capital and in the cases provided by law shall do the above to prevent the bankruptcy of the legal entity. In exchange for such an injection, the contributor of the capital may require that the creditors, the debtor or other persons accept certain undertakings for the benefit of the contributor.

As a measure to prevent bankruptcy, the debtor may be granted financial assistance to the amount sufficient for repaying monetary liabilities and obligatory payments, and for restoring its solvency for account of the budget or non-budgetary funds.

Financial assistance may be accompanied by the debtor or other persons assuming obligations to persons granting the financial assistance[17].

---

[15] Bankruptcy Law, Article 16.

[16] Strictly speaking, sanation is a pre-trial step and not a bankruptcy procedure, but a financial help to the debtor.

Further Stages of the Bankruptcy Procedure

The Bankruptcy Law does not require that the debtor must be liquidated immediately once bankruptcy procedures have started, and offers alternatives to the straightforward liquidation of insolvent entities. These alternatives may be employed at one of the following stages of the bankruptcy procedure:

- Monitoring (observation)
- Financial sanation
- Outside management (trusteeship, external management)
- Receivership (competitive proceedings), and
- Amicable settlement.

Financial sanation, outside management and amicable settlement are real alternatives to the bankruptcy of a debtor, as they are aimed at restoration of solvency of the debtor and the avoidance of liquidation. Monitoring and receivership are rather the procedures aimed at the protection of creditors' rights, as their primary goal is to recover as much of the debtor's property as possible.

All resolutions and rulings hereof shall be inscribed to the Unified Federal Register on Bankruptcy Data as well as being published in the official printed mass media.

Monitoring (Observation)

The goal of monitoring is to secure preservation of the debtor's property, analyse the financial situation of the debtor, compile the register of creditors' claims and hold the first creditors' meeting.

As the principal goal of monitoring is to determine whether the debtor shall not meet the creditors' claims, such a procedure is omitted in cases when there has been a decision made on the liquidation of the debtor[18] or in case of the absence of the debtor[19].

---

[17] The Expert-Consultative Council on Insolvency and Financial Sanation is formed under the MERT, aiming to optimise the legislation on bankruptcy and to prevent bankruptcy.

[18] Bankruptcy Law, Article 225.

[19] Bankruptcy Law, Article 228. The procedures of financial sanation and trusteeship are also ommited. In case of bankruptcy of the absent debtor the claim to the Arbitrazh court may be filed notwithstanding the amount of the creditors' claims.

Monitoring Procedure

Introduction of monitoring by the Arbitrazh court and appointment of a monitor (interim manager) →

Analysing debtor's financial state →

Identifying creditors and determining the amount of their claims →

Notifying creditors that the Arbitrazh court has accepted an application on bankruptcy and on convening the first creditor's meeting →

Establishing the amount of creditors' claims →

Holding the first creditors' meeting →

The Arbitrazh court makes a decision on results of the monitoring: to initiate receivership, to introduce financial sanation or trusteeship, to sign an amicable settlement, or to refuse to adjudicate on bankruptcy.

Once a court has accepted a petition on bankruptcy of a debtor, monitoring is applied to the debtor unless otherwise established by law. Monitoring does not require dismissal or redundancy of the management or employees of the company (though the interim manager may petition to court for the leave to dismiss the management). However, the management is limited in respect to decision-making. From that moment, certain transactions may be entered into only with approval of the monitor. Such transactions include:

- Disposal of any property with a balance sheet value (book value) in excess of 5% of the balance sheet value of the debtor's assets
- Taking or granting loans, credits, guarantees, assignments and giving the debtor's property in trust.

From the date of monitoring, realisation of the pledged property without application to court shall not be admitted[20]. In addition, the following decisions may not be adopted by the debtor under any circumstances:

- On reorganisation or liquidation of the debtor
- On foundation of legal entities, branches or representative offices
- On issuing securities or payment of dividends

[20] Bankruptcy Law, Article 18^1.

- On letting a debtor's shareholders withdraw or on acquisition of shares from shareholders
- On joining associations, holdings and other amalgamations
- On concluding particular partnership contracts.

Monitoring shall incur the following legal consequences:

- Claims to the debtor shall be presented only according to the procedure stipulated in the Bankruptcy Law
- Under the petition of a creditor a court process concerning recovery any property from the debtor shall be stopped
- Under the petition of a creditor an executory process against the debtor shall be stopped
- No claims of participants of the debtor shall be satisfied, e.g. alienation of the share of a participant due to the withdrawal of the participant, payment of the current value of the stake, etc.
- The dividend payments and payments under other emission securities are prohibited
- The termination of offset obligations of the debtor shall not be permitted in case of violation of the priority of the creditors' settlement.

Establishing the Amount of Creditors' Claims

Creditors shall be notified of proceedings on adjudication of bankruptcy being initiated by a monitor or the debtor, who is to notify all creditors he is aware of within 5 days of the date of the Arbitrazh court ruling on accepting an application of bankruptcy.

Creditors shall present their claims within 30 days of the date of the publication regarding the introduction of monitoring[21].

Only creditors with established claims shall take part in the first creditors' meeting. Claims are deemed established if:

- The court has ruled on them
- Documents certifying that the debtor acknowledges these claims are available.

Other claims may be deemed established if:

- The Arbitrazh court has not accepted the debtor's objections, which it may submit within a week of receiving the claim

[21] Ruling of the Arbitrazh Circuit Court of the Central Circuit No.A35-6347/05-g, dated 4 May 2006.

- The debtor has not submitted objections within 15 days from the end of the presentation of claims.

In order to participate in the first creditors' meeting creditors may submit their claims to the debtor within a month's time from the date of receiving the monitor's notification. Established claims shall be submitted to the monitor, those not established – to the debtor and to the Arbitrazh court.

During monitoring, the debtor's financial status is being analysed. At the end of monitoring, the first meeting of creditors is convened to make one of the following decisions:

- To introduce financial sanation (under the agreement with the debtor or the third parties)
- To introduce trusteeship by petition of the first creditors' meeting
    - if the first creditors' meeting has decided on recognising the debtor bankrupt (or has not submitted any decision), but this decision is detrimental to most creditors, and a real opportunity to restore the debtor's solvency has been disclosed
    - if after the meeting circumstances were revealed making the restoration of the debtor's solvency possible
- To recognise the debtor's bankruptcy and initiate receivership by petition of the first creditors' meeting
    - (if bankruptcy symptoms are evident) if the first creditors' meeting has not yielded a decision on introducing trusteeship or on approving an amicable settlement
    - if no decision of the meeting has been submitted
- To sign an amicable settlement and terminate proceedings on adjudication of bankruptcy.

The decision of the creditors' meeting must be approved by the Arbitrazh court. If a decision was not made within a fixed period, the court may make a decision on its own.

The Monitor

The court-appointed monitor does not substitute for the regular corporate government bodies of the debtor *ab initio.* However, if the debtor's manager interferes with actions of the monitor or acts to the detriment of the rights and interests of the debtor and/or its creditors, the court may remove the manager from his duty and authorise the monitor to fulfil the duties of the manager.

The monitor's responsibilities are the following:

- Securing safety of the debtor's property
- Analysing the debtor's financial status in order to establish sufficiency of its property to cover legal costs, monitor's fees and the possibility of solvency restoration
- Identification of fictitious (spurious) or intentional (deliberate) bankruptcy
- Creation of the register of creditors' claims
- Notification of creditors
- Convocation of the first creditors' meeting.

It is up to the first creditors' meeting to decide whether an amicable settlement should be reached, whether the court should appoint a trustee for the debtor or declare the debtor bankrupt and order liquidation to take place.

The First Creditors' Meeting

The first creditors' meeting is convened by the monitor at least 10 days before the end of the monitoring.

The debtor's general director, the representative of the debtor's employees and the monitor take part in the first meeting without voting. The latter is responsible for the course of action at the meeting.

The decision of the first creditors' meeting is to be approved by the Arbitrazh court.

Financial Sanation

Article 76 of the Bankruptcy Law states that during monitoring, the debtor or other interested persons may apply to the Arbitrazh court for the establishment of financial sanation. Such persons shall provide the security, which shall exceed the volume of the debtor's obligations by not less than 20%. The debtor's liability, in accordance with a debt repayment schedule, may be secured with a pledge (mortgage), bank guarantee, state (municipal) guarantee or surety.

If the issue of financial sanation is to be addressed at the creditors' meeting, the application and the enclosed documents must be presented to the monitor and the Arbitrazh court no later than 15 days prior to the date of the creditors' meeting.

When financial sanation is introduced, measures taken earlier to secure creditors' claims are cancelled. Limitations may be imposed on the debtor's right to dispose of his property, but only if such limitations concern the bankruptcy procedure.

At the stage of financial sanation a **schedule for debt repayment** is elaborated and approved. The schedule must provide for:

- Settlements with creditors of the first and second priority turns within six months
- Settlements with all other creditors at least one month before the date of the end of the financial sanation, provided by the financial sanation plan.

Under the decision of the creditors' meeting and approval of the Arbitrazh court it is possible to introduce changes to the schedule for debt repayment.

In case of non-observance of the schedule for debt payment for more than 5 days, the administrative manager shall claim against the persons who provided the security to satisfy obligations of the debtor. Claims of the persons who provided the security shall be satisfied by the debtor after termination of the bankruptcy case or during the receivership, together with the third turn creditors.

Under Article 92 of the Bankruptcy Law, on the results of financial sanation the Arbitrazh court may hold a decision regarding the establishment of a trusteeship in the following cases:

- If it is established that the debtor's solvency can really be restored
- If a petition of the creditors' meeting was filed with the Arbitrazh court on the establishment of the trusteeship
- If the creditors' meeting adopted a decision to file a petition with the Arbitrazh court for declaring the debtor bankrupt and commencing receivership, but there are circumstances certifying that the solvency of the debtor may be restored.

The aggregate term of financial sanation and trusteeship shall not exceed two years.

If more than 18 months have passed between the date of establishment of financial sanation and the date when the Arbitrazh court hears the issue of establishment of the trusteeship, the Arbitrazh court must not hold a decision on the establishment of the trusteeship.

Note that financial sanation is an infrequent procedure due to the fact that more creditors may appear during further bankruptcy procedures.

Trusteeship

The Arbitrazh court establishes a trusteeship, whose task is to restore the debtor's solvency, under the decision of the creditors. At this stage, the settlement of creditors' claims is suspended.

The period of trusteeship must not be more than 18 months. The term may be extended for up to 6 months.

The trustee assumes full responsibility for the management of the debtor and substitutes completely for all bodies of corporate governance of the debtor. Management bodies of the legal entity must transfer all documents, records and other data, as well as stamps and valuables, to the trustee within 3 days of their appointment.

As a result of the establishment of a trusteeship:

- All preceding measures of safeguarding creditor's rights shall be cancelled
- Arrest of the debtor's property or other limitations on the disposal of the debtor's property may be imposed only in the context of the bankruptcy procedures
- All monetary claims against the debtor (except for alimonies, payments to authors of inventions and payments to the insured persons), as well as its obligations to make mandatory payments, shall be frozen
- Claims for payment of damages and fines, including those related to mandatory payments, shall be presented only upon termination of trusteeship and only in the amounts, existing as of the date of introduction of the trusteeship.

Moratorium on Creditors' Claims

While introducing a trusteeship, a moratorium on creditors' claims shall occur.

A moratorium means the suspension of the debtor's execution of monetary liabilities and obligatory payments. It extends to monetary liabilities and obligatory payments with maturity before trusteeship was introduced.

Uncontested recovery on writs of execution shall not be allowed.

Execution of writs on property recovery which came into effect before an application on bankruptcy was accepted shall be suspended (except debts on wages, salaries and some other payments).

Penalties (fines, late charges) and other sanctions shall not be charged, as well as due interest.

Interest shall be accrued in the amount of the creditor's claims under Article 395 of the Civil Code.

Powers of the Trustee

The trustee has a right to:

- Dispose of the debtor's property at his discretion, except for cases when the consent of the creditors' meeting is required. Such cases are the following:
    - Execution of major transactions (property value over 10% of assets book value)
    - Execution of new transactions not stipulated by the outside management plan, if debtor's monetary liabilities exceed 10% of the creditors' total claims
    - Making a decision on increasing consumption expenditures[22], except for cases stipulated by law[23].
- Conclude an amicable settlement on the debtor's behalf
- Within a three month term after the introduction of the trusteeship, announce refusal to perform the debtor's contractual obligations if such performance prevents restoration of the debtor's solvency
- Claim that the Arbitrazh court finds transactions of the debtor invalid.

Only the trustee may invalidate transactions of the debtor. Such transactions are voidable, i.e. it is presumed that the transactions concluded are valid, and only in court is it possible to prove otherwise.

Note

Transactions in the course of the ordinary economic activity of the debtor shall not be appealed if their value is less than 1% of the balance assets of the debtor.

Besides, the law distinguishes between two types of transactions of the debtor that are void, i.e. invalid without necessity to stipulate that fact in court[24]:

- Suspected transactions:

[22] E.g. transactions the result of which is the granting or taking of loans, giving surety, cession of a debt, etc.

[23] Bankruptcy Law, Article 101.

[24] Bankruptcy Law, Chapter III.1.

  - Concluded within 1 year prior to acceptance by the Arbitrazh court of the application on bankruptcy
  - Non-proportional execution of obligations by the parties to the transaction (e.g. price (or other conditions) of the transaction received by the debtor is worse than price (or other conditions) in similar situation in similar transactions)
- Suspected transactions concluded in favour of an interested party:
  - Concluded within the three years prior to acceptance by the Arbitrazh court of the application for bankruptcy
  - Real property damage is caused as a result of the transaction
  - The aim of the transaction is to cause damage to the property rights of the creditors
  - The other party knew that the aim of the transaction was to cause damage to the property interests of the creditors

Note

The term "interested persons" includes the debtor's executives and the chief accountant (including those dismissed within the year prior to the commencement of bankruptcy proceedings), but excludes the debtor's employees.

- Transactions preferable to a particular creditor:
  - Concluded within a month prior to the acceptance by the Arbitrazh court of the application for bankruptcy
  - Aim to secure the execution of obligations by the debtor or any third party (that arose before the conclusion of the transaction in dispute) toward the creditor in question
  - The transaction caused or may cause changes in the priority of creditors' claims under the obligations that arose before the conclusion of the transaction in dispute
  - The transaction caused or may cause the satisfaction of the claims, which are not due as of the moment of conclusion of the transaction, of particular creditors in case of existence of non-executed obligations before other creditors
  - The transaction resulted in a more preferable outcome for a particular creditor in the execution of claims existent prior to conclusion of the transaction, than it would in the case of settlement with the creditors under the legislation of the RF on bankruptcy.

Duties of the Trustee

The trustee must:

- Take the debtor's property under his management and hold its inventory
- Develop an outside management plan and submit it for the approval of the creditors with a month of the appointment. This plan:
    - o Shall contain an overview of measures to restore the debtor's solvency
    - o Shall be approved by the creditors within two months of the trusteeship being introduced
    - o Shall be submitted to the Arbitrazh court within five days of its approval at the creditors' meeting (if the plan has not been submitted six months after the trusteeship was introduced, the court may rule on initiating receivership)
- Review creditors' claims, make objections to them and keep a register of them
- Take steps to recover debts owed to the debtor
- Submit to the creditors a report on the results of the implementation of the outside management plan and exercise other authority as stipulated by law

Article 109 of the Bankruptcy Law suggests that the trustee may use any of the following measures to restore the solvency of the debtor:

- Reorientation of the production process
- Shutting down of unprofitable production lines
- Liquidation of accounts receivable
- Sale of a part of the debtor's property
- Assignment of the debtor's rights
- Having third parties or the state or municipality (with respect to the entities founded by them) perform the debtor's obligations
- Increasing the charter capital of the debtor with contributions of the participants and third parties
- Allocation of additional ordinary shares[25]
- Sale of the debtor's business
- Replacement of the assets of the debtor
- Other measures to restore solvency of the debtor

---

[25] Under the petition of a management body of the debtor, the charter capital of the debtor-J-SC may be increased by the allocation of additional ordinary shares under the closed subscription and within three months. The Prospectus of Emission shall contain the provision that the payment shall be effected only by monetary means.

The Trustee's Report

The trustee is obliged to submit a report on his activities for review to the creditors. Along with the report, the trustee should submit his recommendations as to whether:

- the trusteeship should be prolonged,
- an amicable settlement should be reached
- declaration of bankruptcy and receivership procedures should be requested from the court
- the solvency of the debtor is restored

The report of the trustee should subsequently be submitted for the consideration of the creditors and approval by the Arbitrazh court within 14 days of the expiration of the term of trusteeship. There are several potential outcomes that may follow the submission of the trustee's report:

- The report may be approved by the creditors, in which case their demands will be settled in due course
- If the report is not approved this will invoke receivership and the company will be wound up. The assets of the company will then be sold and the demands of creditors and others met according to the priorities determined by law, or alternatively, the priority of their notices
- An amicable settlement may be agreed at any time during the insolvency procedure
- If approved, this will ultimately result in the creditors' demands being met in due course
- The trusteeship may be prolonged in order to extend the period in which the company may be rescued or creditors' demands met

Receivership (Liquidation)

Receivership is commenced upon the declaration of the debtor's bankruptcy in the Arbitrazh court. The receivership period should not exceed six months, but this period may be extended for up to six months by the Arbitrazh court under the claim of the person participating in the bankruptcy case. Article 124 of the Bankruptcy Law states that any extension of the receivership period by more than an additional six months may be appealed in the Arbitrazh court.

As of the date the receivership is initiated:

- All liabilities and payments are deemed mature
- Financial sanctions are not imposed on any debts

- The information concerning the financial situation of the debtor ceases to be a commercial secret
- All transactions concerning the alienation of the property of the debtor are executed only under Chapter 7 of the Bankruptcy Law
- All limitations imposed on the debtor's property are recalled
- All the debtor's management bodies are dismissed; management is entrusted to the receiver
- The information regarding the declaration of the debtor as bankrupt is subject to mandatory publication in the official mass media, stipulated by the Government of the RF – "The Commersant"

Note

As of the date of the receivership, all sanctions in regard to the debtor shall stop.[26]

The Arbitrazh court shall appoint a receiver, who operates the debtor's property during the receivership.

The Receiver

The receiver is appointed under the same procedure as the trustee. The receiver has all the powers of both a manager and a trustee, and fulfills their duties. The scope of the receiver's tasks depends on the stage of the bankruptcy procedures, but the receiver's actions are aimed at recovering as much of the debtor's property as possible.

The functions of the receiver are the following:

- Operating the debtor's property and ensuring its safety
- Making up an inventory of property
- Involving an independent appraiser to value the debtor's property
- The notification of employees
- Making objections to creditors' claims
- Making claims to the third parties bearing subsidiary liability for the debtor's obligations
- Filing suits to invalidate the transactions of the debtor concluded since the date of submission of the application for bankruptcy or within the six months prior to that date
- Selling the debtor's property and making settlements with creditors
- Other functions stipulated by law

---

[26] Ruling of the Presidium of the High Arbitrazh Court of the RF No.2573/05, dated 23 August 2005.

Sale of the Debtor's Property

The bankruptcy estate consists of two parts:

- All of the debtor's assets as indicated in the balance sheet or similar documents as of the date of the receiver's appointment
- The property revealed during the receivership. Not all of the debtor's property is included in the bankruptcy estate; only that property of which recovery is sought comprises the bankruptcy estate. The following property in the possession of the debtor but not legally owned by the debtor shall be excluded from the bankruptcy estate:
    - Leased property or property in the safe custody of the debtor
    - Personal property of the employees of the enterprise, but not of founders of the legal entity

The debtor's bankruptcy estate includes all property available as of the date the receivership is initiated and any property revealed during the receivership proceedings, except for:

- Certain property, the sale of which is prohibited by law, and exclusive rights, including rights to engage in specific types of debtor's activity
- Residential premises, pre-school institutions and public facilities[27]

After an inventory and appraisal, the property of the bankruptcy estate shall be sold at auction or by bidding unless another procedure has been established by the creditors' meeting or the committee.

Any property of which the sale requires a special permit is sold by closed bidding.

Property not sold during the first bidding is submitted for a second bidding or sold without bidding.

[27] Generally, social facilities and public utilities owned by the debtor, such as housing, child-care and certain other facilities deemed to be significant to the community, are excluded from the debtor's estate and sold by tender to a party which plans to use such social facilities and public utilities for their specified purpose. In cases when the purchaser of the social facilities and public utilities violates the agreement to use social facilities and public utilities for their intended purpose, the social facilities and public utilities shall be transferred to the relevant municipality.

Creditors' Settlement. Priority in Satisfaction of the Creditors' Claims

Article 134 of the Bankruptcy Law stipulates the following priorities in satisfying creditors' claims:

- Top priorities for the accounting of the debtor's estate:
  - Legal costs and the arbitrazh manager's fees
  - Debts in the form of salaries and dismissal payments
  - Current maintenance expenses
  - Other claims on liabilities which emerged during the bankruptcy procedures

Note

Settlements with creditors of each of the top set of priority levels shall be conducted after full settlement with the creditors of the preceding priority. If the claims of creditors on current payments belong to the same priority level, they are satisfied in chronological order.

- First priority – Claims of individuals on payments for harm caused to life and health
- Second priority – Discharge pay and labour remuneration under labour contracts
- Third priority – all other creditors: obligatory payments to the budget and non-budgetary funds and settlements with creditors on any remaining civil law obligations

Note

Pledged property is treated separately from the debtor's other assets, and the disposal of pledged/mortgaged assets will still require the consent of the relevant secured creditor. 70% of the money raised after sale of pledged property goes to the creditor, whose rights are secured by the pledged property. 20% of the money raised after the sale of the property is directed to the special banking account of the debtor for settlements with first and the second priority level claimants, and the rest is used for reimbursement of court expenses and the arbitrazh manager's fees.

In case the creditor secured under pledge is a bankruptcy creditor on a credit agreement, 80% of the money raised from the sale of the pledged property is directed to this bankruptcy creditor. 15% of the money raised is directed to the special banking account of the debtor for settlements with the first and second priority level claimants, and the rest is used for reimbursement of court expenses and the arbitrazh manager's fees.

The receiver is obliged to eliminate all existing bank accounts belonging to the debtor other than the sole bank account whose funds are used to satisfy the claims of the debtor's creditors. The funds in this account are replenished by the proceeds from sales of the debtor's property at public sales (and, failing that, through private contracts), and by collection of the debtor's accounts receivable.

Settlements with creditors of each priority shall be conducted after full settlement with creditors of the preceding priority. If the debtor has insufficient funds to cover the claims of creditors of any priority, remaining funds are allocated *pro rata* to the amounts of the creditors' claims.

If a claim is submitted after settlements have started and this claim has a higher priority compared thant he claims currently being settled, settlements should be postponed until the claim with a higher priority is repaid.

If claims are made after the register of claims has been closed, they have the lowest priority and should be settled only if any of the debtor's property remains. This includes:

- The arbitrazh manager's fees if presented after the closing of the register of claims
- Claims on obligatory payments arising after the opening of the receivership, the term of their presentation notwithstanding [28]

If claims cannot be settled due to insufficient funds, they are deemed cancelled. Creditors may claim from the third parties keeping the debtor's property if the debtor's property has been obtained by these third parties illegally.

The debtor's remaining property after full settlement with all creditors of all priorities, in case of refusal by a creditor to take the property for the execution of obligations, goes to the local self-governing bodies of the RF at the location of the debtor.

If the debtor's property is insufficient to settle the arbitrazh manager's remuneration, such expenses in the part not covered by the debtor's property shall be reimbursed by the creditor-claimant.[29]

---

[28] Ruling of the Federal Arbitrazh Court of the Moscow Circuit No.KG-A40/9322-05, dated 9 November 2005.

[29] Ruling of the Presidium of the High Arbitrazh Court No.6007/08, dated 13 November 2008.

The Arbitrazh Court Ruling on the Termination of Receivership

After settlements with creditors have been effected, the receiver submits a report to the Arbitrazh court, enclosing:

- Documents certifying to the debtor's assets having been sold and creditors' claims having been met
- The register of creditors' claims, indicating the amounts of the repayments

The Arbitrazh court rules on the termination of the receivership, and the decision is submitted to the body responsible for the state registration of legal entities, i.e. the Tax Service.

As of this date, an entry on the liquidation of the debtor is made in the Unified State Register of Legal Entities, the authority of the receiver is over, the receivership is deemed terminated, and the debtor - liquidated.

Amicable Settlement (Compromise, Composition)

An amicable settlement between the debtor and his creditors may be reached at any stage of the bankruptcy procedures.[30] An amicable settlement may be concluded only after the satisfaction of the claims of first and second priority creditors. It is deemed accepted by the bankruptcy creditors if it has been approved by the majority of them.

An amicable settlement must be concluded in writing and is subject to further approval by the Arbitrazh court. An amicable settlement enters into force as of the date of its approval by the court, and is binding to the bankruptcy creditors and the third parties who sign it. Approval of the amicable settlement by the court leads to the termination of the bankruptcy procedures and the powers of the monitor, trustee or receiver. The court, however, may refuse to approve the amicable settlement if its terms contradict the applicable legislation or violate the rights of the third parties.

The amicable settlement may contain provisions on:

- Performance of obligations by installments
- Ceding the debtor's claims
- Performance of the debtor's obligations by third parties
- Debt remission
- Other provisions

[30] Bankruptcy Law, Article 150.

As of the date the amicable settlement is approved:

- The authority of the Arbitrazh manager ceases, and he acts as the debtor's CEO until a new CEO is appointed or elected
- The debtor or Arbitrazh manager starts to repay debts

Note that an amicable settlement is not efficient in cases where there are debts to the federal budget or non-budgetary funds.[31]

The Arbitrazh court may refuse to approve an amicable settlement if:

- Debts of the first and second priorities have not been repaid
- Procedure has been violated or the correct procedure for an amicable settlement has not been complied with
- Third parties' rights have been violated
- The amicable settlement contradicts any legal acts of the RF

Invalidity of an Amicable Settlement

An amicable settlement may be found invalid by the Arbitrazh court if:

- The provisions thereof infringe upon creditors' interests or provide advantages for them
- The execution of the amicable settlement may lead to the debtor's bankruptcy
- Other grounds for the transaction's invalidity are present

An amicable settlement may be found invalid by the Arbitrazh court on the part of all creditors; it may not be found invalid concerning only one of the creditors.[32]

If the amicable settlement is recognised as invalid, bankruptcy procedures shall be resumed.

---

[31] Article 156 of the Bankruptcy Law states that an amicable settlement may not contradict the provisions of the legislation on taxes and levies, under which the indulgence of the federal budget may be provided for not more than one year. Indulgence on federal taxes to the federal budget may be given with the approval of the Government of the RF for a term from one year up to three years. Under the Ruling of the Government of the RF No.257, dated 29 May 2004, the Tax Service is empowered to vote at the creditors' meeting in favour of the conclusion of an amicable settlement only in cases where the debts of the legal entity to the federal budget will be paid within 30 days from the moment of the amicable settlement comes into force. Such provisions make the conclusion of amicable settlements almost impossible.

[32] Bankruptcy Law, Article 164.2.

Dissolution of the Amicable Settlement

An amicable settlement may not be dissolved by agreement between an individual creditor and the debtor.

Note

The amicable settlement shall be concluded not earlier than the date of the first creditors' meeting.

The approval of the amicable settlement must be given by the majority of the total number of bankruptcy creditors, not the majority of the creditors present at the meeting.

The Arbitrazh court is not entitled to change the contents of the amicable settlement.

The amicable settlement may be approved by the Arbitrazh court in case of indebtedness on current payments. The Arbitrazh court shall in this case examine whether the rights and lawful interests of current creditors are infringed.

Non-Execution of the Amicable Settlement

In case of non-execution of the amicable settlement, the creditors are entitled to file their claims in the order provided by procedural legislation without dissolution of the amicable settlement.

In case of initiation of a new bankruptcy case, the volume of the claims of the creditors – participants of the amicable settlement – shall be determined under the provisions of the amicable settlement.

Special Cases of Bankruptcy Procedures

The bankruptcy procedures for banks are determined in the Bankruptcy of Credit Organisations Law, in which the highest emphasis is placed upon bankruptcy prevention. Bankruptcy adjudication for banks may be instigated only after the bank's license for effecting bank transactions has been recalled.

A special order of bankruptcy procedures is set for:

- Insurance organisations
- Professional participants of the securities market
- Town-forming organisations whose employees make up at least 25% of the population of a corresponding locality
- Strategic organisations
- Natural monopolies
- Agricultural organisations

- Individual entrepreneurs
- Absent debtors
- Debtors in the process of liquidation.

Bankruptcy of a Legal Entity in the Process of Liquidation

Under Article 63.3 of the Civil Code and Article 224 of the Bankruptcy Law, if the value of the property of the business entity that is being liquidated proves to be insufficient to satisfy the claims of the business entity's creditors, the legal entity's liquidation commission must file a petition for bankruptcy with the Arbitrazh court.

Monitoring, financial sanation and trusteeship are not established while the legal entity is in the process of liquidation.

Fictitious and Intentional (Premeditated) Bankruptcy

In cases where the Arbitrazh court finds a lack of signs of bankruptcy or discovers a fictitious or intentional bankruptcy, the Arbitrazh court will refuse to declare a debtor bankrupt. Administrative and criminal liability is provided by law for fictitious and intentional bankruptcy and for illegal actions during bankruptcy procedures.

Fictitious Bankruptcy

In cases when a debtor's application has been filed with the Arbitrazh court when the debtor was actually capable of meeting creditors' claims in full, or if the debtor did not take measures to contest a non-grounded claimant's demands, the debtor shall be liable to the creditors for losses incurred due to the opening of the bankruptcy case or the recognition of non-grounded creditors' demands.

Intentional Bankruptcy

In cases of the bankruptcy of a debtor being the fault of the debtor's founders (participants), the owner of the property of the debtor (a unitary enterprise) or other persons - in particular, the fault of the head of the debtor who is entitled to issue instructions binding to the debtor or can otherwise control its activity - founders (participants) of the debtor or other persons may be recognised as subsidiarily liable for the debtor's obligations if the debtor's property is insufficient.

Major damage is the obligatory characteristic of intentional bankruptcy.

The following methods are used in intentional bankruptcy:

- The founding of new business entities and transfer of the charter capital assets of the debtor business entity
- Fictitious sales of property to business entities and individuals, as a result of which the debtor business entity receives long-term obligations of payment for the property
- Withdrawal of participants and transfer of major parts of the property of the legal entity to their ownership
- Sale of capital assets of the legal entity through colourable firms, as a result of which the promissory notes of fictitious firms become company's assets
- Artificial indebtedness of the legal entity to "pocket" creditors to later sell material benefits to these controlled creditors
- Payments to counter agents when it is known in advance that the recourse discharge will not be received
- Credits and loans under unreasonably leonine terms
- The use of money funds for purposes other than covering existing debts

Chapter Roundup

1. A business entity or individual entrepreneur is recognised as bankrupt under the following conditions:

- They cannot meet their creditors' claims
- Three months have passed since the creditors filed their claims
- The sum total of the business entity or individual entrepreneur's obligations exceeds the value of the property owned by them
- The Arbitrazh court has decided upon recognising the business entity or individual entrepreneur as bankrupt

2. The arbitrazh managers have the following roles depending on the stage of the bankruptcy procedures:

- The monitor (the interim manager) in the monitoring stage (observation)
- The administrative manager in financial sanation
- The trustee (the outside manager or external manager) in trusteeship (outside management, external management)
- The receiver in receivership (competitive proceedings)

3. The head of the debtor must file an application for bankruptcy if:

- The debtor is unable to discharge monetary obligations
- The debtor's management body has decided to declare the debtor bankrupt
- The body that is the authorised owner of the property of the debtor has decided to declare the debtor bankrupt
- The debtor is unable to pursue debtors' economic activity

4. Major decisions taken at the creditors' meeting are the following:

- The introduction of financial sanation, outside management or recognition of the debtor's bankruptcy and initiation of receivership
- The approval of the financial sanation and outside management plan and the schedule for debt repayment
- The conclusion of an amicable settlement
- The election of members of the creditor's committee
- The additional requirements for the candidates for administrative manager, external manager and receiver
- The determination of the self-regulated organisation of the arbitrazh managers

- The election of the holder of the register

5. The major stages of bankruptcy procedures are the following:
- Sanation
- Monitoring
- Financial sanation
- Outside management
- Receivership
- Amicable settlement

6. Major steps of the observation procedure are the following:
- Introduction of monitoring by the Arbitrazh court and the appointment of a monitor
- Analysing the debtor's financial status
- Identifying creditors and determining amounts of claims
- Notifying creditors of the acceptance of an application for bankruptcy and on the convening of the first creditor's meeting
- Establishing the amounts of creditors' claims
- Holding the first creditors' meeting
- The Arbitrazh Court makes a decision on the results of the monitoring

7. The following transactions shall not be adopted by the debtor during observation:
- The reorganisation or liquidation of the debtor
- The foundation of legal entities, branches or representative offices
- The issuing of securities or payment of dividends
- Letting a debtor's shareholders withdraw or the acquisition of shares from shareholders
- Joining associations, holdings and other amalgamations
- The conclusion of particular partnership contracts

8. On introduction of external management:
- The management bodies are dismissed
- A moratorium is put on creditors' claims

9. Both the external manager and the receiver may invalidate transactions concluded by the debtor before the initiation of the bankruptcy process.

10. As of the date on which receivership is initiated:

- All liabilities and payments are deemed mature
- Financial sanctions are not imposed on any debts
- The information concerning the financial situation of the debtor ceases to be a commercial secret
- All the transactions concerning the alienation of the property of the debtor are executed only under the Bankruptcy Law
- All limitations imposed on the debtor's property are recalled
- All the debtor's management bodies are dismissed, and management is entrusted to the receiver
- The information about the declaration of the debtor as bankrupt is subject to mandatory publication

11. The priorities for the satisfaction of creditors' claims are as follows:

- Top Priority
    - Legal costs and the arbitrazh manager's Fees
    - Current maintenance expenses
    - Claims on liabilities which emerged during bankruptcy procedures
    - Outstanding salaries and dismissal payments
    - Other current expenses
- First priority - Claims of individuals on payments for harm caused to life and health
- Second priority - Discharge pay and labour remuneration under labour contracts
- Third Priority
    - Obligatory payments to the budget and off-budgetary funds
    - Settlements with creditors regarding remaining civil law obligations

12. An amicable settlement may be agreed at any stage of the bankruptcy process.

13. Types of illegal bankruptcy are the following:

- Fictitious
- Intentional (premeditated)

Questions

1. As regards the monitor (interim manager), which of the following is correct?

- The monitor is introduced by the Arbitrazh court at the end of the observation stage of the insolvency procedure
- The monitor is appointed by the executive management of the company as soon as the first indications of insolvency become apparent
- The monitor is appointed after the Arbitrazh court has accepted an application to declare a company insolvent
- The monitor is introduced by the Arbitrazh court at the beginning of the observation stage of the insolvency procedure

2. A company is trying to avoid insolvency and further liquidation and is submitting an application for financial rehabilitation. Which of the following documents would not be submitted with the application for financial rehabilitation?

- The schedule of repayment of debts
- A list of shareholders or participants who voted in favour of financial rehabilitation
- Information explaining how the shareholders or participants will ensure the payment of the debts of the company
- Information on personal assets

3. In the event of insolvency, which of the following is not likely to be a criminal offence?

- Satisfying the claims of some creditors over those of others
- Deliberately making the insolvency worse
- Making outstanding salary payments to employees
- Falsifying accounting records

4. When the external manager is appointed, what does this effectively signal the end of for the company?

- All employment contracts
- The authority of the management bodies
- Claims by shareholders
- Claims for payment of unpaid wages

5. Which of the following is the correct definition of a legitimate first meeting of creditors?

- The bankruptcy creditors and authorised state bodies present represent more than 25% of the total amount owed to bankruptcy creditors and authorised state bodies
- The bankruptcy creditors and authorised state bodies present represent more than 75% of the total amount owed to bankruptcy creditors and authorised state bodies
- The bankruptcy creditors and authorised state bodies present represent more than 40% of the total amount owed to bankruptcy creditors and authorised state bodies
- The bankruptcy creditors and authorised state bodies present represent more than 50% of the total amount owed to bankruptcy creditors and authorised state bodies

6. In relation to the law of insolvency:

(a) Explain the conditions that must be fulfilled in order to initiate insolvency proceedings against a company.

(b) Explain how the financial interests of creditors are protected during the insolvency process.

7. In 2013, the Open Company Limited by Shares (OAO) "Unona" filed its claim against the Closed Company Limited by Shares (ZAO) "Malaga" to recover debt for heat energy consumed to an amount totalling 3 millon roubles with the arbitration court.

While considering the case, the arbitration court found out that in 2012, bankruptcy adjudication was initiated with respect to ZAO "Malaga", with OAO "Unona" as a creditor. In October 2012, the arbitration court took the decision to approve the composition signed by the debtor and the creditors during the observation procedure, and terminated the proceedings. According to the composition, the debt ZAO "Malaga" owed OAO "Unona" amounted to 150,000 roubles.

Filing the claim with the court in 2013, OAO "Unona" referred to the fact that the arrears stated in the composition did not include money owed for heating a number of premises. Therefore, the right to recover arrears of that type were to be protected by means other than bankruptcy adjudication.

Required:

(a) Explain what is meant by "composition" in bankruptcy adjudication procedures.
(b) Explain whether a composition may be concluded during observation.
(c) Explain whether the claim of OAO "Unona" can be considered a separate claim, not related to bankruptcy adjudication, if that entity was party to a composition.

Further Readings

1. Витрянский В.В. Реформа законодательства о несостоятельности (банкротстве) // Вестник ВАС РФ. 1998. Специальное приложение к № 2.
2. Дубинчин АЛ. Институт несостоятельности и внеконкурсное удовлетворение требований к должнику — юридическому лицу // Хозяйство и право. 1999. № 9—10.
3. Дубинчин А.А. Мировое соглашение в деле о банкротстве: проблемы теории и практики // Хозяйство и право. 2000. № 7.
4. Калнан Р. Мировое соглашение / / Вестник ВАС РФ. 2001. Специальное приложение к №3.
5. Лившиц Н.Г. Мировое соглашение в деле о банкротстве // Вестник ВАС РФ. 1999. №1.
6. Лившиц Н.Г. Разбирательство дел о банкротстве в арбитражном суде // Вестник ВАС РФ. 1998. Специальное приложение к № 2.
7. Машкина Т.Н. О некоторых вопросах практики применения Закона «О несостоятельности (банкротстве)» Арбитражным судом Красноярского края / / Вестник ВАС РФ. 1999. № 10.
8. Никитина О.А. Конкурсное производство // Вестник ВАС РФ. 2001. Специальное приложение к № 3.
9. Никитина О.А. Процедура наблюдения // Вестник ВАС РФ. 1998. Специальное приложение к № 2.
10. Попондопуло В.Ф. Конкурсное право: Правовое регулирование несостоятельности (банкротства) предпринимателей: Учебное пособие. СПб., 1995.
11. Свит Ю. Восстановительные процедуры — способ предотвращения банкротства / / Российская юстиция. 1998. № 3.

CHAPTER FIVE

CORPORATE ETHICAL BEHAVIOUR

Part I. The Idea of Corporate Governance in Russia

"Corporate governance has become an increasingly popular term in Russia since the late 1990s. In Russia corporate governance is not a well-developed concept although the MERT has a corporate governance department. Not only has Russia witnessed a transformation in the role of the private sector in economic development and job creation, but corporate scandals, global competition, and various domestic and international efforts have made corporate governance a household name."[1] The concept of shareholder protection, the ethical conduct of business operations by directors, the involvement of employees and the greater community, transparency in dealing with major transactions, the way information is disclosed and the ways that the management of a company is supervised are well-known. What corporate governance does is to try to bring them all together.

Many legislative provisions concerning corporate governance are directly based on or closely related to "ethical norms". These present a system of behavioural norms and customs of business turnover which are traditionally applied and are not based on legal provisions.

The Organisation for Economic Cooperation and Development (OECD), which in 1999 published its Principles of Corporate Governance, offers a more detailed definition of corporate governance as "the internal means by which corporations are operated and controlled [...], which involve a set of relationships between a company's management, its board, its shareholders and other stakeholders. Corporate governance also provides the structure through which the objectives of the company are set, and the means of attaining those objectives and monitoring performance are determined. Good corporate governance should provide proper incentives for the board and management to pursue objectives that are in

[1] Donald L. Evans, James D. Wolfensohn, Peter L. Woicke, The Russia Corporate Governance Manual, M., 2004, p.4.

the interests of the company and shareholders, and should facilitate effective monitoring, thereby encouraging firms to use resources more efficiently".

The principles of corporate governance apply to all business entities, but are most important for J-SC. This is because it is in J-SC that the separation between ownership and management is the greatest, and thus conflicts related to corporate governance are most likely. The principles of corporate governance should be applied to ensure adequate protection of the interests of all shareholders, regardless of the size of their holdings.

Corporate governance is concerned with the behaviour of those entrusted with the management and direction of corporate entities. Good corporate governance requires such persons to act in a manner that is consistent with the objectives of the stakeholders in the enterprise. The stakeholders are a wide range of persons and groups, including shareholders, customers, suppliers, bankers, the community and the environment.

The first step in achieving good standards of corporate governance is compliance with the law. This is taken for granted in many organisations, but the real life experiences of corporate fraud at Enron, the ponzi scheme of Bernard Madoff and insider dealing by Martha Stewart demonstrate that this is not always the case. In Russia, the Yukos Petroleum Company scandal demonstrates that good corporate governance cannot always be assumed.

Corporate governance is more than simply complying with the law. It implies adherence to a set of standards that should be expected of managers occupying positions of responsibility in which their decisions and actions impact directly and indirectly on others in society.

Good standards of corporate governance include:

- Compliance with the law
- Adherence by management to a set of standards
- Supervision by external bodies, e.g. those that determine stock exchange listing rules

Standards of corporate governance should apply to any legal entity. However, they are most important for J-SCs, especially public companies, as in public companies the separation between owners and management is the greatest and this potentially leads to corporate conflicts and infringements of shareholders' rights.

Examples

Disposal of the company's property in an illegal way, e.g. the sale of the company's assets at a price below the market price or not according to Russian law.

Transfer pricing: the company sells its products at a lower price through company-mediators which accumulate profits.

Additional placement of companies' shares focusing on minimising the stake of the existing minority shareholders.

"Modest" dividend policies of companies.

Corporate law has evolved to ensure that closely connected stakeholders, such as the shareholders and creditors of companies, are duly protected. Federal laws also ensure that directors of companies are accountable in some measure for inappropriate actions that bring harm to others, such as the general laws on non-contractual obligations (set out in the Civil Code) and specific measures governing handling dangerous materials.

Examples

A former chairman and director of the National Association of Securities Dealers (NASDAQ), Bernard Madoff, was arrested for allegedly running a $50bn ponzi scheme. This was reportedly the biggest fraud case ever reported in America.

The scheme ran on a simple principle: the people who invest first get money from people who invest later; in this process the investors who invested last will never get anything. So the concept itself was wrong.

In March 2009, Madoff pleaded guilty to 11 *federal felonies* and admitted to turning his *wealth management* business into a massive ponzi scheme that defrauded thousands of investors of billions of dollars. Bernard Madoff admitted that he had taken $10 million from investors a week before his arrest. He was sentenced to the maximum sentence of 150 years in federal prison.

Investors lost more than $60 billion in the spectacular collapse of Enron, whose books had been audited by accounting firm Arthur Andersen. Various Enron executives and staff were sentenced to prison terms for crimes involving conspiracy, securities fraud, insider trading and lying to auditors.

Before its bankruptcy in late 2001, Enron employed around 22,000 people and was one of the world's leading electricity, natural gas, pulp and paper and communications companies, with claimed revenues of $111 billion in the year 2000.

Directors

Every company must be headed by an effective board which is collectively responsible for the success of the company.

There should be a clear division between responsibility for the running of the board and the executive responsibilities of running the company's business. This principle should be met by splitting the roles of the Chairman of the BD and the CEO:

- The Chairman should be responsible for the working of the board and the agenda for board meetings
- The CEO should have full operational control and the authority to carry out board decisions.

The BD should include a balance of executive and non-executive directors who are independent to ensure that no individual or small group of individuals can dominate the board. There must be a formal, rigorous and transparent procedure for the appointment of new directors.

The BD should be supplied with information in a form and of a quality to enable it to discharge its duties. All directors should receive an induction on joining the board and should regularly update and refresh their skills and knowledge.

The BD should undertake a formal and rigorous annual evaluation of its own performance and that of its committees and individual directors. All directors should submit for re-election at regular intervals, subject to continued satisfactory performance. The board should ensure the planned and progressive refreshing of the board.

Types of Board Structure

The role of the BD is to provide entrepreneurial leadership. It should:

- Set the company's strategic aims, values and standards
- Ensure the necessary financial and human resources are in place for the company to meet its objectives

Unitary board structure is where one board is responsible for both management and governance, and either consists wholly of executive directors or may be a mixture of executive and non-executive. The main problem with this is that executive directors have two competing functions. They are responsible for managing the company and supervising their own performance.

Two-tier board structure is where there is a supervisory board with a Chairman, and a Management Board with a CEO. This is usually found in Germany and France. The Management Board is responsible for managing the company. It reports to the supervisory body. The supervisory board may also be responsible for appointing and removing members of the management board.

Directors' Remuneration

Levels of pay should be sufficient to attract, retain and motivate directors of the quality required to run the company successfully. Companies should avoid paying more than is necessary for this purpose.

A significant proportion should be linked to corporate and individual performance. There should be a formal and transparent procedure for developing policy on executive remuneration and for fixing the remuneration packages of individual directors. No director should be involved in deciding his own remuneration.

Service contracts and periods of notice should not exceed one year.

Accountability and Audit

The BD should present a balanced and understandable assessment of the company's position and prospects.

The board should maintain a sound system of internal control to safeguard shareholders' investment and the company's assets. The board should establish formal and transparent arrangements for considering how they should apply financial reporting and internal control principles, and for maintaining an appropriate relationship with the company's auditors.

The BD should establish an audit committee of at least three members, who should all be independent, non-executive directors. At least one member should have recent and relevant financial experience.

Relationship with Shareholders

The BD must ensure that there is a dialogue with shareholders based on mutual understanding of objectives. The board should use GMs to communicate with shareholders and encourage their participation.

Part II. The International Scope of Corporate Governance

Numerous codes of best practice and corporate governance principles have been developed over the last 10 years. Worldwide, over 100 codes have been written in some 40 countries and regions. Most of these codes focus on the role of the BD in the company. The best known code is that of the Organisation for Economic Co-Operation and Development.

The OECD Principles address both policy makers and businesses, and focus on the entire governance framework (shareholder rights, stakeholders, disclosure, and board practices). The OECD Principles have gained worldwide acceptance as a framework and reference point for corporate governance. Published in 1999 and revised in 2004, they were developed to provide principle-based guidance on good governance.

The principles set out cover six areas:

- Ensuring the basis for an effective corporate governance framework, e.g. the legal and regulatory requirements that affect corporate governance practices in a jurisdiction should be consistent with the rule of law, transparent and enforceable
- The rights of shareholders and key ownership functions, e.g. basic shareholders' rights should include the rights to transfer shares, participate and vote in general shareholder meetings and share in the profits of the company
- Equitable treatment of shareholders, e.g. all shareholders of the same series of a class should be treated equally and minority shareholders should be protected from abusive actions
- The role of stakeholders in corporate governance, e.g. where stakeholder interests are protected by law, stakeholders should have the opportunity to obtain effective redress for violation of their rights
- Disclosure and transparency, e.g. disclosure should include material information on the financial and operating results of the company, majority share holdings and the remuneration policy for members of the board
- Responsibilities of the board, e.g. the board should apply high ethical standards and should take into account the interests of stakeholders

Many national codes of governance, including the Corporate Governance Code adopted in Russia in 2014, have been developed based on the OECD Principles. The OECD Principles serve as an excellent reference point for international practice and are recommended reading for those interested in understanding some of the principles that underlie national standards.

Standards of corporate governance are applicable to all organisational forms of business entity, however, they are most important for companies limited by shares. In such companies, especially public ones, the separation between owners and management is the greatest, and potentially leads to corporate conflicts and infringements of shareholders' rights.

Part III. Fraudulent Behaviour in the Securities Market

According to the estimates of the European Bank for Reconstruction and Development, Russia's securities market legislation demonstrates medium compliance with international standards.

Public offerings of securities, listing and prospectus requirements and the protection of minority shareholders are important elements of a well-functioning securities market.

All operations with securities, including trading, exchange, clearing or settlement, are subject to licensing by the Bank of Russia. Requirements for charter capital and risk management systems must also be met. The Central Bank is a major financial regulator in Russia, the state body that organises control over securities' market activities. The activities of clearing organisations are also subject to supervision and control by the Bank of Russia.

Liability for violations in the securities market is provided by the Securities Market Law, the Code for Administrative Violations and the Criminal Code. The question of liability is most important in this case, as a person may be found liable for administrative or criminal offences only in cases where such violations or crimes have corresponding provisions in law. The case of price manipulation is one of the most complex to be recognised as an offence on the securities markets.

Price Manipulation

The Securities Market Law says that "a fact of price manipulation on the securities market is adjudicated in court".[2] To date we do not know what Russian court practice is with respect to cases brought on charges of price manipulation on the securities market. This does not mean, of course, that price manipulation is non-existent in Russia.

---

[2] Securities Market Law, Article 51.2

Instances that can be described as price manipulation are reported by the media, by witnesses who have seen such practices take place on stock exchanges, and from other hearsay sources.

Law and judicial practices in many western countries such as the USA, Great Britain etc. provide a fairly detailed regulation of the forms and methods that can be used to influence prices. But in Russia, most varieties of manipulation are quite widespread, and they are not restricted, either by laws or by the rules of stock exchanges and other trading outlets.

The only thing Article 51 of the Securities Market Law prescribes is a general ban on price manipulation by professional participants in the securities market, and it generally spells out specific methods of price manipulation (actions whose aim is to make investors believe in an increase and/or decrease in prices and/or trading activity in the securities market to make investors sell or buy publicly placed securities, including

- Circulation of false information: making information available that is likely to give a false or misleading impression of the supply, demand, price or value of an investment. This includes a share buyer posting untrue messages on the internet to drive the share price higher and then selling at a profit
- Transactions involving the securities on the stock exchange or with other professional participants of the securities markets, as a result of which the owner of the securities does not change
- Simultaneous offers to buy and sell the securities at prices significantly different from the current market prices of similar transactions
- Agreement by two or more participants to offer the purchase/sale of the securities at prices significantly different from the current market prices of similar transactions).

Price manipulation incurs the liability of the professional participants of the securities market; such actions by professional participants of the securities market can be grounds for suspending or cancelling their licenses.

A system for the control of placed orders introduces a ceiling limit on price fluctuations during a trading session, and also pre- and post-trading periods, including control of trading large blocks of securities. For example, when a buy order is made in the Trading System for a price that is lower than the limit price, this order is automatically rejected; the same treatment is given to a sell order (i.e. prices may not be higher than a certain limit).

Some manipulative practices are not mentioned in the above quotations, for example, deriving profit from knowledge of the intentions of customers regarding the purchase/sale of securities (when a broker performs operations for his own account when there are instructions from investors to buy/sell securities or the opposite. Specifically, when a broker buys securities from an investor or on the open market to resell them to another broker at a profit for himself) and neglecting customer interests or misleading customers in the course of carrying out transactions (making orders and carrying out transactions on a customer's account on terms disadvantageous to the customer, or an unauthorised use of a customer's account), but they are indirectly covered by other laws and regulations. For example, Article 992 of the Civil Code says that a commission agent must carry out customers' instructions on terms that are as beneficial as possible for the principal and in accordance with the principal's directions; if the agency agreement does not specify any such directions, in accordance with the customs of business turnover or other usual and standard requirements.

The Securities Market Law, in Article 3, which governs brokerage operations, lays down the following requirements relating to a broker's performance of his duties: "a broker should carry out his customers' instructions conscientiously and on a "first-come-first-served" basis, unless a different procedure is prescribed in the broker-customer agreement or in the customer's instructions. In all cases transactions made at the customer's instructions have priority over the dealer operations of the broker himself when such broker doubles as a dealer. If a broker has an interest that prevents him from carrying out customer's instructions on terms of maximum benefit to the customer, the broker must notify the customer immediately that he has such an interest. If a conflict of interests between a broker and his customer, of which the customer is not notified prior to the reception by the broker of appropriate instructions, results in [the broker's] carrying out such instructions in a manner detrimental to the customer's interests, the broker must reimburse the [customer's] losses at their own expense in a manner prescribed by the civil law of the RF."

It is worth noting that it is extremely difficult to establish the facts of price manipulation on the securities market because it is difficult to identify and record such practices. This calls for high-price software to monitor sharp price fluctuations in real time. Nor is it less difficult to investigate instances of price manipulation, because the Bank of Russia has no powers to carry out such investigations, and the information an investigator needs is not always made available to the regulators as there are many possible ways to avoid making it available (e.g. it is defined as confidential, or bans by the Central Bank on the disclosure of certain kinds of information are cited). It is also of note that the Criminal Code and the Code for Administrative Violations contain no rules defining such practices as unlawful.

Examples

The Guinness share-trading fraud was a famous *British business scandal* of the 1980s. It involved an attempt to manipulate the *stock market* on a massive scale to inflate the price of *Guinness* shares and thereby assist a £2.7 billion take-over bid for the *Scottish* drinks company *Distillers.* The European Court of Human Rights in Strasbourg later found that the trial violated the defendants' human rights by making improper use of statements. The scandal was discovered after testimony as part of a plea bargain by the US stock trader *Ivan Boesky. Ernest Saunders, Gerald Ronson, Jack Lyons* and *Anthony Parnes,* the so-called "Guinness four", were charged, paid heavy fines and, with the exception of Lyons, who was suffering from ill-health, served prison sentences later reduced on appeal.

A person buys a large number of a particular share near the end of the day, aiming to drive the stock price higher to improve the performance of their investment. The market price is pushed to an artificial level and investors get a false impression of the price of those shares and their value, then making a wrong investment decision.

Insider Dealing

Insider information is price sensitive information relating to the issuer of securities, i.e. information which if made public would significantly affect the market price of those securities (e.g. an insider buying securities, knowing that soon the take-over of the company will increase its shares, will make a considerable sum of money). Such information should be included in the commercial secrets of the company.

A special Federal Law regulating insider dealing was adopted by the RF in July 2010.[3] Together with this law, legal norms on fighting against inappropriate use of insider information were introduced to such legislative acts of the RF as the Securities Market Law, the Code for Administrative Violations, and the Criminal Code. The law gives a definition of insider information and insider dealing, puts exceptions on the volume of insider information, and introduces particular cases of price manipulation.

---

[3] Federal Law No.224-FZ "On Counteracting the Illegitimate Use of Insider Information and Market Manipulation and on Amendments to Certain Laws of the Russian Federation", dated 27 July 2010.

Insiders

Insiders – people who have inside information from an inside source are determined by the law to be:

- Directors, employees, shareholders or debt-holders gaining direct access to the information
- Professional advisers (e.g. lawyers or external auditors) who obtain the information using their position
- Those who obtained the information directly or indirectly from any of the above
- Any person who is aware of confidential information, the undue disclosure of which could influence the prices of financial instruments, currency or goods

Three groups of insiders may be distinguished:

- "Primary" insiders – people who get insider information directly
- "Secondary" insiders – people who get insider information from "primary" insiders
- Insiders – natural people

The law also sets the ways in which insider information may not be used and the procedure for the disclosure of such information. Business entities must carry a list of insiders, and these insiders must inform the entities of their financial operations. The law puts a ban on the transfer of insider information (not specifying the type of transfer, i.e. transfer for or without reward). The Bank of Russia will fight against the inappropriate use of insider information. It must be informed by business entities about insiders, but the terms of submission of that information is not given.

The Offence

The prosecution must prove that the insider:

- Dealt in the price-affected securities
- Encouraged someone else to deal in them
- Disclosed information and enabled it to be used by a person dealing in them

Encouragement is an offence if the individual encouraging another knew or had reasonable cause to believe that dealing would take place, regardless of:

- Whether or not the person encouraged knows that the securities are price-affacted
- How the encouragement is given
- Whether the deal actually took place

Examples

Martha Stewart, an American business magnate, was under a civil case by the US Securities and Exchange Commission, stating that Stewart avoided a loss of $4,567,300 by selling all 3,928 shares of her ImClone stock using insider information. The day following her sale, the stock value fell 16%. After her release from prison in 2005 she published a book called "The Martha Rules" on starting and managing a new business with good corporate governance.

An employee finds out that his company is about to become the target of a takeover bid. Before the information is made public, he buys shares in his company, because he knows the bid may be imminent.

This behaviour creates insider dealing and may incur a claim for damages from the person who sold the shares to the employee, as this person might not have done so if he had known of the potential takeover.

Defences

An individual accused of insider dealing may put forward any of the following defences:

- He did not expect to make a profit for himself or avoid losses
- He had reasonable grounds to believe that the information was already public
- He would have dealt in the securities anyway without the information
- In disclosing the information to another, he did not expect that person to act on it or make a profit/avoid losses.

Other Violations in the Securities Market

Other violations provided by the Code for Administrative Violations and which incur administrative liability are the following:[4]

[4] Code for Administrative Violations, Articles 15.17 – 15.31.

- Presentation of deliberately false information on securities, the issuers of the securities or prices for the securities, including information in advertisements
- Illegal emission of securities. In cases of such violations the Securities Market Law stipulates the rights of the state body regulating the securities market – the Bank of Russia – which include:
    - Inform in written form of the elimination of violations; file an order to the legal entity demanding it stop breaching legislation on the securities market
    - Suspend further placement of securities, and limit or prohibit particular operations concerning securities
    - Publish in the mass media details about the unfair issuance of securities
    - Give written permission for further placement of securities in cases of elimination of violations
    - Apply to court regarding the validity of the issuance of securities
- Illegal transactions with securities
- Professional activity on the securities market without license. In this case, the Bank of Russia shall:
    - Suspend the unlicensed activity because a license is needed
    - Cancel the license of the legal entity/professional participant of the securities market
    - File an action with the Arbitrazh court for the recovery of profits obtained through the unlicensed activity
    - File an action with the Arbitrazh court regarding the liquidation of the participant in the securities market in case of the license not being obtained within the stipulated period
- Breach of legislation on public information on the issue of securities
- Breach of rules on holding the register of shareholders
- Breach of secondary legislation: currency legislation, legislation on banks and banking activity and money laundering, etc.

Violations of legislation on banks and banking activity shall incur for individuals administrative fines[5] or criminal liability.[6]

---

[5] From 40,000 to 50,000 roubles. Code for Administrative Violations, Article 15.26.

The issuance of securities may also be found invalid under the suit of the Bank of Russia, Federal Tax Service or its regional branches, the Prosecutor and other state bodies executing their powers in the securities market.

All decisions of the Central Bank must be formalised with an Order, which must be sent to the legal entity within three days of the date the Order was made. In cases where there is an examination of the activity of the business entity, but no violations are found, no decisions shall be taken.

Example

An empty cargo ship that is used to transport a particular commodity is moved. This could create a false impression of changes in the supply of, or demand for, that commodity or the related futures contract. It could also artificially change the price of that commodity or the futures contract, and lead to people making the wrong investment decisions.

Aims of Combatting Insider Information and Market Manipulation

The Insider Information Law puts forward the following aims:

- To ensure that market-based pricing mechanisms are used in the financial and commercial markets
- To increase investor confidence
- To improve the protection of investors' interests
- To facilitate the efficient development and international competitiveness of the financial and commercial markets
- To reveal and stop any abuse on the regulated markets in the forms of unlawful use of insider information and market manipulation

Part IV. The Nature and Control Over Money Laundring

"Money laundering" is defined as processing the proceeds of criminal activities to disguise their origins. It is used to legalise cash from illegal arms sales, smuggling, and organised crime activities such as drugs trafficking and prostitution rings, as well as embezzlement, insider trading, bribery and computer fraud schemes. The volume of money laundering transactions performed worldwide is estimated by the International

[6] In case of criminal offence, this offence will incur large-scale damage, exceeding 1 million roubles. The volume of a criminal fine varies from 100,000 to 500,000 roubles. An imprisonment up to three years is also handed down in case of abuses with securities. Criminal Code, Article 185.2.

Monetary Fund (IMF) to be anywhere between $600 billion and $1.5 trillion. This is between two and five times Russia's Gross Domestic Product (GDP).

The terrorist attacks of September 11th 2001 started a new round of anti-money laundering regulation initiatives around the world. As authorities are seeking to adjust the control of the financial system to enable it to filter out money transfers by terrorist organisations, it is becoming essential for Russian banks and corporate treasuries to understand how international anti-money laundering regulation works.

National governments sought to adjust the control of the financial system to enable it to filter out money transfers by terrorist groups. While Russian companies and banks in particular, are hardly sponsoring terrorists, Russia's financial system is thought to be used to launder large amounts of money generated by bribery, drug cartels and illegal international arms trading.

As American, British and Western European financial institutions see their compliance costs soaring, they are sure to shift some of the burden onto their Russian correspondent banks. For that reason it is now becoming essential for Russian banks and corporate treasuries to understand how international anti-money laundering regulation works and how it is going to impact their business.

Long before the September 11th attacks, banks were already facing intensified regulatory scrutiny of their anti-money laundering activities. Now they have been conscripted into the war against terrorism in a major way, as regulators and law enforcement officials seek their assistance in identifying and freezing the assets of terrorists.

Example

> On September 14th, 2011, in Buffalo, N.Y., Guy W. Gane, Jr., of Williamsville, N.Y., was sentenced to 156 months in prison and ordered to pay $6 million in restitution to the victims of his scheme. Gane was convicted on mail fraud and money laundering charges. According to court documents, Gane was President of Watermark M One Financial Services, which was shut down in May 2008 as a result of action by the United States Postal Inspection Service and the Securities and Exchange Commission. The scheme began in early 2006 when Gane and his employees began selling "debentures" to trusting clients, claiming to be using the money to invest in waterfront real estate. The defendant promised a 10 percent return after a year to his investors. However, no investments were ever made. Gane used new investor funds to pay off the earlier investors. 94 victims lost over $6 million.

With the ratification of the 1990 Council of Europe Convention on Laundering, Search, Seizure and Confiscation of the Proceeds from Crime (the Strasbourg Convention), Russia adopted the Anti-Money Laundering Law of 2001. This law broadly corresponds to the Financial Task Force on Money Laundering's (FATF) recommendations, even if some provisions appear ambiguous. Therefore, the Anti-Money Laundering Law establishes in Russia the legal base for the creation of a system for fighting against money laundering.

This system includes: the criminalisation of money laundering; providing law enforcement bodies with information about actions and persons connected with money laundering that is received from financial and other organisations, in accordance with a special law, and also during operational and search activities; the confiscation of criminal proceeds (special confiscation); special administrative and control measures which complicate money laundering, and international cooperation.

Russian legislation on money laundering basically corresponds to international standards.

There are also some problems that complicate the enforcement of the Anti-Money Laundering Law. These are such problems as: protection of information; realisation of the principle "know your client" by credit organisations that have a lot of clients, and the training of skilled personnel for working in the internal control service. The list of suspicious operations should be increased.

The relevant organisations are lending establishments, professional players on the securities market, insurance, lease, mail and telegraph communications companies, and other non-lending organisations that transfer money, as well as pawn shops. The law stipulates that transactions involving upwards of 600,000 roubles are to be controlled, and in case of transactions with real estate, upwards of 3 million roubles. In 2012 transactions to be mandatorily controlled were amended by operations concerning receiving by a non-commercial organisation of the sum over 200,000 roubles.

Note

The Bank of Russia explains that money transfers through non-credit organisations, as well as the refilling of deposits for sums exceeding 600,000 roubles, will not be subject to mandatory control.[7]

---

[7] Information Letter of the Bank of Russia No.21, dated 28 December 2012.

The Bank of Russia, which is a megaregulator of the RF, collects, processes and analyses information about financial transactions. If it finds reason to suspect money laundering, it forwards the relevant information to law enforcement agencies.

This is nothing less than a system of financial intelligence similar to the one used in the US. As a result, Russia was removed from the FATF black list in 2002 and became a full member of the organisation in 2003. In 2005, the FSFM filed 800 money-laundering suits, and forwarded cases worth $20 billion to law enforcement agencies.

Russia also created a Eurasian Group to combat money laundering and terrorism financing (Eurasian Antiterrorist Group, EAG). The 2005 plans of its members – Russia, Belarus, Kazakhstan, Kyrgyzstan, China and Tajikistan – include the proliferation of the FATF Forty Recommendations on combating money laundering and Eight Special Recommendations on terrorism financing.

Russia created an interdepartmental commission on combating money laundering and terrorism financing to coordinate effective interaction between the federal authorities and the Central Bank of Russia in this sphere. The President's Decree No.596 "On Long-Term State Economic Perspective", dated 7 May 2012, aims to de-offshore the Russian Economy.

The Russian Ministry of Internal Affairs reports that some 150-160 billion roubles are laundered in Russia annually, though international financial institutions give a different figure for annual money laundering in Russia: 100 billion dollars. Money laundering remains an acute problem in Russia. It is directly connected to combating terrorism and crime financing and seriously affects market stabilisation and the attraction of foreign investment.

Violations of legislation on anti-money laundering activity incur administrative fines[8] or criminal liability punished by up to seven years of imprisonment with a fine for up to one million roubles.[9]

The most serious obstacle in fighting against money laundering remains the presence of off shore centres in different areas of the world and also Russia. In this situation we need the coordinated political and economic influence of international society on these off shore centers.

Russia's efforts have earned international recognition. The US State Department's report on money laundering and financial crimes gave the country high marks for its efforts to combat the scourge at the root of both terrorism and the drugs trade. The report, released in March 2006, cited in

---

[8] Code for Administrative Violations, Article 15.27.

[9] Criminal Code, Article 174.4.

particular Russia's development of a legislative and regulatory foundation for combating money laundering and terrorism financing.

Meanwhile, Russia received low marks in a Transparancy International Corruption Index. A report from 2014 ranked Russia 92nd out of 189 economies. The corruption market in Russia is considered to be worth $240 billion.

With those types of scores, especially for a major economy, Russia has a long way to go in its struggle to combat money laundering, counter graft and crack down on economic crime.

Criminal proceeds are laundered in three stages:

- Placement – currency enters the financial system (e.g. illicit monies deposited at a financial institution on the purchase of money orders using stolen cards)
- Layering – the trail which left by "dirty" money is obscured. A series of financial transactions build layers between the funds and their illicit source (e.g. a series of bank-to-bank funds transfers)
- Integration – with monies from legitimate commercial activities as they enter the mainstream economy. The illicit funds take on the appearance of legitimacy

"Criminal property" includes, for example, the proceeds from tax evasion, and benefits obtained through bribery or corruption.

Note

In contrast to European countries and the USA, in the the RF tax evasion is a separate crime not yet included in the list of money-laundering offences.

The main aims of anti-money laundering legislation are the following:

- Prevention of the involvement of income derived from illegal activities in bank operations
- Timely identification of customers and transactions bearing signs of possible money laundering activities
- Collection and storage of information pertaining to such customers and transactions to facilitate efficient assistance of the state bodies of the RF within the framework of the current legislation

The organisations obliged to control monetary operations are the following:

- Credit organisations
- Professional participants in the securities market
- Insurance and leasing companies

- Federal postal service organisations
- Pawn shops
- Mediators in sale and purchase operations, etc.

The following distinct instruments may be used to fight money laundering:

- The "know your customer" program, requiring banks to collect, update and verify information about their customers
- Investigations into suspicious customers' transactions
- Identification of transactions which might be connected with money laundering, such as export/import transactions, insurance schemes or contracts of factoring where commercial legal entities act as agents
- Reporting of banks' customers' transactions to state bodies
- Documentation and data storage programs
- Personnel training with respect to anti-money laundering issues

Regulatory Framework on Money Laundering

The following acts directly or indirectly regulate anti-money laundering dealings:

- The Criminal Code
- The Anti-Money Laundering Law
- Information Letters of the Bank of Russia
- Orders of the Financial Monitoring Service.

Part V. Bribery

Bribery is an act implying the giving of money or a gift that alters the behaviour of the recipient. It is the offering, giving, receiving, or soliciting of any item of value to influence the actions of an official or other person in charge of a public or legal duty.

According to the OECD, bribery and corruption:

- Undermine corporate governance
- Threaten economic development, sustainable development and fair business practices

In 2003, 140 countries (though only 80 ratified), signed the United Nations Convention against Corruption (UNCAC), whose aim is the enforcement of international cooperation in tackling corruption. This document is the basic anti-corruption document on the international level.

Legislation

The United Kingdom Bribery Act was adopted in 2010 and came into force in the year 2011.

The Act created four offences:

- Bribing a person to induce or reward them performing a relevant function improperly (active bribery)
- Requesting, accepting or receiving a bribe as a reward for performing a relevant function improperly (passive bribery)
- Using a bribe to influence a foreign official to gain a business advantage
- A new form of corporate liability for failing to prevent bribery on behalf of a commercial organisation

"Commercial organisation" has a wide meaning and includes partnerships, limited liability partnerships and companies which carry out business.

Commercial organisations can defend themselves by having in place "adequate procedures" to prevent bribery. This may include implementing antibribery procedures. It is important that firms consider what procedures are most appropriate for their firm given the risks they face and the way they run their business. The procedures should be proportionate to the risk posed.

For some firms there will be no need to put bribery prevention procedures in place, as there is no risk of bribery on their behalf. Other firms may need to put in place measures in key areas, such as gifts and hospitality, as this is the area where they have identified a risk.

The penalty for individuals is a maximum sentence of 10 years. For commercial organisations there may be an unlimited fine.

Note

The UK Bribery Act does not apply to bribery committed outside the UK by a foreign person.

Six Guiding Principles

The guidance in the United Kingdom is not prescriptive and is based around six guiding principles:

- Proportionate procedures
  The procedures put in place by an organisation should be proportionate to the risks it faces and the nature, scale and complexity of its activities. A small organisation would require different procedures to a large multinational organisation.
- Top-level commitment
  The top-level management should be committed to preventing bribery and fostering a culture within the organisation in which bribery is unacceptable.
- Risk assessment
  Organisations should assess the nature and extent of their exposure to risks of bribery, including potential external and internal risks of bribery. For example, some industries are considered higher risk than others, such as the extractive industries; some overseas markets may be higher risk where there is an absence of anti-bribery legislation.
- Due diligence
  The organisation should apply due diligence regarding people who perform services for – or on behalf of – the organisation in order to mitigate bribery risks.
- Communication
  The organisation should ensure its bribery prevention policies and procedures are embedded and understood throughout the organisation through internal and external communication, including training, proportionate to the risks it faces. Communication and training enhances awareness and helps to deter bribery.
- Monitoring and review
  An organisation should monitor and review procedures designed to prevent bribery and make improvements where necessary. The risks an organisation faces may change and, therefore, an organisation should evaluate the effectiveness of its anti-bribery procedures and adapt where necessary.[10]

[10] http://www.accaglobal.com/content/dam/acca/global/pdf/sa_june11_bribery.pdf

The Russian Federation

Bribery Law adopted in the RF at the end of the year 2008 states that the supervising state body shall be the Audit Chamber of the RF.

In 2011, a new provision on mediation in bribery was introduced to the Criminal Code of the RF to go alongside bribing and accepting a bribe.[11] Punishments for these crimes include multiple fines (calculated from the amount of the bribe), disqualification for a period of up to three years and up to 15 years of imprisonment.

In 2013, the Labour Ministry published recommendations on the appropriate behaviour of civil servants in communications with customers. The measures offered are dedicated to the prevention of bribery. This includes refraining from using such phrases as "thanks does not pay bills", etc.[12]

---

[11] Criminal Code, Article 291.1.

[12] Information of the Labour Ministry "Recommendations' Review on Execution of the Complex of Organisational, Explanatory and Other Measures…on Bribery", dated 19 February 2013.

Chapter Roundup

1. Corporate governance may be defined as:

- A system of relationships defined by structures and processes
- These relationships may involve parties with different and sometimes contrasting interests
- All parties are involved in the direction and control of the company
- This is done to properly distribute rights and responsibilities, and thus increase long-term shareholder value

2. The main purposes of corporate governance are the following:

- To ensure the balance of power is maintained (monitor those who control recourses belonging to investors)
- To ensure fair remuneration of executive directors
- To ensure the independence of external auditors
- To make the BD responsible for management
- To ensure business ethics are practiced

3. The main violations in the securities market are the following:

- Insider dealing
- Price manipulation
- Illegal emission of securities
- Illegal transactions involving securities
- Breaches of legislation on public information about the issue of securities
- Breaches of rules on holding the register of shareholders
- Breaches of currency legislation, legislation on banks and banking activity and money laundering

4. The main aims of anti-money laundering legislation are the following:

- Prevention of the involvement of income derived from illegal activities in bank operations
- Timely identification of customers and transactions bearing signs of possible money laundering activities
- Collection and storage of information pertaining to such customers and transactions in order to facilitate efficient assistance of the state bodies of the RF within the framework of the current legislation

5. The four offences related to bribery under UK law are:

- Bribing a person to induce them to perform a relevant function improperly or reward them for doing so
- Requesting, accepting or receiving a bribe as a reward for performing a relevant function improperly
- Using a bribe to influence a foreign official to gain a business advantage
- A new form of corporate liability for failing to prevent bribery on behalf of a commercial organisation

Questions

1. Which group of people is corporate governance concerned with?

- Shareholders only
- Management only
- Employees only
- All stakeholders

2. Which of the following is the correct definition of money laundering?

- Tax evasion
- Black wages
- Legitimising illegal cash flows
- Paying bribes to government officials

3. Russian law states that major transactions should (broadly speaking) be approved by the GM. Good corporate governance practice recommends that which of the following parties should be involved in all major transactions?

- Employees
- An independent appraiser
- Customers affected by the major transaction
- Suppliers affected by the transaction

4. What are ethics?

- Business practices
- Regulations governing business activities
- Assumptions used when determining accounting policies
- High moral imperatives that go beyond business regulations

5. Money laundering legislation has three main objectives. Which of the following is not one of the objectives?

- The control of foreign currency cash flows
- To prevent the involvement of banks and other institutions in the illegal legitimisation of cash flows
- Timely identification of suspicious movements of cash
- Collecting information on suspicious movements of cash

6. In relation to company law and corporate governance:

(a) Explain the meaning and significance of a legal entity having a separate legal personality.

(b) Discuss the implications of separate legal personalities for effective corporate governance.

7. OAO Trucking is a large distribution company that runs a fleet of heavy goods vehicles delivering goods throughout Russia and other central and eastern European countries. The company has 1,200 shareholders, but most of the shares are owned by four individuals.

The company has found it difficult to compete in recent times, with falling profits and recurrent cash flow crises. Peter is one of the major shareholders, owning 25% of the ordinary shares. He blames the company's difficulties on having to maintain expensive premises in Moscow and having to bear the costs of vehicle maintenance, repair and replacement.

The company is again experiencing a crisis, and Peter has met with Rosa, one of the other major shareholders, who also owns 25% of the ordinary shares, to propose a radical action plan. Their proposal is to sell off the head office premises of the company in order to release cash. The company will then relocate to leased premises and land on the outskirts of Moscow. They also intend to sell a large proportion of the company's vehicle fleet to a willing buyer and lease vehicles instead.

The other two major shareholders own 40% of the equity between them. They are outraged by the proposal to sell off land and vehicles. They believe that, as well as being the main fixed asset of the company, the real estate is an appreciating asset that should be retained at all costs. Their understanding is that Peter and Rosa will sell the land for a price substantially below its market value. One shareholder also believes that Peter is only prepared to sell the vehicles because his brother is a major shareholder in the company that is willing to buy them.

Required:

(a) Explain the criteria that must be applied by the company to determine whether the proposal to sell off the head office premises is a major transaction.

(b) Explain the factors that will determine whether the proposal to sell off a large proportion of the company's vehicle fleet will be a transaction in which there is an interest.

(c) Explain the consequences of the directors agreeing to a major transaction or a transaction in which there is an interest without following due process.

Further Reading

1. Adwemuni, Wole: Fraud in Banks. Nigerian Institute of Bankers, Landmark Publications Ltd.. 1986.
2. Bagella M., Becchetti L. Esternalita Regionali ed Effetti Economici della Regolamentazione contro il Riciclaggio. VI Rapporto Fondazione Rosselli. Dalla banca alla eurobank: Nuevo mercati e regole. Edibank. Ed. 2. 2001.
3. Bagella M., Becchetti. Regional externalities and direct effects of legislation against money laundering: A test on excess money balances in the five Andean countries. Journal of Money Laundering Control. Ed. 7 (4).
4. Bank fraud, Bulletin of Fraud and Risk Management, Bank Administration Institute Foundation, Chicago.
5. Bequali, August: White Collar Crime: A 20th Century Crisis. Lexington Books, Lexington, Massachusetts, 1978.
6. Bose, Mihir. Fraud. Unwin Hyman Ltd., London.
7. Coeman, James W. The Criminal Elite. St. Martin's Press. New York, 1985.
8. Commercial crime international, IMB Publishing Ltd., Barking, Essex, England.
9. Conway, Barbara. Maritime Fraud. Lloyds of London Press, London, 1990.
10. Dunn, Donald H. Ponzithe Boston Fraudster. MeGraw Hill, New York, 1975.
11. Durnev A. and Guriev S. The Resourse Curse: A Corporate Transperancy Channe.l
12. Ellen, Eric. International Maritime Fraud. Sweet and Maxwell, London, 1981.
13. Francis, Diane. Contrepreneurs. Macrnillan of Canada, Toronto, 1988.

14. Guriev S., Yakovlev E., Zhuravskaya E. Inter-State Spillovers and Lobbying. // WP13/2007/16. – Moscow: Publishing house of SU HSE, 2007.
15. Трунов И.Л. Адвокатская тайна в свете реформ правового регулирования / Трунов И.Л., Трунова Л.К. // Закон и право. 2002. № 4. С. 18.
16. Устинов В.С. Понятие и криминологическая характеристика организованной преступности. – Н. Новгород: НВШ МВД РФ, 1993.
17. Фатьянов А.А. Тайна как социальное и правовое явление: ее виды // Государство и право. 1998. № 6.
18. Черных П.Я. Историко-этимологический словарь современного русского языка. Т. 2. М., 1993.
19. Чечетин А.Е. Опыт борьбы с наркобизнесом в США. / МВД России. – Омск: Омская высшая школа милиции, 1992.
20. Шатлен Ж. Международные конвенции по борьбе с незаконной торговлей культурными ценностями // Информационный бюллетень Национального центрального бюро Интерпола в РФ.- 1992.- № 2-3.
21. Шашкова А.В. Предпринимательское право РФ: курс лекций. – М., 2007.
22. Шашкова А.В.. Russian Business Law / А.В. Шашкова // Линкор. – М., 2007.
23. Шестаков А.В. Теневая экономика: учеб. пособие. – М.: Издательский дом «Дашков и Ко». - 2000.
24. Шкредов В.П. Экономика и право: опыт экономико-юридического исследования общественного производства. 2-е изд. М., 1990.
25. Шлыков В.В. Комплексное обеспечение экономической безопасности предприятия. – СПб: Алетейя, - 1999.
26. Шубин Д.А. Сохранение адвокатской тайны: реальность и перспектива // Ваш налоговый адвокат. 2005. № 3.
27. Шустерман С. На садиста объявили облаву // Федерация еврейских общин России. 2005. 6 сентября.
28. Щенникова Л.В. Правовая охрана культурных ценностей в России // Государство и право.- 1994.- № 3.
29. Экспорт мафии // Информационный бюллетень НЦБ Интерпола в РФ,- 1992, – № 1.
30. Эндерсон Э. Организованная преступность, мафия и правительства // ЭКО. 1994. № 3. С. 160-173.
31. Юркина О. Банковская тайна: все карты спутаны / О. Юркина // Наша газета. – 2010. - 1 февраля.

32. Яковлев А. Методические подходы к оценке величины неучтенного наличного оборота / Яковлев А., Воронцова О. // Вопросы экономики. 1997. № 7.
33. Ярочкин В.И. Секьюритология – наука о безопасности жизнедеятельности. – М. : Ось-89. - 2000.

ANSWERS TO QUESTIONS FROM THE CHAPTERS

Essential Elements of the Russian Legal System

1. A person may be deprived of his rights only:

- *Under a court decision*

If a person is in debt, only the court may recover that debt.

2. Under the Constitution of the RF, civil legislation is under the jurisdiction:

- *Of the RF*

In the RF there is only one Civil Code. A Code of Moscow, or of any other subject of the RF, does not exist.

3. In case of a contradiction between the Decree of the President of the RF and the Civil Code of the RF, the following is applied:

- *The Civil Code of the RF*

Laws are acts which enjoy priority over any other types of act issued in the territory of the RF.

4. The law comes into force after relations between the parties have arisen. This law is applied to the relations between the parties:

- *After the law comes into force*

As a general rule, the law does not have retroactive effect. Thus it shall be applied to the relations between the parties only after the law comes into force. As the law has more legal force than the agreement of the parties, it shall be applied to the relations between the parties, the existence of the agreement notwithstanding.

5. The universally recognised norms and principles of international law are:

- *Part of the legal system of the RF*

The universally recognised norms and principles of international law have direct power in the territory of the RF, and immediately after they are signed they become part of the legal system of the RF.

6. This question tests the candidates' knowledge of the structure and functions of the courts of arbitration and the extent to which previously decided cases affect the outcomes of subsequent cases.

(a) The key term here is "economic disputes", as it differentiates the main purpose of the courts of arbitration from those of the Constitutional Court and the courts of general jurisdiction. The courts therefore regulate and resolve disputes arising from legal relations concerning legal entities such as companies, partnerships and semi-state bodies, as well as individual entrepreneurs.

However, the courts do not deal with commercial actions that may give rise to criminal (penal) liability, nor do they deal with the economic activities of individuals not registered as individual entrepreneurs.

It is also important to point out that it is the nature of the subject matter or dispute before the court, and not the status of the person or entity, that may determine the jurisdiction of the case. For example, losses arising from a traffic accident between two professional drivers who are on their way home at night would be dealt with by the courts of general jurisdiction.

The types of case considered by the courts of arbitration are broadly varied, though nothing like as diverse as the cases heard by the courts of general jurisdiction.

The courts of arbitration consider disputes arising from contractual relations. These include those relating to the formation, variation or discharge of contracts, breaches of contract, violation of rights and undue fulfilment of obligations.

The courts of arbitration deal with many matters relating to companies, including state registration (or refusal to register), shareholders' rights, and the reorganisation and liquidation of enterprises. Increasingly, the courts are asked to consider cases relating to the goodwill of the organisation and torts, or non-contractual obligations. The courts also deal with the enforcement of judgements made by foreign courts.

The courts of arbitration are structured in a hierarchical manner.

At the first (lowest) level are the federal arbitration courts of the subjects of the RF. These are the courts of first instance within their jurisdiction and deal with the majority of cases.

The second level is that of the appellate courts. As their name suggests, these are courts of appeal, or second instance, whose primary role is to re-examine cases already dealt with by the first level courts.

The third level is the federal arbitration circuit court. This also serves as a court of second instance – cassation appeals are heard in it.

The highest level is the Supreme Arbitration Court. This court also has powers in business and economic activities. The court also has a supervisory role in respect of the lower courts, and has the right of legislative initiative. It also deals with cases involving disputes relating to normative legal acts of the president, the government and federal executive bodies relevant to business and economic activities in the first instance. It hears cases concerning non-normative acts of the same bodies that claimants consider to be non-compliant with existing laws. It considers cases involving disputes between the RF and subjects of the RF and between subjects of the RF.

As a court of final appeal, it can set aside the decisions of the lower courts, though it will do so on points of law rather than the facts or circumstances involved in the relevant case.

(b) The doctrine of judicial precedent is a feature of common law systems such as those of the USA and the UK. Under the common law system, judges can create laws by making judgements on cases that then become standards for future decisions that require the application of the same or very similar principles.

As the RF has a codified law system in which legislation is the main source of law, judicial precedent has no formal place in the system. As a consequence, the primary role of judges is to interpret and apply the law. Judges do not create new laws.

This does not mean that previous cases are wholly irrelevant once decided. The decisions of courts are formally documented and there is a vast archive of material available for perusal by judges and legal professionals. In order to foster consistency in the application of the law, the courts will inevitably need to refer to previous decisions. The rationale applied in previously decided cases may also influence the content of the occasional information letters issued by the Supreme Court.

7. This question tests the ability to apply relevant sources of law to both theoretical and practical situations.

(a) The rule concerning the interpretation of statutes of the RF states that in case of a contradiction of legal acts of the same level, the more recent legal act shall be applied.

In case of a contradiction of legal acts of different levels, the legal act of the higher level shall be applied.

Therefore, the Civil Code shall be applied, as the dispute is between legal acts of the same level and it is the more recent legal act.

(b) Under the Civil Code, acts of civil legislation do not have retroactive effect and shall be applied only to relationships which started after they came into force. Only in cases directly provided for by law can a legislative act be applied to relationships which started before that act came into force.

Therefore in this case, relations are regulated by the Rules on Reimbursement of the Injury to the Employee, as the Rules were valid as of the date of the last injury and as of the date of filing the claim.

The court shall satisfy the claim of the defendant to abolish, in part, the decision of the Court of Permskaya Oblast, as the court applied an inappropriate law.

The Law of Obligations

1. The unilateral transaction is the following:

- *Refusal of the inheritance*

All other transactions are contracts, i.e., bilateral transactions.

2. Transactions between a legal entity and an individual shall be carried out in the following form:

- *In simple written form*

The Russian law provides for written form of transactions in case at least one party to the transaction is a legal entity.

3. Transactions between individuals for sums exceeding 10 minimum monthly amounts in the form of wages and salaries shall be concluded in the following form:

- *In simple written form*

Oral transactions may be concluded between individuals for the sum up to 10 minimum monthly amounts in the form of wages and salaries. If the sum of the transaction exceeds this, the transaction should have a simple written form.

4. Non-observance of the simple written form deprives the parties of the right in confirmation of the transaction to refer to:

- *Witness evidence*

Non-observance of the form of the transaction, which should be concluded under the Russian law in simple written form, does not invalidate the transaction. However, in order to prove the existence of the transaction, the parties shall be deprived of the right to refer to witness evidence.

5. A transaction is deemed to be invalid from the moment of:

- *Its conclusion*

Generally, a transaction should be deemed invalid from the moment of its conclusion. In a few certain cases, when we speak of a voidable transaction, it may be recognised as invalid from the moment of the court's decision on its invalidity.

6. This question tests the applicants' knowledge of how a contract is created and terminated.

(a) Article 421 of the Civil Code of the RF confers a right upon citizens and legal entities to enter into legally binding agreements between themselves. The Code is essentially permissive in this respect, in that the freedom to contract is constrained only by specific instances dictated by law.

In order to enter into a contract, it is necessary for a party to have the capacity to do so. In this context, "capacity" simply refers to the ability to do something that has legal consequences. The Civil Code makes provisions for both natural and artificial legal persons in this respect. Article 17 of the Code deals with the capacity of individuals. Private individuals obtain full active capacity at 18 years of age, or over 16 years of age if married. The Code goes on to limit but not totally restrict the legal capacity of persons between six and 14 years of age and those between 14 and 18 years of age. Once an individual has full active capacity, that person is only restricted insofar as the state restricts or prohibits certain activities. In rare instances a court may decide to take away the right of a citizen to act on his or her own behalf, such as in the event of mental incapacity or where a person has brought hardship on the family due to inappropriate lifestyle choices. In cases of personal insolvency, the freedom to contract becomes limited, as the individual is prevented from entering into certain transactions.

For enterprises, Article 48 of the Civil Code identifies three different generic organisational models. The three typologies are differentiated by their capacity to own assets and definitions of their property rights. Therefore, while a partnership or company can do almost anything that a human can do, bodies such as state owned organisations, schools, hospitals and charities, associations and clubs do not have the corresponding freedom to act.

The capacity of an enterprise can further be restricted by conditions set out in the Charter at the behest of the founders.

As in the case of personal bankruptcy, the freedom to contract of an insolvent company that is subject to supervision by the court of arbitration is restricted.

Various laws restrict the freedom to contract when it is considered to be in the interests of the state or society as a whole. For example, it is forbidden for persons not properly licensed to deal in illegal drugs. Restrictions may also apply to certain foreign transactions to protect the currency or regulate trading activities with some countries.

(b) A contract may be terminated in four generic ways (Chapter 29, Civil Code):

Firstly, a contract is terminated when its provisions have been performed in their entirety. This is the most common way in which a contract is discharged. For example, a hotel guest agrees to pay 5,000 roubles for a room for the night. Once the guest has stayed in the hotel and paid in full for the accommodation, the contract is terminated, its objects having been fulfilled.

Secondly, a contract is terminated if the parties to the contract decide that they are prepared to walk away from the agreement.

In this case it may not be necessary to take any action, provided that both parties are prepared to accept the consequences and take the matter no further. For example, the hotel guest may telephone to cancel the reservation at the hotel and the hotel manager may be prepared to forego the business, confident that the room can be re-booked.

Thirdly, a contract may be cancelled due to the impossibility of its fulfilment. This is sometimes called frustration of the contract. If the hotel guest arrives at the hotel only to find that it has burnt to the ground, it is clearly impossible to fulfil the contract due to supervening forces. It is common in Russia for contracts to include *force majeure* clauses that enable withdrawal by one party. Such clauses usually attempt to envisage catastrophic events or incidents that would render termination of the contract unavoidable. Some contracts become impossible to fulfil because of changes in the law that make fulfilment illegal.

Fourthly, a contract may be terminated by breach. This occurs when one party breaks the terms agreed. It normally triggers the right of the other party to pursue financial or other redress. Therefore, if the hotel guest fails to arrive and does not cancel the contract, the hotel management may be able to charge a cancellation fee if specified in the contract.

7. Hypothesis

Five days from the conclusion of the agreement, the J-SC's warehouse has been robbed. We consider the theft to have occurred on the fifth day.
The definition of the owner's risks and the transfer of property.

- According to the Article 211 of the Civil Code, the risk of accidental destruction of the property or of accidental damage inflicted on it is borne by its owner, unless otherwise stipulated by the law or by the contract.
- According to the general rule the risk of accidental loss or damage of the property is transferred to the purchaser simultaneously with the transfer of the right of ownership.

The pledged goods stolen, worth the sum of 20,000 roubles and the goods stolen, valued at 100,000 roubles remain the J-SC's property.

We have no precise details about the contract, so because an agreement has been signed we consider it valid. In this case the bank has a due execution of obligations towards the J-SC.

The pledged goods were the property of the J-SC.

Because there is no place at the bank's warehouse, the bank didn't respect the pledge by demanding the J-SC to keep them safe in its own warehouse (the creditor is overdue).
The pledge, and the security of the pledged property.

- The pledger shall take the risks of the accidental loss or accidental damage of the pledged property, unless otherwise stipulated by the contract of pledge.
- The pledgee is liable for the full or partial loss or damage of the pledge transferred to him, which happened through his or her own fault (through intention or negligence), and for loss or damage which occurred in the course of entrepreneurial activity, unless the loss or damage is caused by force majeure.

The pledger or the pledgee is obliged:

- To insure for account of the pledger the pledged property.
- To take the measures necessary to guarantee the security of the pledged property

- To immediately notify the other party about the arising of a threat of the loss or the damage of the pledged property.

The goods provided by the J-SC were not insured. Measures necessary to guarantee the security of the pledged property have not therefore been taken. The J-SC did not respect its obligations (improper discharge of the obligations of the debtor).

The court decision:

Considering that the contract is valid, that the goods have been stolen on the fifth day, and because the pledged goods (and the pledged goods only) were under the property of the J-SC, the court considers that the goods were under the responsibility of the J-SC. Because we are under a settlement relating to the security of the pledged property, and because measures necessary to guarantee the security of the property have not been taken (no insurance); the court shall consider that the J-SC is responsible.

In other words, the J-SC is liable for the full loss or damage of the goods stolen, worth 100,000 roubles, and is also liable for the partial loss or damage of the other goods stolen, worth 20,000 roubles. On the other side, the bank is liable for the partial loss or damage of the goods stolen, valued at 20,000 roubles.

Here we have a case of the delay of the creditor (the bank). There is fault of both parties, therefore the court will decrease the liability of the creditor.

Formation and Constitution of Business Organisations

1. Legal capacity of a legal entity arises from the moment of:

- *Formation*

A legal entity is an "artificial person" gaining its legal capacity from the moment of formation.

2. The moment of creation of a legal entity is the moment of its:

- *State registration*

The moment of creation of the legal entity is the moment of the inscription of the legal entity to the Unified State Register of Legal Entities – state registration by the Federal Tax Service of the RF.

3. A legal entity is deemed to be reorganised, except in the form of takeover, from the moment of:

- *State registration of newly created legal entities*

Reorganisation of the legal entity is termination of the legal entity. However, rights and duties of the legal entity do not terminate, they are transferred to other legal entities participating in the reorganisation.

4. The term to present creditors' claims may not be less than the following term from the moment of publication on liquidation of a legal entity:

- *2 months*

Creditors have a right to participate in reorganisation or liquidation of the legal entity. They may file claims on anticipatory execution of obligations before them in case of reorganisation within 30 days, in case of liquidation – within 2 months from the moment of termination of the period for information of creditors.

5. While liquidating a legal entity the following creditors' claims are satisfied in the first turn:

- *Claims of the individuals, to whom the liquidated legal entity bears responsibility for causing harm to life or health, by way of capitalisation of the corresponding regular payments*

Special four priority turns are set for creditors participating in liquidation. Claims of the individuals to whom the liquidated legal entity bears responsibility for causing harm to life or health, by way of capitalisation of the corresponding regular payments, enjoy the first turn.

6. The question asks the applicants to explain the nature of a limited liability company and to set out the matters that must be included in the constitutional documents of a limited liability company.

(a) The Civil Code envisages three generic types of economic entity. Limited companies are organisations that have a personality separate from that of their owners and have the right to hold assets, incur liabilities and engage in entrepreneurial activity in their own name. The limited liability company is an economic entity that is formed under the Federal Law on Limited Liability Companies. It may be distinguished from open and closed companies limited by shares, or joint stock companies, which are governed by the Federal Law on Companies Limited by Shares.

The limited liability company is the simplest type of limited company, and is generally subject to less stringent regulatory requirements than those imposed on companies limited by shares. This reflects a greater level of direct involvement of the participants in the affairs of the company. The capital contributions are not permanent capital and there is greater ease of exit for participants.

Limited liability companies have less complex formation requirements than other types of limited company, such as a lower statutory capital threshold and the right to adopt a relatively simple Charter.

The limited liability company is owned by participants who contribute to the Charter capital. This capital is divided into participating shares representing their equity in the business. The minimum number of participants is one person. The maximum number of participants is 50 persons. If the company wishes to attract capital from a larger number of investors it should be reorganised as a company limited by shares.

In common with other types of limited company, the liability of participants is limited to the value of their contribution to the Charter capital. Participants may contribute in cash or *in specie*, provided that the non-cash contribution can be appraised in monetary terms. However, unlike the other forms of a limited company, the participants in a limited liability company may withdraw from the company at any time by transferring their stake in the business. The remaining participants in the company have a pre-emptive right to purchase the stake before it can be offered to outsiders.

(b) When a limited liability company is formed, the promoters must prepare an agreement of the establishing of a company and a Charter. Necessity of the agreement of the establishing of a company was provided by Amendments to the Limited Liability Companies' Law valid from 1 July 2009. The prescribed content of the Charter is set out in the Law on Limited Liability Companies.

The Charter must state the following:

- The name and registered address of the company
- The statutory capital, the contributions of the participants and the form these will take
- How the company will be managed, powers of management bodies and decision-making protocols.

There is no need to prepare detailed inner rules, though the participants may choose to do so.

If the participants choose to draft internal rules, the Law on Limited Liability Companies provides that these may include matters such as how general meetings will be conducted, voting methods and internal controls, such as the procedures to be followed by internal auditors.

7. The question tests the candidates' knowledge on acting under the power of attorney and executing acts, which are not ultra vires.

(a) The power of attorney empowers the person only for the execution of deeds and/or actions directly provided for in the power of attorney.

The examined power of attorney empowers Yaroslav for receiving goods and production due to OOO "Ust" but not for concluding contracts. OOO "Ust" will be responsible on the contract with OOO "Renessanse" only in case of subsequent approval of the contract concluded by Yaroslav by OOO "Ust". Otherwise, the contract will create rights and obligations directly for the person who signed it; namely Yaroslav. That means it will be Yaroslav in person who will be responsible for the fulfilment and non-fulfilment of obligations under the contract (exercise of pre-payment included).

(b) **(i)** No. The change of ownership of the company does not directly influence the personality of General Director. However, appointment of General Director is the competence of the general participants' meeting, and the new 100% owner has the possibility to convoke the meeting and cease Vladimir's powers as a General Director.

(ii) No. The power of attorney was issued by the company OOO "Ust" and the change of owner of the company does not influence the validity of deeds executed and concluded by the company.

(c) *No. The power of attorney was issued by the company OOO "Ust" and the change of owner of the company does not influence the validity of deeds executed and concluded by the previous director of the company. However, the power of attorney may be dissolved by the person who issued the power of attorney, and namely by OOO "Ust".*

Legal Implications Relating to Companies in Difficulty or in Crisis

1. As regards the monitor (interim manager) which of the following is correct?

- *The monitor is introduced by the Arbitrazh court at the beginning of the observation stage of the insolvency procedure*

After the Arbitrazh court accepts an application to declare a company insolvent, the Arbitrazh court considers such an application and appoints a monitor if there are reasonable grounds to initiate bankruptcy.

2. The company is trying to avoid insolvency and further liquidation and is submitting an application for financial rehabilitation. Which of the following documents would not be submitted with the application for financial rehabilitation?

- *Information on the personal assets of the shareholders or participants*

Under the general rule the company is not responsible under the obligations of the shareholders of the company and the shareholders of the company are not responsible under obligations of the company. Thus, information on the personal assets of the shareholders or participants of the company is not required.

3. In the event of insolvency, which of the following is not likely to be a criminal offence:

- *Making outstanding salary payments to employees*

Satisfying creditors of the following priority before the preceding priority shall be a criminal offence. Though, in the present case making outstanding salary payments to employees is the least offence, not likely involving criminal charges.

4. When the external manager is appointed what does this effectively signal the end of for the company?

- *The authority of the management bodies*

When external management begins, all management bodies of the company shall terminate and transfer their powers to the external manager.

5. Which of the following is the correct definition of a legitimate first meeting of creditors?

- *The bankruptcy creditors and authorised state bodies present represent more than 50% of the total amount owed to bankruptcy creditors and authorised state bodies*

The presence of creditors whose claims amount to 50% of the total amount owed to bankruptcy creditors and authorised state bodies according to the Register of creditors' claims, is required to hold the first creditors' meeting.

6. The question asks the applicants to explain the conditions that must be fulfilled in order for insolvency proceedings to be instigated against a company, and to explain the protection provided by law for creditors during the insolvency process.

(a) Article 2 of the Law on Bankruptcy states that a legal entity is considered to be bankrupt when the Court of Arbitration recognises that it cannot fully meet the claims of creditors. This supports the provisions under Articles 25 and 65 of the Civil Code which state that any individual entrepreneur or legal entity may be regarded as bankrupt if it is incapable of satisfying creditors' claims.

Both of these legal sources are somewhat broader in definition than the stricter accounting concept of insolvency, which considers insolvency to occur when total liabilities exceed total assets. Under either the Civil Code interpretation or the Law on Bankruptcy interpretation, the court may regard the entity to be bankrupt if it cannot meet its obligations within a reasonable period of them falling due. This may occur if the entity is not bankrupt at all, but simply illiquid.

Article 3 of the Law on Bankruptcy refers to "signs of bankruptcy". It states that the entity shall be considered to be incapable of meeting the claims of third parties if it does not discharge these obligations within three months of the date on which they fall due. The obligations that may be considered as relevant to the entity's financial position are debts for delivered goods, completed works and services, outstanding loans (capital and interest) and debts arising from damage to property and under non-grounded enrichment. Certain obligations are disregarded for the purposes of assessing whether the entity is insolvent, including forfeits and other penalties, interest for deferred obligations and liabilities arising from inflicting harm to third parties.

If the sum total of the obligations exceeds the value of property owned by the entity, the court will regard it as insolvent.

(b) The Law on Bankruptcy protects creditors of insolvent organisations in numerous ways:

Oversight and management:

When an organisation is declared bankrupt its affairs are placed in the hands of an arbitration manager. The Law on Insolvency lays down specific minimum requirements in respect of this official, who must be a member of one of the self-regulated organisations for arbitration managers and have higher educational qualifications. The manager must have a specified minimum level of experience and no criminal record. Professional indemnity insurance is mandatory.

The court ensures that the arbitration manager is independent in respect of monies due to any of the creditors of the organisation for which he or she is accountable. In this way, the process ensures that the arbitration manager should act objectively at all times, in the best interests of the creditors.

Once the procedure commences, the Law on Bankruptcy requires a specific monitoring procedure to be followed which ensures the involvement of creditors at key stages.

Restrictions on transactions:

During the process of insolvency the arbitration manager is limited in respect of transactions that may be carried out on behalf of the company. This serves as a safeguard for the assets of the company and provides short-term protection for creditors, even though their claims are frozen for the time being.

Accountability to the court:

The Court of Arbitration has both a regulatory and administrative role in the entire bankruptcy process. For example, if at any stage of the proceedings it is considered to be in the best interests of everyone to conclude a composition, this requires the sanction of the court.

Creditors' meeting:

The creditors' meeting has several functions. It can decide to introduce and subsequently approve financial sanation, adopt an external management plan, initiate receivership or conclude an amicable settlement.

The creditors' meeting represents creditors of all categories, with decisions vested in the creditors *pro rata* the monetary sums due to them. The meeting can also elect a creditors' committee.

Creditors' committee:

If there are more than 50 creditors, a committee may be formed to represent the interests of the broader body of creditors, control and monitor the insolvency process and discharge any other duties delegated to it by the creditors' meeting. The committee is elected by the meeting and comprises of between three and eleven persons. The committee may appoint one of their number to act as its representative in litigation.

External management:

External management seeks to restore the solvency of the business. As in the case of the arbitration manager, the court lays down duties and obligations of the external manager whilst offering several discretionary options to enable the company to recover.

Receivership and settlements:

Article 134 of the Law on Bankruptcy lays down a strict order for the settlement of the obligations of the insolvent company.

7. (a) Composition – is a specific type of deal that may be concluded between the debtor and creditors at any phase of an arbitration court's consideration of bankruptcy. Composition is to be approved by the Arbitration court. Unilateral renunciation of composition which is already effective, is inadmissible.

Composition is to contain provisions on the amount, order and terms of performing the debtor's obligations and/or on terminating the debtor's obligations by cancellation of compensation, novation of obligation or by other means stipulated by the Civil Code of the RF.

Besides this, composition may contain provisions on:

- Deferral of performance of the obligation (performance by instalments)
- Cession of the debtor's right of claim
- Performance of the debtor's obligations by third parties
- Discount on the debt
- Exchanging claims for shares
- Meeting creditors' claims by other means not contradicting legal acts of the RF.

An Arbitration court may rule on refusal to approve composition, on recognising it void or on dissolving composition.

(b) *Composition is one of the grounds to terminate the bankruptcy procedure. According to the law on insolvency, composition is the grounds for terminating court proceedings on bankruptcy. Composition may be concluded at any stage of court bankruptcy adjudication, including the observation stage.*

(c) *The volume of creditor's claims, who concluded composition with the debtor, is determined by terms stipulated in composition.*

In the given case, in 2012 the Arbitration court approved composition concluded by the debtor and creditors in the course of observation, and terminated the proceedings by judging ZAO "Malaga" to be bankrupt. According to composition, the debt of ZAO "Malaga" to OAO "Unona" amounted to 150,000 roubles. Therefore, OAO "Unona" could not file claims on debt recovery to the amount of 3 mln. roubles from ZAO

"Malaga" after composition was signed and the bankruptcy procedure terminated, since it was unlawful.

Corporate Ethical Behaviour

1. Which group of people is corporate governance concerned with?

- *All stakeholders*

In case of good corporate governance agency relations are substituted by stakeholder relations. Corporate governance is concerned with not only shareholders of the company, but all parties which may influence the company or which may be influenced by the company.

2. Which of the following is the correct definition of money laundering?

- *Legitimising illegal cash flows*

Money laundering is the legitimisation of illegal cash flows, which includes tax evasion, black wages and paying bribes to government officials.

3. Russian law provides that major transactions should (broadly speaking) be approved by the GM. Which of the following parties are recommended by good corporate governance practice to be involved in all major transactions?

- *An independent appraiser*

Corporate governance recommends that rights of all creditors and shareholders of the company (notwithstanding the share) be observed. Depending on the volume of the major transaction, different management bodies of the company shall participate in its approval. Thus, independent appraisal is recommended.

4. What are ethics?

- *High moral imperatives that go beyond business regulations*

Ethics goes beyond business regulations. Ethics is never a must. Ethical requirements are executed absolutely at the discretion of the company.

5. Anti-Money laundering legislation has 3 main objectives. Which of the following is not one of the objectives?

- *The control of foreign currency cash flows*

There are three main objectives of the Anti-Money laundering legislation, which do not include the control of foreign currency cash flows.

6. The purpose of this question is to test the knowledge of the meaning and significance of a separate legal personality and its implications for effective corporate governance.

(a) The term "separate legal personality" refers to the nature of a legal entity as having its own identity, separate from those who own it (the shareholders) and those who manage it (the directors and other executives). As such, the entity becomes an "artificial person" once it is registered with the state authorities, and as such it has most of the attributes of a natural person (Article 51 of the Civil Code). Just as a natural person is born, a company is born once it is registered. Just as a natural person can own assets and incur liabilities, so too can an artificial person. Extending the analogy, an artificial person can marry (merge), divorce (demerge), become bankrupt (insolvent) and eventually die (be liquidated).

The creation of a separate legal personality is rooted in the provisions of Article 48 of the Civil Code, which defines three models of legal entities, categorised according to their rights of estate, the extent of their powers and whether their operations are commercial or non-commercial in nature.

There are several significant features that emerge from the creation of bodies with a separate legal personality.

Firstly, the legal entity owns its own property and incurs its own obligations. Therefore, those who do business with the entity should be aware that any contracts entered into can usually only be enforced against the entity itself and not the individuals who make the decisions.

Secondly, many types of legal entity have limited liability. Although the entity itself actually has unlimited liability for the obligations it incurs, the owners (shareholders) are only liable to the extent of their monetary contributions to the capital. This is an important advantage for shareholders, who can be confident that they can incur no further obligations, even if their shares eventually become worthless.

Thirdly, the entity has perpetual succession. Although those who run the company may leave, retire or die, the entity has an ongoing existence until steps are taken to bring this to an end. One implication of this is that investments such as shares in a company represent potential wealth and income for future generations.

Fourthly, the capacity of a legal entity is dictated by a constitution, such as the Charter of a company. This may be permissive or restrictive in nature, depending on the wishes of those who first draft it or subsequently choose to amend it.

Furthermore, accountability for the actions of the management and their consequences lie with the entity and not the decision makers themselves.

If a third party wishes to litigate, it must do so against the entity and not the directors.

(b) Corporate governance is the system through which a company is directed and controlled (Cadbury Report, 1992).

The Organisation for Economic Cooperation and Development (OECD) elaborates by stating that it is: "…a set of relationships between a company's directors, its shareholders and other stakeholders. It also provides the structure through which the objectives of the company are set, and the means of achieving those objectives and monitoring performance, are determined."

This answer adopts the OECD framework for discussing the implications of a separate legal personality for corporate governance. It should be noted that the points made in this answer could be discussed using any alternative framework or approach that identifies the key factors.

Rights of shareholders:

The corporate governance framework should protect shareholders and facilitate their rights in the company. Companies are obliged to generate investment returns for the risk capital put up by the shareholders. Directors should be accountable to shareholders in this respect.

The fact that a company is a separate entity exposes the shareholders to some degree of risk. Generally, the degree of separation increases as the size of the shareholder base increases. Historically, in the RF this separation has been less important in the past as companies tended to be directed and controlled by their owners. This is reflected in the relatively powerful position of the GM in the decision making hierarchy in comparison with western European countries. However, this is changing rapidly and it is unlikely that the dominance of concentrated ownership and complex holding structures will persist in the longer term.

The rights of shareholders are protected by provisions in the Civil Code relating to formation, organisational models and liquidation, and also by the detailed provisions of the Federal Law on Companies Limited by Shares (and parallel legislation for limited liability companies).

Equitable treatment of shareholders:

All shareholders should be treated equitably (fairly), including those who constitute a minority, individuals and foreign shareholders. Shareholders should have redress when their rights are contravened or where an individual shareholder or group of shareholders is oppressed by the majority.

In the RF it is recognised that the majority have the right to exert power but due regard should also be paid to the minority. Therefore, the law protects shareholders in numerous ways including major transactions, interested transactions, reorganisation and constitutional rights (such as the right to propose items for the agenda of GMs).

Stakeholders:

The corporate governance framework should recognise the legal rights of stakeholders. The company should facilitate cooperation with stakeholders in order to create wealth, employment and sustainable enterprises.

There are several examples of how having a separate legal personality impacts on stakeholders, particularly creditors and employees.

For example, a supplier to a company may be dealing with an extremely wealthy individual who is responsible for the operations of the company, but it is the company and not the individual that will incur the obligation.

Disclosure and transparency:

Companies should make relevant and timely disclosures on matters affecting financial performance, management and ownership of the business.

As the entity is a separate person, its true financial position at any given time will only be known to a relatively small group of persons. Existing laws require companies to prepare accounts on an annual basis and make reports on significant issues to the shareholders. There is increasing pressure for disclosures to be more frank, more full and more frequent, especially in respect of issues that impact on the community and the environment.

Board of directors:

The board of directors is responsible for setting the direction of the company and monitoring the management of the company in order to achieve its stated objectives. The corporate governance framework should underpin the board's accountability to the company and its members.

Directors act as agents of the owners. This exacerbates the problem of separation as the shareholders are reliant on the actions of the directors to act in their best interests. It should also be remembered that supervisory boards are a relatively new concept in the RF.

7. The purpose of this question was to test the candidates' understanding of the decision making powers in a company and apply these to a scenario.

(a) The rules relating to major transactions are applied under the J-SC Law and the Civil Code. The purpose of the rules is to safeguard the assets of a company, thereby reducing risk to shareholders' wealth.

A major transaction is any transaction of a company, dealing with a value of 25% or more of the book value of the company's assets as at the end of the last accounting period. In addition, the Charter of the company may specify transactions that will be regarded as major transactions. The value of the transaction is estimated with reference to the market value. A major transaction may be a large, one-off disposal or acquisition or a series of related transactions. It may relate to acquisition or disposal of property or the company entering into a credit agreement, such as a pledge, guarantee or surety.

If the book value of the transaction is more than 25% but less than 50% of the company's assets, the decision on the confirmation of the major transaction may be made by the board of directors. This must be unanimous. However, if all of the members of the board cannot agree on the transaction the decision passes to the shareholders in a GM. Their decision on the matter is made by simple majority.

The ability of Peter and Rosa to secure the required level of support would determine whether the transaction could go ahead. However, they own 50% of the shares in the company, so it would be necessary for the holder of just one more share to sanction the transaction and therefore back their plan. The question of whether the proposed sale of the real estate will be regarded as a major transaction turns on whether the value of the fixed assets fall within the thresholds determined by the law. Even if the transaction is small enough not to be regarded as a major transaction, Peter and Rosa may bear subsidiary responsibility if the disposal price is clearly below the market value of the assets as this would constitute a fraud against the company.

(b) Transactions in which there is an interest are governed by the J-SC Law. The purpose of the rules on this matter is to reduce the prospect of "interested persons" from securing personal gain from the company's transactions at the expense of the shareholders. Transactions in which there is an interest are not forbidden, but it is necessary to follow the legal requirements on disclosure and decision making.

There are various parties who are considered to be able to establish an interest. These include the directors of the company, CEO or senior management, shareholders and their associates, who may individually or collectively hold 20% or more of the shares of the company, and persons authorised to give instructions on behalf of the company. In this case it appears that the vehicle fleet will be sold to a company in which Peter's brother has an interest. If so, this would be regarded as a transaction in which he has an interest and he would be excluded from voting on the matter.

The law deems these persons to be interested if they, their close relatives or affiliates are a party to the transaction or benefit from it. They are also deemed interested if they own 20% or more of the shares in an entity that is a party to the transaction, or if they hold managerial positions in an entity that is a party to the transaction. Those who have an interest are required to notify the board of directors, internal audit commission or external auditor of their interests as defined above.

There are some exclusions to the rules. If there is a sole shareholder who also makes decisions on behalf of the company, the transaction is not a major one. This also applies if all of the shareholders of the company have an interest, where the company is buying back or redeeming its own shares and in the event of a merger or acquisition where the counterparty company owns 75% or more of the company being reorganised.

As the company in the scenario has more than 1,000 shareholders, the decision on the transaction may be taken by a majority vote of independent directors of the board of directors. If all of the directors are deemed not to be independent persons, the decision must be taken by a majority of the shareholders voting in a general meeting. This is a requirement if the book value of the transaction exceeds 2% of the company's assets as at the last accounting date.

(c) If the major transaction is approved without following the necessary procedures this is a violation of the Civil Code. This may apply even if the transaction is subsequently ratified by the board of directors or the general meeting of shareholders. The persons responsible for the transaction may bear subsidiary responsibility for the transaction. Furthermore, under the minority protection provisions, the shareholders who are entitled to vote may demand redemption of their shares if dissatisfied with the outcome of the transaction, provided they voted against the transaction or abstained from voting.

If the company contravenes the rules on the proposed transaction in which there is an interest, those objecting to the transaction may petition the court to declare the transaction null and void and implement remedial measures. Shareholders possessing not less than 1% of the shares may file a claim against individual members of the board of directors or against the board as a collective body in order to obtain compensation for losses suffered.

MULTIPLE CHOICE QUESTIONS

1. The property of a commercial partnership acquired in the process of its activity belongs under the right of ownership to which of the following?
   (i) The commercial partnership
   (ii) The founders of the commercial partnership
   (iii) The founders of the commercial partnership, in proportion to their stakes in the charter capital
   (iv) The commercial partnership and every founder

2. Participants of the general (unlimited) partnership may be whom?
   (i) Commercial legal entities and state bodies
   (ii) Individual entrepreneurs and commercial legal entities
   (iii) Commercial legal entities and municipal bodies
   (iv) State and municipal bodies

3. A participant who has withdrawn from a general partnership is liable for the obligations of the partnership, arisen before the moment of the withdrawal, on par with the rest of the participants, within a period of how much time?
   (i) 5 years
   (ii) 3 years
   (iii) 2 years
   (iv) 1 year

4. Upon the registration of a general partnership, what must each of its participants pay?
   (i) Half of its contribution to the charter capital
   (ii) A third of its contribution to the charter capital
   (iii) A quarter of its contribution to the charter capital
   (iv) Two thirds of its contribution to the charter capital

5. A participant of a commandite partnership has which of the following rights?

(i) To participate in the management of the partnership
(ii) To receive part of the partnership's profits
(iii) To participate in the business activity of the partnership
(iv) To challenge actions of general partners on management and business activity of the partnership

6. A commandite partnership is not subject to liquidation if there remain at least what?

(i) Two general partners and one limited partner
(ii) One general partner and two limited partners
(iii) One general partner and one limited partner
(iv) Two general partners and two limited partners

7.When liquidating a commandite partnership from its property, which of the following is paid in the first case?

(i) Indebtedness to the state budget
(ii) Indebtedness to the creditors
(iii) The share of the participants
(iv) The share of the general partners

8. Which of the following is not an obligation of a monitor?

(i) To sell assets to raise funds to pay salaries
(ii) To carry out an analysis of the financial position
(iii) To notify creditors about commencement of observation
(iv) To call and hold the first meeting of creditors

9. During financial sanation which of the following does the company have a right to do?

(i) Make transactions in which there is an interest (with no consent of the creditors)
(ii) Decide to reorganise the company
(iii) Enter into loans, warranties and guarantees
(iv) Dispose of an asset which comprises 2% of the balance sheet at the most recent date

10. If a company is placed into trusteeship which of the following would not help restore solvency?

(i) Speeding up collection of receivables
(ii) Speeding up payment of payables
(iii) Closing down the loss making section of the business
(iv) Selling part of the business operations

PRACTICAL ASSIGNMENTS

Essential Elements of the Russian Legal System

1 The Russian Legal System: Elements and their Roles

In relation to the Russian Legal System:

(a) Explain the role of the legislature.
(b) Explain the role of the courts.
(c) Explain the role of the administration.

2 The Russian Legal System: Hierarchy of Laws and their Implementation

In relation to Sources of law explain the following:

(a) Laws (statutes) and other legislative acts, their hierarchy and its legal meaning.

(b) Implementation of legislative acts in time.

(c) Implementation of provisions of international treaties and conventions, the means of resolving conflicts between provisions of national legislative acts and provisions of international treaties and conventions.

3 The Russian Legal System: Sources of Law

In terms of the Russian legal system describe:

(a) The system of the law and the system of legislation.
(b) Major characteristics and examples of public and private law.
(c) The role of international legal acts in the Russian legal system.

4 Implementation of the law in the Russian Federation

In relation to the general principles of the implementation of laws of the Russian Federation, explain what is meant by the following terms, giving brief examples of each:

(a) Accomplishment
(b) Execution
(c) Observance
(d) Enforcement

5 In relation to the Russian legal system:

(a) Explain the purposes and scope of the Constitution of the Russian Federation.

(b) Explain the consequences of a conflict between the provisions of the Constitution and the provisions of international laws.

(c) Explain the role of codes within the overall framework of Russian law.

6 In relation to the Russian legal system:

(a) Explain the process through which a proposal for new legislation becomes a federal law.

(b) Describe the factors that limit the powers of Russian legislature to enact new federal laws.

7 The Russian Legal System: Courts and Jurisdictions

In relation to the Russian Legal System:

(a) Explain the types of legal action considered by the courts of general jurisdiction.

(b) Explain the types of legal action considered by the arbitration courts.

8 In relation to the Russian legal system:

(a) Describe the role and structure of the courts of general jurisdiction.

(b) Explain the circumstances that would make it appropriate for a case to be dealt with by the court of arbitration.

The Law of Obligations

9 Obligation Security: Bank Guarantee

In relation to the means of obligation security:

(a) Explain the nature of a bank guarantee and the rights and obligations of the parties involved.

(b) State and explain how a guarantor's obligation may be terminated.

10 Obligation Security: Mortgages

In relation to the Law of Contract:

(a) State what is meant by the term 'mortgage' and explain the form that a mortgage contract should take.

(b) State to what extent it is possible for more than one obligation to be secured on the same property.

(c) Describe how a commitment secured by mortgage can be further supported by a personal obligation entered into by a third party.

11 Obligation Security: Forfeit & Pledge

In relation to the law of obligations, explain the meaning and operation of the following:

(a) Forfeit
(b) Pledge

12 In relation to means of securing obligations:

(a) Define 'surety'.
(b) Explain the rights and responsibilities of a surety.
(c) Explain how the responsibilities of a surety are terminated.

13 Obligation Security: Forfeit and Earnest Money

In relation to contract law:

(a) Define what is meant by a Forfeit and describe the different types of forfeit that may be stipulated in a contract.

(b) Define what is meant by earnest money and describe its functions.

14 Contracts: Moment of Conclusion, Proper Form and Execution

In respect to contract law explain the following:

(a) Determining the moment of the conclusion of a contract.

(b) The form of the contract and the legal consequences of a breach of contract form.

(c) Due execution of a contract (time, place, subject, way, currency).

15 Contracts: Changes, Termination and Transfer of Rights and Duties

In respect to contract law explain the following:

(a) The possibility and cases of introducing changes to a contract.
(b) The possibility and cases of dissolving a contract.
(c) The transfer of Creditor's rights to another person.
(d) The transfer of Obligor's duties to another person.

16 Proper Discharge of a Contract

In relation to contract law, explain the provisions of the Civil Code in relation to the Proper Discharge of a Contract.

17 Termination of a Contract

In respect of contract law explain the following:

(a) The termination of a contract and the parties' responsibilities hereunder (grounds for termination). The termination of a contract by means of fulfilment, documents proving fulfilment.

(b) Set off (zachet) and cases of impossibility of set off.

(c) Novation and cases of impossibility of novation.

(d) Compensation (otstupnoye) for termination of contract.

18 Freedom of Contract

In relation to contract law:

(a) Describe what is meant by 'freedom to contract' and explain the limitations that exist under Russian law in respect of this freedom.

(b) Explain the ways in which a contract may be terminated.

Formation and Constitution of Business Organisations

19 Legal Entities: LLC (OOO) vs. JSC (ZAO or OAO)

In relation to Legal Entities:

(a) Explain the main differences between a limited liability company and a company limited by shares.

(b) Explain the main differences between an open company limited by shares and a closed company limited by shares.

20 Limited Liability Companies

In relation to limited liability companies:

(a) Explain the characteristics of a limited liability company.

(b) Explain the provisions of the Civil Code in respect of the matters that can only be decided by the shareholders of a limited liability company acting collectively in a general meeting.

21 Legal Entities: Commandite Partnerships

In relation to the forms of a legal entity:

(a) Compare and contrast the characteristics of a Commandite Partnership with those of an unlimited partnership.

(b) Explain the advantages and disadvantages for the members of a commandite partnership ceasing this form of trading in favour of establishing a limited liability company.

22 Legal Entities: Separate Legal Personality

In relation to legal entities:

(a) Explain the meaning and consequences of a 'Separate Legal Personality'.

(b) Explain the extent to which the concept of limited liability applies to the shareholders, directors and the company itself in a company limited by shares.

23 Statutory Capital

In relation to Statutory Capital:

(a) Explain what is meant by statutory capital and describe its purposes. (b) Explain the minimum legal requirements in relation to statutory capital for open and closed companies limited by shares.

(c) What are the consequences for any company that fails to adhere to the minimum legal requirements in relation to statutory capital?

24 Company Formation

In relation to limited liability companies and companies limited by shares explain the following:

(a) Formalities involved in registering a company, determining the moment of creation of the company, legal meaning of the moment of creation of the company.

(b) Formation of the initial capital of the company, the minimum amount necessary to create a company.

(c) Existing restrictions on the number of shareholders/participants of the company.

(d) Constitutional documents of the company and inner documentation (obligatory and optional).

25 Company Formation

In relation to the formation of a company limited by shares, explain the provisions of the Federal Law on Companies Limited by Shares applicable to:

(a) The founders of a company.
(b) The name and location of a company.

26 Reorganisation of Companies Limited by Shares

In relation to the Reorganisation of Companies limited by Shares:

(a) Explain the five ways in which a company limited by shares may be reorganised.

(b) Explain the procedure for decision making in respect of the reorganisation of a company limited by shares.

(c) State the protection provided by the law in relation to the creditors of a company that is to be reorganised.

27 Reorganisation of Legal Entities

In relation to the Reorganisation of Legal Entities:

(a) State and explain the ways in which a company limited by shares may be reorganised.

(b) Explain the effects of reorganisation on the rights and obligations of the company that is reorganised.

(c) Explain the circumstances under which a company must be reorganised and the alternative outcomes of reorganisation.

Legal Implications Relating to Companies in Difficulty or in Crisis

28 Insolvency

In relation to the law of insolvency:

(a) Explain the conditions that must be fulfilled in order to initiate insolvency proceedings against a company.

(b) Explain how the financial interests of creditors are protected during the insolvency process.

29 Corporate Insolvency

In relation to Corporate Insolvency:

(a) Explain the role and responsibilities of an external manager.

(b) Explain the alternative outcomes that may follow the submission of an external manager's report.

30 Bankruptcy and Insolvency

In respect of bankruptcy procedures explain the following:

(a) The signs (symptoms) of bankruptcy of an individual and a legal entity.

(b) The determination of monetary obligations and the amount thereof.

(c) The body (person) responsible for examining the case of bankruptcy and the person empowered and/or obliged to initiate the bankruptcy procedures.

(d) Deliberate and fictitious bankruptcy and the responsibility therefore.

31 Bankruptcy and Insolvency

In relation to bankruptcy and insolvency explain the following:

(a) Conditions for initiating insolvency and bankruptcy procedures (who may initiate the procedure, under what conditions, who determines the case of bankruptcy etc.).

(b) Enumerate and describe the main stages of the bankruptcy procedure and their legal meaning.

(c) In what turn are the creditors demands to an individual entrepreneur settled.

32 Observation Process

In relation to company insolvency:

(a) Explain the purposes of observation.

(b) Explain the limitations imposed by law once the observation process commences.

(c) Explain the alternative outcomes of the observation process.

Corporate Ethical Behaviour

33 Concept of Corporate Governance

In relation to corporate governance:

(a) Explain the matters that fall within the exclusive competence of the general meeting of shareholders of a company limited by shares.

(b) Explain how the powers and accountabilities of a sole executive body of a company limited by shares are determined.

34 Corporate Governance

Describe how senior management and the statutory internal bodies of a company limited by shares promote effective corporate governance.

35 Corporate Governance: Companies Limited by Shares

In relation to corporate governance:

(a) Define what is meant by corporate governance.

(b) Explain the significance of corporate governance for open companies limited by shares.

36 Corporate Governance and Audit

(a) Explain the meaning and scope of the term ‘corporate governance’.

(b) Describe the role of the following bodies in relation to promoting best practices in corporate governance:

(i) The internal auditors.

(ii) The external auditors.

LIST OF ABBREVIATIONS FOR MAJOR ISSUING AUTHORITIES OF THE RUSSIAN FEDERATION

Federal Ministries and Bodies under the President of the RF ***Федеральные министерства и службы, руководство которыми осуществляет президент РФ***	
Ministry of Internal Affairs of the RF (http://www.mvd.ru/) *Министерство внутренних дел Российской Федерации*	Ministry of Internal Affairs *МВД*
Ministry of the RF for Civil Defense, Emergencies and Elimination of Consequences of Natural Disasters (http://www.mchs.gov.ru/) *Министерство Российской Федерации по делам гражданской обороны, чрезвычайным ситуациям и ликвидации последствий стихийных бедствий*	EMERCOM *МЧС*
Ministry of Foreign Affairs of the RF (http://www.mid.ru/) *Министерство иностранных дел Российской Федерации* • *Федеральное агентство по делам Содружества Независимых Государств*	MID *МИД*
Ministry of Defense of the RF (http://www.mil.ru/) *Министерство обороны Российской Федерации*	Ministry of Defense *Минобороны*
Ministry of Justice of the RF (http://www.minjust.ru/) *Министерство юстиции Российской Федерации* • Federal Service on Execution of Punishments	Ministry of Justice *Минюст* Execution of Punishments' Service *ФСИН*

Федеральная служба исполнения наказаний • Federal Service of Court Bailiffs *Федеральная служба судебных приставов*	Court Bailiffs' Service *ФССП*
State Courier Service of the RF (Federal Service) (http://www.gfs.ru/) *Государственная фельдъегерская служба Российской Федерации (федеральная служба)*	Courier Service *ГФС*
External Intelligence Service of the RF (Federal Service) (http://svr.gov.ru/) *Служба внешней разведки Российской Федерации (федеральная служба)*	External Intelligence Service *СВР*
Federal Security Service of the RF (Federal Service) (http://www.fsb.ru/) *Федеральная служба безопасности Российской Федерации (федеральная служба)*	Security Service *ФСБ*
Federal Drug Control Service of the RF (Federal Service) (http://fskn.gov.ru/) *Федеральная служба Российской Федерации по контролю за оборотом наркотиков (федеральная служба)*	Drug Service *ФСКН*
Federal Guarding Service of the RF (Federal Service) (http://www.fso.gov.ru/) *Федеральная служба охраны Российской Федерации (федеральная служба)*	Guarding Service *ФСО*
Senior Management on Special Programmes of the President of the RF (Federal Agency) (http://www.gusp.gov.ru/) *Главное управление специальных программ Президента Российской Федерации (федеральное агентство)*	Senior Management on Special Programmes of the President *ГУСП*

Management of Affairs of the President of the RF (Federal Agency) (http://www.udprf.ru/) *Управление делами Президента Российской Федерации (федеральное агентство)*	Management of Presidential Affairs *Управление делами*
Federal Financial Monitoring Service (http://www.fedsfm.ru/) *Федеральная служба по финансовому мониторингу (федеральная служба)*	Financial Monitoring Service Rosfinmonitoring *Росфинмониторинг*
Federal Ministries and Bodies under the Government of the RF ***Федеральные министерства, руководство которыми осуществляет правительство РФ***	
Ministry of Health of the RF (http://www.minzdravsoc.ru) *Министерство здравоохранения и социального развития Российской Федерации* • Federal Service on Supervising Health Care *Федеральная служба по надзору в сфере здравоохранения* • Federal Medico-Biological Agency *Федеральное медико-биологическое агентство*	Ministry of Health *Минздрав* Health Care Supervising Service *Росздравнадзор* Medico-Biological Agency *ФМБА*
Ministry of Labour and Social Defence of the RF (http://mintrud.gov.by) *Министерство труда и социальной защиты Российской Федерации* • Federal Labour and Employment Service *Федеральная служба по труду и занятости*	Labour Ministry *Минтруд* Rostrud *Роструд*
Ministry of Culture of the RF (http://www.mkrf.ru) *Министерство культуры Российской Федерации*	Ministry of Culture *Минкультуры*

Ministry of Education and Science of the RF (http://www.mon.gov.ru) *Министерство образования и науки Российской Федерации*	Ministry of Education and Science *Минобрнауки*
Ministry of Natural Resources and Environment of the RF (http://www.mnr.gov.ru) *Министерство природных ресурсов и экологии Российской Федерации* • *Федеральная служба по гидрометеорологии и мониторингу окружающей среды* • *Федеральная служба по надзору в сфере природопользования* • *Федеральное агентство водных ресурсов* • *Федеральное агентство лесного хозяйства* • *Федеральное агентство по недропользованию*	Ministry of Natural Resources *Минприроды*
Ministry of Industry and Trade of the RF (http://www.minprom.gov.ru) *Министерство промышленности и торговли Российской Федерации*	Ministry of Industry *Минпромторг*
Ministry of Relations and Mass Communications of the RF (http://www.minsvyaz.ru) *Министерство связи и массовых коммуникаций Российской Федерации*	Ministry of Mass Communications *Минкомсвязь*
Ministry of Agriculture of the RF (http://www.mcx.ru) *Министерство сельского хозяйства Российской Федерации*	Ministry of Agriculture *Минсельхоз*
Ministry of Sport of the RF (http://www.minstm.gov.ru) *Министерство спорта Российской Федерации*	Ministry of Sport *Минспорт*
Ministry of Transportation of the RF (http://www.mintrans.ru) *Министерство транспорта Российской Федерации*	Ministry of Transportation *Минтранс*

Ministry of Finance of the RF (http://www.minfin.ru) *Министерство финансов Российской Федерации* • Federal Tax Service *Федеральная налоговая служба* • Federal Service of Financial-Budgetary Supervision *Федеральная служба финансово-бюджетного надзора* • Federal Treasury (Federal Service) *Федеральное казначейство (федеральная служба)*	MinFin *Минфин* Tax Service *ФНС* Financial-Budgetary Supervision Service *Росфиннадзор* Federal Treasury *Казначейство России*
Ministry of Economic Development of the RF (http://www.economy.gov.ru) *Министерство экономического развития Российской Федерации* • Federal Accreditation Service *Федеральная служба по аккредитации* • Federal Service for State Registration, Cadastre and Cartography *Федеральная служба государственной регистрации, кадастра и картографии* • Federal Agency of State Reserves *Федеральное агентство по государственным резервам* • Federal Agency on Administration of Federal Property *Федеральное агентство по управлению государственным имуществом* • Federal Service on Intellectual Property *Федеральная служба по интеллектуальной собственности*	MERT *Минэкономразвития* Accreditation Service *Служба по аккредитации* Rosreestr *Росреестр* State Reserves Agency *Росрезерв* Federal Property Agency *Росимущество* Rospatent *Роспатент*

Ministry of Energy of the RF (http://minenergo.gov.ru) *Министерство энергетики Российской Федерации*	Ministry of Energy *Минэнерго*
Ministry of Crimean Affairs *Министерство Российской Федерации по делам Крыма*	Ministry of Crimea
Ministry for North Caucasus Affairs *Министерство Российской Федерации по делам Северного Кавказа*	Ministry of the Caucasus
Ministry of Far East Development (http://minvostokrazvitia.ru) *Министерство Российской Федерации по развитию Дальнего Востока*	Ministry of Far East Development *Минвостокразвития*
Ministry of Construction and Housing and Communal Services (http://www.minstroyrf.ru) *Министерство строительства и жилищно-коммунального хозяйства*	Ministry of Construction *Минстрой*
Federal Bodies under the Government of the RF ***Федеральные службы, руководство которыми осуществляет правительство РФ***	
Federal Service on Supervising Consumer Rights and Human Prosperity (http://www.26.rospotrebnadzor.ru/) *Федеральная служба по надзору в сфере защиты прав потребителей и благополучия человека*	Rospotrebnadzor *Роспотребнадзор*
Federal Migration Service (http://www.fms.gov.ru/) *Федеральная миграционная служба*	FMS *ФМС*
Federal Anti-Monopoly Service of the RF (http://www.fas.gov.ru/) *Федеральная антимонопольная служба*	Anti-Monopoly Service *ФАС*
Federal Customs Service (http://www.customs.ru/) *Федеральная таможенная служба*	Customs Service *ФТС*

Federal Tariff Service (http://www.fstrf.ru/) *Федеральная служба по тарифам*	Tariff Service *ФСТ*
Federal Financial Markets Service (http://www.ffms.ru/) *Федеральная служба по финансовым рынкам*	Financial Markets Service *ФСФР*
Russian Federal Space Agency (http://www.federalspace.ru) *Федеральное космическое агентство*	Roscosmos *Роскосмос*
Federal Agency for the Development of the State Border Facilities of the RF (http://www.rosgranitsa.ru/) *Федеральное агентство по обустройству государственной границы Российской Федерации*	Rosgranitsa *Росграница*
Federal Service for Ecological, Technological & Atomic Supervision (http://gosnadzor.ru/) *Федеральная служба по экологическому, технологическому и атомному надзору*	Technadzor *Ростехнадзор*
Federal Service on Regulation of the Alcoholic Market (http://www.fsrar.ru/) *Федеральная служба по регулированию алкогольного рынка*	Alcoholic Market Service *Росалкогольрегулирование*
Federal Service for Defense Contracts (http://www.fsoz.gov.ru/) *Федеральная служба по оборонному заказу*	Rosoboronzakaz *Рособоронзаказ*
Federal Service of State Statistics (http://www.gks.ru/) *Федеральная служба государственной статистики*	Rosstat *Росстат*
Federal Agency of Scientific Organisations (http://fano.gov.ru/) Федеральное агентство научных организаций	FANO *ФАНО*

Other Issuing Authorities of the RF	
Central Bank of the RF (http://www.cbr.ru) *Центральный банк Российской Федерации*	Bank of Russia *Банк России*
Fund of Mandatory Medical Insurance of the RF (http://www.ffoms.ru/) *Федеральный фонд обязательного медицинского страхования*	Medical Fund *ФОМС*
Fund of Social Insurance of the RF (http://www.fss.ru/) *Фонд социального страхования Российской Федерации*	Social Fund *ФСС*
Federal Notary Chamber (http://www.notariat.ru/) *Федеральная нотариальная палата*	Notary Chamber *ФНП*
Pension Fund of the RF (http://www.pfrf.ru/) *Пенсионный фонд Российской Федерации*	Pension Fund *ПФР*

KEY LEGISLATION REFERENCED IN THE MANUAL

- Constitution

The Constitution of the RF, dated 12 December 1993

- Arbitrazh Procedural Code

The Arbitrazh Procedural Code of the RF No.95-FZ, dated 24 July 2002

- Tax Code

The Tax Code of the RF, Part I No.146-FZ, dated 31 July 1998, Part II No.117-FZ, dated 5 August 2000

- Civil Code

The Civil Code of the RF, Part I No.51-FZ, dated 30 November 1994, Part II No.14-FZ, dated 26 January 1996, Part III No.146-FZ, dated 26 November 2001, Part IV No.230-FZ, dated 24 November 2006

- Criminal Code

The Criminal Code of the RF No.63-FZ, dated 13 June 1996

- Code for Administrative Violations

The Code for Administrative Violations of the RF No.195-FZ, dated 30 December 2001

- Land Code

The Land Code of the RF No.136-FZ, dated 25 October 2001

- Competition Law

The Federal Law No.135-FZ "On Competition Protection", dated 26 July 2006

- Anti-Monopoly Law

The Law of the RSFSR No.948-1 “On Competition and Restriction of Monopoly Activity on Commodity Markets”, dated 22 March 1991

- Bankruptcy Law

The Federal Law of the RF No.127-FZ “On Insolvency (Bankruptcy)”, dated 26 October 2002

- Bankruptcy of Credit Organisations Law

The Federal Law No.40-FZ “On Insolvency (Bankruptcy) of Credit Organisations”, dated 25 February 1999

- Foreign Investments Law

The Federal Law No.160-FZ “On Foreign Investments in the RF”, dated 9 July 1999

- J-SC Law

The Federal Law No.208-FZ “On Joint-Stock Companies”, dated 26 December 1995

- LLC Law

The Federal Law No.14-FZ “On Limited Liability Companies”, dated 8 February 1998

- Privatisation Law

The Federal Law No.178-FZ “On the Privatisation of State and Municipal Property”, dated 21 December 2001

- Securities Market Law

The Federal Law No.39-FZ “On the Securities Market”, dated 22 April 1996

- Law on Accounting

The Federal Law No.129-FZ “On Accounting”, dated 21 November 1996

- Law on International Treaties

The Federal Law No.101-FZ “On International Treaties of the RF”, dated 15 July 1995

- Law on Banks and Banking Activity

The Federal Law of the RF No.395-1 "On Banks and Banking Activity", dated 2 December 1990

- Law on Autonomous Institutions

The Federal Law No.174-FZ "On Autonomous Institutions", dated 3 November 2006

- Law on Subsoil Resources

The Law of the RF No.2395-1 "On Subsoil Resources", dated 21 February 1992

- Law on Non-Commercial Organisations

The Federal Law No.7-FZ "On Non-Commercial Organisations", dated 12 January 1996

- Law on Consumer Cooperation

The Law of the RF No.3085-1 "On Consumer Cooperation", dated 19 June 1992

- Law on Public Organisations

The Federal Law No.82-FZ "On Public Organisations", dated 19 May 1995

- Law on Charity Organisations

The Federal Law No.135-FZ "On Charity Activity and Charity Organisations", dated 11 August 1995

- Law on Production Cooperatives

The Federal Law No.41-FZ "On Production Cooperatives", dated 8 May 1996

- Law on Agricultural Cooperation

The Federal Law No.193-FZ "On Agricultural Cooperation", dated 8 December 1995

- Law on State and Municipal Unitary Enterprises

The Federal Law No.161-FZ "On State and Municipal Unitary Enterprises", dated 14 November 2002

- Law on Minimum Wages

The Federal Law No.82-FZ "On Minimum Wages and Salaries", dated 19 June 2000

- Law on Investment Funds

The Federal Law No.156-FZ "On Investment Funds", dated 29 November 2001

- Law on People's Enterprises

The Federal Law No.115-FZ "On the Status of Workers' Joint-Stock Companies (People's Enterprises)", dated 19 July 1998

- Law on the Rights of Investors in the Securities Market

The Federal Law No.46-FZ "On the Protection of the Rights of Investors in the Securities Market", dated 5 March 1999

- Law on Audit Activity

The Federal Law of the RF No.307-FZ "On Audit Activity", dated 30 December 2008

- Law on Appraisal Activity

The Federal Law No.135-FZ "On Appraisal Activity in the RF", dated 29 July 1998

- Law on the Registration of Legal Entities

The Federal Law No.129-FZ "On the State Registration of Legal Entities and Individual Entrepreneurs", dated 8 August 2001

- Law on Small Business Entities

The Federal Law No.88-FZ "On the State Support of Small Business Entities in the RF", dated 14 June 1995

- Law On Self-Regulated Organisations

The Federal Law No.315-FZ "On Self-Regulated Organisations", dated 1 December 2007

- Insider Information Law

The Federal Law No.224-FZ "On Counteracting the Illegitimate Use of Insider Information and Market Manipulation and on Amendments to Certain Laws of the Russian Federation", dated 27 July 2010

- Partnerships' Law

The Federal Law No.380-FZ "On Ecomonic Partnerships", dated 3 December 2011.

- Investment Partnership Law

The Federal Law No.335-FZ "On the Investment Partnership", dated 28 November 2011.

- Law on the Central Depositary

The Federal Law No.414-FZ "On the Central Depositary", dated 7 December 2011.

- Bribery Law

The Federal Law No.273-FZ "On Combating Corruption", dated 25 December 2008.

GLOSSARY

A

ab initio
prep. lawyer Latin for "from the start," as "it was legal ab initio."

abandon
v. to intentionally and permanently give up, surrender, leave, desert or relinquish all interest or ownership in property, a home or other premises, a right of way, and even a spouse, family, or children.

able-bodied
adj. physically capable of working at a job or in the military. It is often used to describe a person as capable of earning a living and, therefore, of paying alimony or child support.

abstract
n. in general, a summary of a record or document, such as an abstract of judgment or abstract of title to real property.

absolute necessity
n. removing a direct danger to a person or to rights and lawful interests of other persons with infliction of harm if such danger could not be eliminated by other means.

accept
v. to receive something with approval and intention to keep it. This use often arises on the question of accepting a payment which is late or not complete or accepting the "service" (delivery) of legal papers.

acceptance
n. 1) receiving something from another with the intent to keep it, and showing that this was based on a previous agreement. 2) agreeing verbally or in writing to the terms of a contract, which is one of the requirements to show there was a contract (an offer and an acceptance of that offer). A written offer can be accepted only in writing. 3) receiving goods with the

intention of paying for them if a sale has been agreed to. 4) agreement to pay a bill of exchange, which can be an "absolute acceptance" (to pay as the bill is written) or "conditional acceptance" (to pay only when some condition actually occurs such as the shipment or delivery of certain goods). "Acceptance" is most often used in the factual determination of whether a contract was entered into.

access
n. in real estate the right and ability to get to the property.

account
n. detailed record of a particular asset, liability, owners' equity, revenue or expense.

accrue
v. 1) growing or adding to, such as interest on a debt or investment which continues to accumulate. 2) the coming into being of the right to bring a lawsuit. For example, the right to sue on a contract only accrues when the contract is breached (not on mere suspicion that it might be breached) or when the other party repudiates the contract (anticipatory breach).

acknowledge
v. 1) generally to admit something, whether bad, good or indifferent. 2) to verify to a notary public or other officer that the signer executed (wrote, signed) the document like a deed, lease, or power of attorney, to make it certified as legal and suitable for recording.

acquisition
n. one company taking over controlling interest in another company.

act of God (force majeure)
n. a natural catastrophe which no one can prevent such as an earthquake, a tidal wave, a volcanic eruption, a hurricane or a tornado.

action
n. a lawsuit in which one party (or parties) sues another.
actionable
adj. when enough facts or circumstances exist to meet the legal requirements to file a legitimate lawsuit

active legal capacity
n. the capability of an individual/legal entity to acquire and exercise civil rights by his/its actions, to create for himself/itself civil duties and to discharge them

addendum
n. an addition to a completed written document.

additional paid in capital
n. the amounts paid for stock in excess of its par value; included are other amounts paid by stockholders and charged to equity accounts other than capital stock.

adequate remedy
n. a remedy (money or performance) awarded by a court or through private action (including compromise) which affords "complete" satisfaction, and is "practical, efficient and appropriate" in the circumstances.

adhesion contract
n. a contract (often a signed form) so imbalanced in favor of one party over the other that there is a strong implication it was not freely bargained.

administer
v. 1) to conduct the duties of a job or position. 2) particularly, to manage the affairs of the estate of a person who has died under supervision of the local court. 3) to give an oath, as in "administer the oath."

admit
v. 1) to state something is true in answering a complaint filed in a lawsuit. The defendant will admit or deny each allegation in his or her answer filed with the court. If he or she agrees and states that he/she did what he/she is accused of, then the allegation need not be proved in trial. 2) in criminal law, to agree a fact is true or confess guilt. 3) to allow as evidence in a trial, as the judge says: "Exhibit D, the letter, is admitted."

adopt
v. 1) to take on the relationship of parent to child of another person, particularly (but not necessarily) a minor, by official legal action. 2) to accept or make use of, such as to adopt another party's argument in a lawsuit.

advance
n. a payment which is made before it is legally due, such as before shipment is made, a sale is completed, a book is completed by the author, or a note is due to be paid.

adverse
adj. clearly contrary, such as an adverse party being the one suing you.

affiliate
n. a relationship between two companies when one company owns substantial interest, but less than a majority of the voting stock of another company, or when two companies are both subsidiaries of a third company.

affirm
v. what an appeals court does if it agrees with and confirms a lower court's decision.

aggregate
n. the sum or total

agreement
1) n. any meeting of the minds, even without legal obligation. 2) in law, another name for a contract including all the elements of a legal contract: offer, acceptance, and consideration (payment or performance), based on specific terms.

alienation
n. the transfer of title to real property, voluntarily and completely. It does not apply to interests other than title, such as a mortgage.

alimony
n. support paid by one ex-spouse to the other as ordered by a court in a divorce (dissolution) case.

allocate
v. distribute according to a plan or set apart for a special purpose.

amalgamation
n. union

ambiguity
n. when language has more than one meaning.

amend
v. to alter or change by adding, subtracting, or substituting.

amicable settlement (compromise)
n. an agreement between opposing parties to settle a dispute or reach a settlement in which each gives some ground, rather than continue the dispute or go to trial. Judges encourage compromise and settlement, which is often economically sensible, since it avoids mounting attorneys' fees and costs.

amortization
n. a periodic payment plan to pay a debt in which the interest and a portion of the principal are included in each payment by an established mathematical formula.

annual report
n. the requirement for all public companies to file an annual report detailing the preceding year's financial results and plans for the upcoming year.

annuity
n. 1) an annual sum paid from a policy or gift. 2) short for a purchased annuity policy which will pay dividends to the owner regularly for years or for life.

anticipatory breach
n. when a party to a contract repudiates his/her obligations under that contract before fully performing those obligations.

appeal
1) v. to ask a higher court to reverse the decision of a trial court after final judgment or other legal ruling. 2) n. the name for the process of appealing, as in "he has filed an appeal."

appear
v. for a party or an attorney to show up in court.

appellant
n. the party who appeals a trial court decision he/she/it has lost.

appraise
v. to professionally evaluate the value of property including real estate, jewelry, antique furniture, securities, or in certain cases the loss of value (or cost of replacement) due to damage.

appraiser
n. a professional who makes appraisals of the value of property.

appreciate
v. to increase in value over a period of time through the natural course of events, including inflation, greater rarity, or public acceptance. This can include real property, jewelry, rare books, art works or securities.

acquisitive prescription (adverse possession)
n. a means to acquire title to property through obvious, continued and regular possession of the property, while claiming ownership for the period of years set by the law of the state where the property exists (generally, five years for movable property and fifteen years for immovable property).

arbiter
n. in some jurisdictions the name for a referee appointed by the court to decide a question and report back to the court, which must confirm the arbiter's finding before it is binding on the parties.

arbitration
n. a mini-trial, which may be for a lawsuit ready to go to trial, held in an attempt to avoid a court trial and conducted by a person or a panel of people who are not judges. The arbitration may be agreed to by the parties, may be required by a provision in a contract for settling disputes, or may be provided for by law.

arbitrator
n. one who conducts an arbitration, and serves as a judge who conducts a "mini-trial," somewhat less formally than a court trial.

arbitrazh
n. a special court for economic disputes usually between legal entities and individual entrepreneurs

arbitrazh manager
n. an individual entrepreneur approved by the Arbitrazh court to guide bankruptcy procedures and to carry out other duties imposed by law.

arrest
v. 1) to take or hold a suspected criminal with legal authority, as by a law enforcement officer. 2) to delay the enforcement of a judgment by a judge while errors in the record are corrected.

article
n. a paragraph or section of any writing such as each portion of a will, corporate charter (articles of incorporation), or different sections of a statute.

articles of incorporation
n. the basic charter of a corporation which spells out the name, basic purpose, incorporators, amount and types of stock which may be issued, and any special characteristics such as being non-profit.

as is
adj. description of a condition in a sales contract in which the buyer agrees to take the property (e.g. house, horse, auto, or appliance) without the right to complain if it is faulty.

assess
v. to set a value on property, usually for the purpose of calculating real property taxes.

asset
n. generally any item of property that has monetary value, including articles with only sentimental value (particularly in the estates of the dead).

assign
1) v. to transfer to another person any asset such as real property or a valuable right such as a contract or promissory note. 2) n. the person

(assignee) who receives a piece of property by purchase, gift or by will. The word often shows up in contracts and wills.

association
n. any group of people who have joined together for a particular purpose, ranging from social to business, and usually meant to be a continuing organization.

assume
v. to take over the liability for a debt on a promissory note, which is often done by the buyer of real property which has a secured debt upon it.

attached
adj. 1) referring to two buildings which are connected, or equipment which is solidly incorporated into a structure such as bolted to the floor or wired to the ceiling (and not capable of being removed without damage to the structure). 2) referring to money or an object which is taken by court order based on a sworn claim by a plaintiff (person suing) that the owner-defendant being sued may soon depart to avoid payment of the debt.

attorney
n. 1) an agent or someone authorized to act for another. 2) a person who has been qualified to provide legal services, including appearing in court.
audit
n. an examination by a trained accountant of the financial records of a business or governmental entity, including noting improper or careless practices, recommendations for improvements, and a balancing of the books. An audit performed by employees is called "internal audit," and one done by an independent (outside) accountant is an "independent audit."

auditor
n. an accountant who conducts an audit to verify the accuracy of the financial records and accounting practices of a business or government. A proper audit will point out deficiencies in accounting and other financial operations. The term "auditor" is often misused as meaning any accountant.

authorities
n. a common term for law enforcement, as in "I'm going to call the authorities" (i.e. police).

authorize
v. to officially empower someone to act.

authorized capital stock
n. is the maximum number of shares of common stock that can be issued under a company's Articles of Incorporation (charter). Issued shares are normally less than the number of authorized shares.

average cost
n. total cost for all units bought (or produced) divided by the number of units.

award
1) n. the decision of an arbitrator or commissioner (or any non-judicial arbiter) of a controversy. 2) v. to give a judgment of money to a party to a lawsuit, arbitration, or administrative claim. Example: "Plaintiff is awarded $27,000."

B

bad faith
1) n. intentional dishonest act by not fulfilling legal or contractual obligations, misleading another, entering into an agreement without the intention or means to fulfill it, or violating basic standards of honesty in dealing with others. 2) adj. when there is bad faith then a transaction is called a "bad faith" contract or "bad faith" offer.

bail
1) n. the money or bond put up to secure the release of a person who has been charged with a crime. 2) v. to post money or bond to secure an accused defendant's release. This is generally called "bailing out" a prisoner.

bailiff
n. a court official, who keeps order in the courtroom and executes court decisions.

balance due
n. the amount of a debt still owed on an account or the principal owed on a promissory note.

balance sheet
n. the statement of the assets and the liabilities (amounts owed) of a business at a particular time usually prepared each month, quarter of a year, annually, or upon sale of the business. It is intended to show the overall condition of the business. A balance sheet should not be confused with a profit and loss statement, which is an indicator of the current activity and health of the business.

bank guarantee
n. an irrevocable commitment by a bank to pay a specified sum of money in the event that the party requesting the guarantee fails to perform the promise or discharge the liability to a third person in case of the requestor's default.

bankruptcy
n. a federal system which permits persons and businesses which are insolvent (debtors) or face potential insolvency, to place his/her/its financial affairs under the control of the Arbitrazh court.

bar
1) n. collectively all attorneys, as "the bar". 2) v. to prevent some legal maneuver, as in "barring" a lawsuit due to the running out of the time to file. 3) to prohibit and keep someone from entering a room, building, or real property.

bar association
n. an organization of lawyers.

bargain
n. 1) a mutual agreement or contract between two parties which is voluntary and involves the exchange of consideration (money, goods, services, or a promise for a promise). 2) a supposed good deal.

basis
n. the original cost of an asset to be used to determine the amount of capital gain tax upon its sale.

bearer
n. anyone holding something, such as a check, promissory note, bank draft, or bond. This becomes important when the document (generally

called a "negotiable instrument") states it is "payable to bearer," which means whoever holds this paper can receive the funds due on it.

beneficiary
n. a broad definition for any person or entity (like a charity) who is to receive assets or profits from an estate, a trust, an insurance policy or any instrument in which there is distribution.

benefit
1) n. any profit or acquired right or privilege, primarily through a contract. 2) in worker's compensation the term "benefit" is the insurance payment resulting from a fatal accident on the job, while "compensation" is for injury without death. 3) in income taxation, anything that brings economic gain. 4) "fringe benefits" may be part of the compensation for employment other than salary or wages, and may include health or disability insurance. 5) v. to gain something, as "This sale will benefit X."

bias
n. the predisposition of a judge, arbitrator, prospective juror, or anyone making a judicial decision, against or in favor of one of the parties or a class of persons.

bid
n. an offer to purchase with a specific price stated. It includes offers during an auction in which people compete by raising the bid until there is no more bidding, or contractors offer to contract to build a project or sell goods or services at a given price, with usually the lowest bidder getting the job.

bilateral contract
n. an agreement in which the parties exchange promises for each to do something in the future. "Seller promises to sell her house to Buyer and Buyer promises to pay Seller $100,000 for it

bill
n. 1) what is commonly called a "check" by which the signer requires the bank to pay a third party a sum of money. This is a holdover from the days when a person would draw up a "bill of exchange." 2) a statement of what is owed. 3) any paper money. 4) a legislative proposal for enactment of a law. It is called a bill until it is passed and signed, at which time it is a law (statute) and is no longer referred to as a bill (a draft law). 5) an old-

fashioned term for various filed documents in lawsuits or criminal prosecutions, which is falling into disuse.

board of directors
n. the policy managers of a corporation or organization elected by the shareholders or participants.

bona fide
adj. Latin for "good faith," it signifies honesty, the "real thing" and, in the case of a party claiming title as bona fide purchaser or holder, it indicates innocence or lack of knowledge of any fact that would cast doubt on the right to hold title.

bona fide purchaser
n. commonly called BFP in legal and banking circles; a person who has purchased an asset (including a promissory note, bond or other negotiable instrument) for stated value, innocent of any fact which would cast doubt on the right of the seller to have sold it in good faith. This is vital if the true owner shows up to claim title, since the BFP will be able to keep the asset, and the real owner will have to look to the fraudulent seller for recompense.

bond
n. written evidence of debt issued by a company with the terms of payment spelled out. A bond differs from corporate shares of stock since bond payments are pre-determined and provide a final payoff date, while stock dividends vary depending on profitability and corporate decisions to distribute. There are two types of such bonds: "registered," in which the name of the owner is recorded by the company and "bearer," in which interest payments are made to whomever is holding the bond.

breach
1) n. literally, a break. A breach may be a failure to perform a contract (breaking its terms), failure to do one's duty (breach of duty, or breach of trust), causing a disturbance, threatening, or other violent acts which break public tranquility (breach of peace), illegally entering property (breach of close), not telling the truth-knowingly or innocently-about title to property (breach of warranty), or, in past times, refusal to honor a promise to marry (breach of promise). 2) v. the act of failing to perform one's agreement, breaking one's word, or otherwise actively violating one's duty to other.

burden
n. anything that results in a restrictive load upon something. This is not meant in a tangible sense, but includes a "burden" on interstate commerce (which is any matter which limits, restricts or is onerous such as a license or fee for passage), and "burdens" on land such as zoning restrictions or the right of a neighbor to pass over the property to reach his home (easement).

business (legal) entity
n. an itemized listing of the amount of all estimated revenue which a given business anticipates receiving, along with a listing of the amount of all estimated costs and expenses that will be incurred in obtaining the above mentioned income during a given period of time.

bylaws (internal documents)
n. the written rules for conduct of a corporation, association, partnership or any organization.

C

cancel
v. to cross out, annul, destroy, void and/or rescind a document.

capitalization
n. 1) the act of counting anticipated earnings and expenses as capital assets (property, equipment, fixtures) for accounting purposes. 2) the amount of anticipated net earnings which hypothetically can be used for conversion into capital assets.

care
n. in law, to be attentive, prudent and vigilant.

careless
adj., adv. 1) negligent. 2) the opposite of careful. A careless act can result in liability for damages to others.

case
n. short for a cause of action, lawsuit, or the right to sue (as in "does he have a case against X?").

cause
from Latin causa 1) v. to make something happen. 2) n. the reason something happens. 3) n. short for cause of action.

certificate of incorporation
n. document which the state issues to prove a corporation's existence upon the filing of articles of incorporation (charter) and other necessary documents.

charge
n. 1) in a criminal case, the specific statement of what crime the party is accused (charged with) contained in the indictment or criminal complaint. 2) a fee for services.

charity
n. 1) in general the sentiment of benevolence, doing good works, assisting the less fortunate, philanthropy and contributing to the general public. 2) an organization which exists to help those in need or provide educational, scientific, religious and artistic assistance to members of the public.

charter
n. the name for articles of incorporation.

charter capital
n. the aggregate capital of a legal entity put to the bank account in order to register a legal entity, which guarantees the rights of creditors of the legal entity

child
n. 1) a person's natural offspring. 2) a person 14 years and under. A "child" should be distinguished from a "minor" who is anyone under 18.

citizen
n. person who by place of birth, nationality of one or both parents, or by going through the naturalization process has sworn loyalty to a nation.

civil
adj. 1) that part of the law that encompasses business, contracts, estates, domestic (family) relations, accidents, negligence and everything related to legal issues, statutes and lawsuits, that is not criminal law. In a few areas civil and criminal law may overlap or coincide. 2) referring to one's

basic rights guaranteed under the Constitution (and the interpretations and statutes intended to implement the enforcement of those rights) such as voting, equitable taxation, freedom of speech, press, religion and assembly.

claim
1) v. to make a demand for money, for property, or for enforcement of a right provided by law. 2) n. the making of a demand (asserting a claim) for money due, for property, from damages or for enforcement of a right. If such a demand is not honored, it may result in a lawsuit.

code
n. a collection of written laws gathered together, usually covering specific subject matter.

collateral
1) n. property pledged to secure a loan or debt, usually funds or personal property as distinguished from real property (but technically collateral can include real estate). 2) adj. referring to something that is going on at the same time parallel to the main issue in a lawsuit or controversy which may affect the outcome of the case, such as adoption of a new federal regulation or a criminal trial of one of the parties

commission fee
n. a fee paid under the contract of commission by the principal to the commission agent.

common ownership
n. ownership of two or more persons.

common property
n. 1) real property owned by "tenants in common," who each have an "undivided interest" in the entire property. 2) property managed by a homeowners' association in a condominium project or a subdivision development, which all owners may use and each owns a percentage interest in. 3) lands owned by the government for public (common) use, like parks and national forests.

common (ordinary) stock
n. stock in a corporation in which dividends (payouts) are calculated upon a percentage of net profits, with distribution determined by the board of

directors. Usually holders of common stock have voting rights. These are distinguished from preferred stock in which the profits are a predetermined percentage and are paid before the common shareholders who gamble on higher profits, and collectively have voting control of the corporation.

company
n. any formal business entity for profit.

compensation
n. 1) payment for work performed, by salary, wages, commission or otherwise. It can include giving goods rather than money. 2) the amount received to "make one whole" (or at least better) after an injury or loss, particularly that paid by an insurance company either of the party causing the damage or by one's own insurer.

competent
adj. 1) in general, able to act in the circumstances, including the ability to perform a job or occupation, or to reason or make decisions. 2) in wills, trusts and contracts, sufficiently mentally able to understand and execute a document. 3) in criminal law, sufficiently mentally able to stand trial, if he/she understands the proceedings and can rationally deal with his/her lawyer. 4) in evidence, "competent" means "relevant" and/or "material."

complainant
n. a person or entity who begins a lawsuit by filing a complaint and is usually called the plaintiff, or in some cases the petitioner.

complaint
n. the document filed with the court by a person or entity claiming legal rights against another.

conclusion
n. 1) in general, the end. 2) in a trial, when all evidence has been introduced and final arguments made, so nothing more can be presented, even if a lawyer thinks of something new or forgotten. 3) in a trial or court hearing, a final determination of the facts by the trier of fact (jury or judge) and/or a judge's decision on the law.

condition
n. a term or requirement stated in a contract, which must be met for the other party to have the duty to fulfill his/her obligations.

condition precedent
n. in a contract, an event which must take place before a party to a contract must perform or do their part.

condition subsequent
n. in a contract, a happening which terminates the duty of a party to perform or do his/her part.

consent
1) n. a voluntary agreement to another's proposition. 2) v. to voluntarily agree to an act or proposal of another, which may range from contracts to sexual relations.

consideration
n. 1) payment or money. 2) a vital element in the law of contracts, consideration is a benefit which must be bargained for between the parties, and is the essential reason for a party entering into a contract.

constituent agreement
n. an agreement between founders of a legal entity on foundation of a legal entity.

constituent documents
n. foundation documents of a legal entity approved by the founders, which are required for state registration of a legal entity. Usually, charter and constituent agreement or charter.

constitution
n. the fundamental, underlying document which establishes the government of a nation.

construe (interpret)
v. to determine the meaning of the words of a written document, statute or legal decision, based upon rules of legal interpretation as well as normal, widely accepted meanings.

contract
1) n. an agreement with specific terms between two or more persons or entities in which there is a promise to do something in return for a valuable benefit known as consideration. Since the law of contracts is at the heart of most business dealings, it is one of the three or four most significant areas

of legal concern and can involve variations on circumstances and complexities.

contribution
n. 1) donation to a charity or political campaign. 2) the sharing of a loss by each of several persons who may have been jointly responsible for injury to a third party, who entered into a business which lost money or who owe a debt jointly. Quite often this arises when one responsible party pays more than his share and then demands contribution from the others in proportion to their share of the obligation. 3) payment of one of the participants of a legal entity of its part of the charter capital. 4) payment or non-monetary transfer to the charter capital of a legal entity of its participant or a third party.

controversy
n. 1) disagreement, argument or quarrel. 2) a dispute, which must be an actual contested issue between parties in order to be heard by a court.

copyright
1) n. the exclusive right of the author or creator of a literary or artistic property (such as a book, movie or musical composition) to print, copy, sell, license, distribute, transform to another medium, translate, record or perform or otherwise use (or not use) and to give it to another by will. As soon as a work is created and is in a tangible form (such as writing or taping) the work automatically has federal copyright protection.

counsel
1) n. a lawyer, attorney, attorney-at-law, counsellor, counsellor-at-law, solicitor, barrister, advocate, etc. 2) v. to give legal advice.

counter offer
n. an offer made in response to a previous offer by the other party during negotiations for a final contract. Making a counter offer automatically rejects the prior offer, and requires an acceptance under the terms of the counter offer or there is no contract. Example: X (Seller) offers to sell her house for $150,000, to be paid in 60 days; Y (Buyer) receives the offer and gives Seller a counter offer of $140,000, payable in 45 days. The original offer is dead, despite the shorter time for payment since the price is lower. Seller then can choose to accept at $140,000, counter again at some compromise price, reject the counter offer, or let it expire.

counterclaim
n. a retaliatory claim by a defendant against a plaintiff in a lawsuit included in the defendant's answer and intending to off-set and/or reduce the amount of the plaintiff's original claim against the defendant.

court
n. 1) the judge, as in "The court rules in favor of the plaintiff." 2) any official tribunal (court) presided over by a judge or judges in which legal issues and claims are heard and determined.

cumulative preference share
n. a preference share a dividend on which shall be accumulated and disbursed within a term determined by the charter of the joint-stock company.

cumulative voting
n. in corporations, a system of voting by shareholders for directors in which the shareholder can multiply his voting shares by the number of candidates and vote them all for one person for director. This is intended to give minority shareholders a chance to elect at least one director whom they favor. For example, there are five directors to be elected, and 10 000 shares issued, a shareholder with 1 000 shares could vote 5 000 for his candidate rather than being limited to 1 000 for each of five candidates, always outvoted by shareholders with 1 001 or more shares.

D

damages
n. the amount of money which a plaintiff (the person suing) may be awarded in a lawsuit.

de facto
adj. Latin for "in fact." Often used in place of "actual".

de jure
adj. Latin for "lawful," as distinguished from de facto (actual).

debenture
n. a form of bond certificate issued by a corporation to show funds invested, repayment of which is guaranteed by the overall capital value of the company under certain specific terms.

debt
n. 1) a sum of money due to another. 2) obligation to deliver particular goods or perform certain acts according to an agreement, such as returning a favor. 3) a cause of action in a lawsuit for a particular amount owed.

deceased
1) adj. dead. 2) n. the person who has died, as used in the handling of his/her estate, probate of will and other proceedings after death, or in reference to the victim of a homicide (as: "The deceased had been shot three times.")

deceit
n. dishonesty, fraudulent conduct, false statements made knowing them to be untrue, by which the liar intends to deceive a party receiving the statements and expects the party to believe and rely on them.

decide
v. for a judge, arbitrator, court of appeals or other magistrate or tribunal to reach a determination (decision) by choosing what is right and wrong according to the law as he/she sees it.

deduction
n. an expenditure which an income tax payer may subtract from gross (total) income to determine taxable income.

default
1) n. failure to respond to a summons and complaint served on a party in the time required by law. 2) the failure to make a payment when due, which can lead to a notice of default and the start of foreclosure proceedings if the debt is secured by a mortgage. 3) v. to fail to file an answer or other response to a summons and complaint, or fail to make a payment when due.

defect
n. an imperfection, quite often so great that the machinery or written document cannot be used.

defendant
n. the party sued in a civil lawsuit or the party charged with a crime in a criminal prosecution. In some types of cases (such as divorce) a defendant may be called a respondent.

defense
n. 1) a general term for the effort of an attorney representing a defendant during trial and in pre-trial maneuvers to defeat the party suing or the prosecution in a criminal case. 2) a response to a complaint, called an affirmative defense, to counter, defeat or remove all or a part of the contentions of the plaintiff.

defraud
v. to use deceit, falsehoods or trickery to obtain money, an object, rights or anything of value belonging to another.

degree of kinship
n. the level of relationship between two persons related by blood, such as parent to child, one sibling to another, grandparent to grandchild or uncle to nephew, first cousins, etc., calculated as one degree for each step from a common ancestor. This may become important when determining the heirs of an estate when there is no will.

del credere
n. in the contract of commission the surety of the commission agent for the execution of the transaction by the third party

delegate
1) v. to assign authority to another. 2) n. a person chosen to attend a convention, conference or meeting on behalf of an organization, constituency, interest group or business.

deliberate (intentional)
1) adj. (dee-lib-er-et) done with care and intention or premeditated. 2) v. (dee-lib-er-ate) to consider the facts, the laws and/or other matters, particularly by members of a jury, a panel of judges or by any group including a legislature.

demand
1) v. to claim as a need, requirement or entitlement, as in to demand payment or performance under a contract. In a lawsuit for payment of a debt or performance of an act, the party suing (plaintiff) should allege that he/she/it demanded payment or performance. 2) n. a claim, such as an unqualified request for payment or other action. 3) the amount requested by a plaintiff (usually in writing) during negotiations to settle a lawsuit. 4) adj. referring to a note payable at any time a request to pay is made.

dependent
1) n. a person receiving support from another person (such as a parent), which may qualify the party supporting the dependent for an exemption to reduce his/her income taxes. 2) adj. requiring an event to occur, as the fulfillment of a contract is dependent on the expert being available.

depreciate
v. in accounting, to reduce the value of an asset each year theoretically on the basis that the assets (such as equipment, vehicles or structures) will eventually become obsolete, worn out and of little value.

diligence
n. reasonable care or attention to a matter, which is good enough to avoid a claim of negligence, or is a fair attempt (as in due diligence in a process server's attempt to locate someone).

director
n. a sole executive body of a company or a member of the governing board of a company elected or re-elected at annual meetings of participants (shareholders).

disabled people (invalids)
n. people which are prevented from performing all usual physical or mental functions

disability
n. 1) a condition which prevents one from performing all usual physical or mental functions. This usually means a permanent state, like blindness, but in some cases is temporary. 2) a legal impediment, including being a minor who cannot make a contract, or being insane or incompetent.

discharge
v. 1) to perform one's duties. 2) to dismiss someone from a job. 3) to pay one's debts or obligations.

discretion
n. the power of a judge, public official or a private party (under authority given by contract, trust or will) to make decisions on various matters based on his/her opinion within general legal guidelines.

dissolution of company
n. termination of a company.

distribute
v. 1) the dividing up of those assets of an estate or trust when someone has died according to the terms of the deceased's will or trust, or in absence of a will, according to the laws of descent and distribution. 2) division of profits or assets of a corporation or business.

dividend
n. a portion of profit, usually based on the number of shares of stock in a corporation and the rate of distribution approved by the board of directors, that is paid to shareholders for each share they own.

double taxation
n. taxation of the same property for the same purpose twice in one year.

draft
1) n. a bill of exchange or check in which one party (including a bank) is directed by the party drafting (writing) the bill or check to take money from the drafter's (writer's) bank account and pay it to another person or entity. 2) v. to prepare and sign a bill of exchange or check. 3) n. a less than final document, which is ready for discussion, rewriting and/or editing, such as a book, a proposal, or a legislative bill.

due
n. and adj. owed as of a specific date. A popular legal redundancy is that a debt is "due, owing and unpaid." Unpaid does not necessarily mean that a debt is due.

duress
n. the use of force, false imprisonment or threats (and possibly psychological torture or "brainwashing") to compel someone to act contrary to his/her wishes or interests.

duty
n. 1) a legal obligation, the breach of which can result in liability. In a lawsuit a plaintiff must claim and prove that there was a duty by defendant to plaintiff. This can be a duty of care in a negligence case or a duty to perform in a contract case. 2) a tax on imports.

E

earnest payment (earnest money)
n. a deposit paid to demonstrate commitment and to bind a contract, with the remainder due at a particular time. If the contract is breached by failure to pay, then the earnest payment is kept by the recipient as pre-determined (liquidated) or committed damages.

ejectment (replevin)
n. a lawsuit brought to remove a party who is occupying real property.

emancipation
n. freeing a minor of more than 16 years of age from the control of parents and declaring him to have full active legal capacity. Emancipation may also end the responsibility of a parent for the acts of a child, including debts, negligence or criminal acts.

emergency
n. a sudden, unforeseen happening which requires action to correct or to protect lives and/or property.

eminent domain (requisition; nationalization)
n. the power of a governmental entity to take private real estate for public use under the court decision, with or without the permission of the owner.

emotional distress (moral damages)
n. an increasingly popular basis for a claim of damages in lawsuits for injury due to the negligence or intentional acts of another. Originally damages for emotional distress were only awardable in conjunction with damages for actual physical harm.

encumbrance
n. a general term for any claim or lien on a parcel of real property. These include: mortgages, pledges, easements (servitudes).

endorse (indorse)
v. 1) to sign one's name to the back of a check, bill of exchange or other negotiable instrument with the intention of making it cashable or transferable. 2) to pledge support to a program, proposal or candidate.

enterprise
n. property complex used for performance of business activity.

entity
n. a general term for any institution, company, corporation, partnership, government agency, university or any other organization which is distinguished from individuals.

equitable
adj. 1) just, based on fairness and not legal technicalities. 2) refers to positive remedies (orders to do something, not money damages) employed by the courts to solve disputes or give relief.

error
n. a mistake by a judge in procedure or in substantive law, during a hearing, upon petitions or motions, denial of rights, during the conduct of a trial (either granting or denying objections), on approving or denying jury instructions, on a judgment not supported by facts or applicable law or any other step in the judicial process.

estate
n. 1) all that one owns in real estate and other assets. 2) commonly, all the possessions of one who has died and are subject to probate (administration supervised by the court) and distribution to heirs and beneficiaries, all the possessions which a guardian manages for a ward (young person requiring protection and administration of affairs). 3) an alternative term for real property interest which is used in conjunction with another defining word, like "life estate," "estate for years," or "real estate."

estimate
n. accounting aspect of a separate property when a company has property at operative management.

excise tax
n. a tax imposed by federal, state, and local governments on an act, occupation, privilege, manufacture, sale, or consumption that is not deductible (e.g., tobacco, gasoline and spirits).

execute
v. 1) to finish, complete or perform as required, as in fulfilling one's obligations under a contract or a court order. 2) to sign and otherwise

complete a document, such as acknowledging the signature if required to make the document valid. 3) to seize property under court order. 4) to put to death pursuant to a sentence rendered by a court.

executed
1) adj. to have been completed. (Example: "it is an executed contract") 2) v. to have completed or fully performed. (Example: "he executed all the promises made in the contract") 3) v. completed and formally signed a document, such as a deed, contract or lease. 4) v. to have been put to death for a crime pursuant to a death sentence.

execution
n. 1) the act of getting an officer of the court to take possession of the property of a losing party in a lawsuit (judgment debtor) on behalf of the winner (judgment creditor), sell it and use the proceeds to pay the judgment. 2) carrying out a death sentence.

executory
adj. something not yet performed or done. Examples: an executory contract is one in which all or part of the required performance has not been done; an executory bequest is a gift under a will which has not been distributed to the beneficiary.

expenditure
n. a cost incurred in the normal course of business to generate revenues.

expense
n. in business accounting and business taxation, any current cost of operation, such as rent, utilities and payroll, as distinguished from capital expenditure for long-term property and equipment.

express
adj. direct, unambiguous, distinct language, particularly in a contract, which does not require thought, guessing, inference or implication to determine the meaning.

express contract
n. a contract in which all elements are specifically stated (offer, acceptance, consideration), and the terms are stated, as compared to an "implied" contract in which the existence of the contract is assumed by the circumstances.

external audit
n. an audit conducted by an individual or firm that is independent of the company being audited. These independent auditors audit the books of a company generally once per year after the completion of the company's fiscal year.

external auditor
n. an auditor, usually working for an audit firm, that is completely independent of the company it is auditing. External auditors should always be certified by a professional association of accountants, and should be selected by, and report to, the corporation's general meeting.

F

face value (par value)
n. in shares of stock, the original cost of the stock shown on the certificate, or "par value."

fee
n. a charge for services.

fiduciary
1) n. from the Latin fiducia, meaning "trust," a person (or a business like a bank or stock brokerage) who has the power and obligation to act for another (often called the beneficiary) under circumstances which require total trust, good faith and honesty. 2) adj. defining a situation or relationship in which a person is acting as a fiduciary for another.

file
1) v. to deposit with the clerk of the court a written complaint or petition which is the opening step in a lawsuit and subsequent documents, including an answer, demurrer, motions, petitions and orders. 2) n. the master folder of a lawsuit kept by the clerk of the court, including all legal pleadings (documents) filed by both sides. 3) n. the record an attorney keeps on a case.

fiscal year
n. the declared accounting year for a company, but it is not necessarily in conformance to a calendar year (January through December). However, it does cover twelve months, 52 weeks, 365 days.

float
n. 1) the time between the deposit of checks in a bank and when the amount is truly accessible; 2) the amount of funds represented by checks that have been written but not yet presented for payment. v. 3) to issue new securities through an underwriter.

forfeit
v. to lose property or rights involuntarily as a penalty for violation of law.

fraud
n. the intentional use of deceit, a trick or some dishonest means to deprive another of his/her/its money, property or a legal right.

fungible things
n. sometimes merely called "fungibles," goods which are interchangeable, often sold or delivered in bulk, since any one of them is as good as another.

G

GA
n. an acronym for General Accountant.

Generally Accepted Accounting Principles (GAAP)
n. a recognized common set of accounting principles, standards, and procedures. GAAP is a combination of accepted methods of doing accounting and policy board set authoritative standards.

gift
n. the voluntary transfer of property (including money) to another person completely free of payment or strings while both the giver and the recipient are still alive.

goal
n. the milestone the organization aims to achieve that evolves from the strategic issues.

good faith
n. honest intent to act without taking an unfair advantage over another person or to fulfill a promise to act, even when some legal technicality is not fulfilled. The term is applied to all kinds of transactions.

good title
n. ownership of real property which is totally free of claims against it and therefore can be sold, transferred or put up as security (placing a mortgage or deed of trust on the property).

goods
n. items held for sale in the regular course of business, as in a retail store.

grandfather clause
n. a clause in a statute or zoning ordinance (particularly a city ordinance) which permits the operator of a business or a land owner to be exempt from restrictions on use if the business or property continues to be used as it was when the law was adopted.

grant
v. to transfer real property from a title holder (grantor) or holders to another (grantee) with or without payment.

gratuitous
adj. or adv. voluntary or free.

gross
n. 1) the entire amount of income before any deductions are made. 2) any total amount before any deductions (examples: gross income or gross labor).

guarantee
1) v. to pledge or agree to be responsible for another's debt or contractual performance if that other person does not pay or perform. 2) the promise to pay another's debt or fulfill contract obligations if that party fails to pay or perform. 3) n. occasionally, the person to whom the guarantee is made. 4) a promise to make a product good if it has some defect.

guardian
n. a person who has been appointed by a judge to take care of a minor up to 14 years of age.

guardianship (child custody)
n. supervision over children and over individuals, who have been recognized by the court as legally incapable as a result of a mental derangement.

guilty
adj. having been convicted of a crime or having admitted the commission of a crime by pleading "guilty" (saying you did it).

H

hearing
n. any proceeding before a judge in which evidence and/or argument is presented to determine some issue of fact or both issues of fact and law.

heir
n. one who acquires property upon the death of another, based on the rules of descent and distribution, namely, being the child, descendant or other closest relative of the deceased.

holding
1) n. any ruling or decision of a court. 2) n. any real property to which one has title. 3) n. investment in a business. 4) v. keeping in one's possession.

holding company
n. a company, usually a corporation, which is created to own the stock of other corporations, thereby often controlling the management and policies of all of them.

I

i.e.
prep. abbreviation for id est, which is Latin for "that is" or "that is to say." It is used to expand or explain a general term as in "his children (i.e. Matthew, Mark, Luke and Joan)." It should not be confused with "e.g.," which means "for example."

illegal
1) adj. in violation of statute, regulation or ordinance, which may be criminal or merely not in conformity. 2) status of a person residing in a country of which he/she is not a citizen and who has no official permission to be there.

immunity
n. exemption from penalties, payments or legal requirements, granted by authorities or statutes.

immovable property
n. objects which cannot be shifted without causing the enormous damage to their purpose

implied
adj., adv. referring to circumstances, conduct or statements of one or both parties which substitute for explicit language to prove authority to act, warranty, promise, trust, agreement, consent or easement, among other things.

in perpetuity
adj. forever, as in one's right to keep the profits from the land in perpetuity.

in rem
adj. from Latin "against or about a thing," referring to a lawsuit or other legal action directed toward property, rather than toward a particular person. Thus, if title to property is the issue, the action is "in rem." The term is important since the location of the property determines which court has jurisdiction and enforcement of a judgment must be upon the property and does not follow a person. "In rem" is different from "in personam," which is directed toward a particular person.

income
n. money, goods or other economic benefit received.

incompetent
adj. 1) referring to a person who is not able to manage his/her affairs due to mental deficiency or sometimes physical disability. 2) in criminal law, the inability to understand the nature of a trial. 3) a generalized reference to evidence which cannot be introduced because it violates various rules against being allowed, particularly because it has no bearing on the case. It may be irrelevant (not sufficiently significant) or immaterial (does not matter to the issues).

incorporeal (intangible)
adj. referring to a thing which is not physical, such as a right. Examples are things like copyrights, patents, intellectual property, or goodwill. This is distinguished from tangible.

incur
v. acquiring or getting into something undesirable. In business it usually is referencing a liability, e.g., incurring a loss or to incur a debt.

indemnify
v. to guarantee against any loss which another might suffer. Example: two parties settle a dispute over a contract, and one of them may agree to pay any claims which may arise from the contract, holding the other harmless.

independent contractor
n. a person or business which performs services for another person or entity under a contract between them, with the terms spelled out such as duties, pay, the amount and type of work and other matters. An independent contractor is distinguished from an employee, who works regularly for an employer.

individual entrepreneur
n. an individual, which is registered in the Tax Service as an entrepreneur

inflation
n. an increase in the general price level of goods and services; alternatively, a decrease in the purchasing power of the dollar or other currency.

injury
n. any harm done to a person by the acts or omissions of another. Injury may include physical hurt as well as damage to reputation or dignity, loss of a legal right or breach of contract. If the party causing the injury was either willful (intentionally causing harm) or negligent then he/she is responsible (liable) for payment of damages for the harm caused.

insanity
n. mental illness of such a severe nature that a person cannot distinguish fantasy from reality, cannot conduct her/his affairs due to psychosis, or is subject to uncontrollable impulsive behavior.

insider
n. someone who has a position in a business or stock brokerage, which allows him/her to be privy to confidential information (such as future changes in management, upcoming profit and loss reports, secret sales

figures and merger negotiations) which will affect the value of stocks or bonds.

insolvency
n. 1) the condition of having more debts (liabilities) than total assets which might be available to pay them, even if the assets were mortgaged or sold. 2) a determination by a bankruptcy court that a person or business cannot raise the funds to pay all of his/her debts.

installment contract
n. an agreement in which payments of money, delivery of goods or performance of services are to be made in a series of payments, deliveries or performances, usually on specific dates or upon certain happenings.

intent
n. mental desire and will to act in a particular way, including wishing not to participate.

inter alia
(in-tur eh-lee-ah) prep. Latin for "among other things." This phrase is often found in legal pleadings and writings to specify one example out of many possibilities. Example: "The judge said, inter alia, that the time to file the action had passed."

inter se
(in-tur say)prep. Latin for "among themselves," meaning that, for instance, certain corporate rights are limited only to the shareholders or only to the trustees as a group.

interest
n. 1) any and all, partial or total right to property or for the use of property, including an easement to pass over a neighboring parcel of land, the right to drill for oil, a possibility of acquiring title upon the happening of some event, or outright title. 2) the financial amount (money) paid by someone else for the use of a person's money, as on a loan or debt, on a savings account in a bank, on a certificate of deposit, promissory note or the amount due on a judgment. 3) one's involvement in business, activities or with an individual which is sufficient to create doubt about a witness being objective-damaging his/her credibility. 4) one's involvement in business, activities or with an individual which is sufficient connection to give a person "standing" (the right based on interest in the outcome of the lawsuit

or petition) to bring a lawsuit on a particular matter or act on behalf of other people.

interest rate
n. the rate of interest charged for the use of money, usually expressed as an annual rate.

interested transaction
n. a transaction, in which a member of the company's board of directors or supervisory board or a person who discharges functions of the sole executive body, or a member of the company's collective executive body take interest, or transactions of a participant of the company having together with affiliated persons 20 or more per cent of votes of the company's total number of votes. It may not be performed by the company without the prior consent of the general meeting of the company's participants

internal audit
n. an appraisal function established within an organization to examine and evaluate its activities as a service to the organization, which is performed by internal audit commission or inspector. The objective of internal auditing is to assist members of the organization in the effective discharge of their responsibilities. The third parties may be participants of the internal audit commission but the internal audit commission may not include members of the board of directors and executive bodies. The functions of the internal audit commission or the inspector may also be performed by an independent auditor.

interpretation
n. determination of the meaning of the words of a written document, statute or legal decision, based upon rules of legal construction as well as normal, widely accepted meanings.

J

joint
adj., adv. referring to property, rights or obligations which are united, undivided and shared by two or more persons or entities.

joint and several
adj. referring to a debt or a judgment for negligence, in which each debtor (one who owes) or each judgment defendant (one who has a judgment against him/her) is responsible (liable) for the entire amount of the debt or judgment. Such term may also refer to joint creditors.

joint liability
n. when two or more persons are both responsible for a debt, claim or judgment. It can be important to the person making the claim, as well as to a person who is sued, who can demand that anyone with joint liability for the alleged debt or claim for damages be joined in (brought into) the lawsuit.

joint ownership
n. the common ownership of two or more persons cannot be divided without changing the intended purpose of the property (indivisible things) or which is not subject to division by force of law.

joint-stock company (J-SC)
n. this type of company is a company, whose charter capital is divided into a definite number of shares. It is the only type of Russian legal entity which may issue shares. The participants of the J-SC (the shareholders) are not liable under its obligations and take the risks, involved in the losses in connection with its activity, within the cost of the shares in their possession. A J-SC may be founded by one or more persons.

joint venture
n. an enterprise entered into by two or more people for profit, for a limited purpose, such as purchase, improvement and sale or leasing of real estate.

jurisdiction
n. the authority given by law to a court to try cases and rule on legal matters within a particular geographic area and/or over certain types of legal cases.

jury
n. it is a group of citizens called to hear a trial of a criminal prosecution or a lawsuit, decide the factual questions of guilt or innocence or determine the prevailing party (winner) in a lawsuit and the amount to be paid, if any, by the loser.

justifiable defense
n. defense in case of protection of personality and rights of a defending person or other persons from a socially-dangerous attack if such attack involves violence, threatening life of a defending person or other persons, or an immediate threat of such violence.

K

kin
n. blood relative.

L

lapse
1) v. to fail to occur, particularly a gift made in a will. 2) v. to become non-operative.

latent defect
n. a hidden flaw, weakness or imperfection in an article which a seller knows about, but the buyer cannot discover by reasonable inspection.

law
n. 1) any system of regulations to govern the conduct of the people of a community, society or nation, in response to the need for regularity, consistency and justice based upon collective human experience. 2) n. a statute, ordinance or regulation enacted by the legislative branch of a government and signed into law, or in some nations created by decree without any democratic process. 3) n. a generic term for any body of regulations for conduct, including specialized rules (military law), moral conduct under various religions and for organizations, usually called "bylaws."

legal
adj., adv. according to law, not in violation of law or anything related to the law.

legal entity (business entity)
n. an organization that has the legal standing to enter into contracts and may be sued for failure to perform as agreed in the contract.

legitimate
adj., adv1) legal, proper, real. 2) referring to a child born to parents who are married. A baby born to parents who are not married is illegitimate, but can be made legitimate (legitimatized) by the subsequent marriage of the parents. 3) v. to make proper and/or legal.

liability
n. one of the most significant words in the field of law, liability means legal responsibility for one's acts or omissions.

license
1) n. governmental permission to perform a particular act (like getting married), conduct a particular business or occupation, operate machinery or vehicles after proving ability to do so safely or use property for a certain purpose. 2) n. the certificate that proves one has been granted authority to do something under governmental license. 3) n. a private grant of right to use real property for a particular purpose, such as putting on a concert. 4) n. a private grant of the right to use some intellectual property such as a patent or musical composition. 5) v. to grant permission by governmental authority or private agreement.

lien
n. any official claim or charge against property or funds for payment of a debt or an amount owed for services rendered.

limitation period (limitation of actions)
n. the period of time in which a person has to file to the court or appropriate agency what he/she believes is a valid lawsuit or claim.

limited liability company (LLC)
n. a type of company, where the charter capital of a LLC is divided into participatory stakes, as indicated in its constituent documents - the charter and the constituent agreement. The participants of the LLC are not liable under its obligations and take the risks, involved in the losses in connection with its activity, within the cost of the stake in their possession. A LLC may be established by one or more individuals or legal entities (participants). However, if the number of participants exceeds fifty, then the entity must be reorganized into an open J-SC or a production cooperative within one-year, or be liquidated. In addition, a LLC cannot have as its sole founder a legal entity which is 100% owned by another legal entity.

liquidated damages
n. an amount of money agreed upon by both parties to a contract which one will pay to the other upon breaching (breaking or backing out of) the agreement or if a lawsuit arises due to the breach.

litigant
n. any party to a lawsuit. This means plaintiff, defendant, petitioner, respondent, third parties to the suit or the claim, but not a witness or attorney.

loan
n. an agreement under which an owner of assets (the lender) allows another entity (the borrower) to use the assets for a specified time period. In return, the borrower agrees to pay the lender a payment (interest) and return the assets (cash) at the end of the agreed upon time period.

lockout
n. dismissal of an employee under the initiative of the employer due to participation of the employee in a collective labour dispute or a strike

loss
n. 1) the value placed on injury or damages due to an accident caused by another's negligence, a breach of contract or other wrongdoing. The amount of monetary damages can be determined in a lawsuit. 2) when expenses are greater than profits, the difference between the amount of money spent and the income.

M

maintenance
n. the activity involved in maintaining something in good working order. May include replacement of signifcant portions of the item(s) being maintained.

major transaction
n. a transaction with acquisition or alienation and with possibility of the direct or indirect alienation by the company of the assets whose value comprises over 25 per cent of the value of the company's property, estimated on the basis of the data of accountancy over the last reporting period that precedes the date of the adoption of a decision on the

completion of such transactions, unless the company's charter provides for a higher scale of the major transaction

majority
n. 1) the age when a person can exercise all normal legal rights, including contracting and voting. It is 18 for most purposes. 2) 50 percent, plus one of votes cast.

mandatory
adj., adv. absolutely demanded or required.

market value
n. the price which a seller of property would receive in an open market by negotiation, as distinguished from a "distress" price on a forced or foreclosure sale, or from an auction. Market value of real property is normally determined by a professional appraiser who makes comparisons to similar property sales in the area, which are often called "comparables."

material
adj. relevant and significant.

maturity
n. 1) the date when the payment of the principal amount owed under the terms of a promissory note or bill of exchange becomes due. Quite often a note states that failure to pay interest or installment payments when due "accelerates" the note, making the "maturity date" immediate if such payments are demanded and not paid. 2) the age when one becomes an adult, which is 18 for most purposes.

memorandum
n. a brief writing, note, summary or outline.

mental derangement (distress)
n. mental disorder.

mental suffering
n. emotional pain synonymous with "mental anguish."

merger
n. in corporate law, the joining together of two corporations in which one corporation transfers all of its assets to the other, which continues to exist.

In effect one corporation "swallows" the other, but the shareholders of the swallowed company receive shares of the surviving corporation.

minor
n. anyone under 18.

minority
n. 1) in voting, a side with less than half the votes. 2) the period of life under legal age.

minority interest
n. the interest or percentage ownership of a group of stockholders who, in total, own less than 50% of the shares in the corporation.

minutes
n. the written record of meetings, particularly of boards of directors and/or shareholders of corporations, kept by the secretary of the corporation or organization.

monetary unit
n. the unit used to measure economic activity (e.g., U.S. $).

monopoly
n. a business or inter-related group of businesses which controls so much of the production or sale of a product or kind of product as to control the market, including prices and distribution. Business practices, combinations and/or acquisitions which tend to create a monopoly may violate various federal statutes which regulate or prohibit business trusts and monopolies or prohibit restraint of trade.

mortgage
n. a document in which the owner pledges his/her/its title to real property to a lender as security for a loan.

movable property
n. things (including money and securities), which have not been referred by the Civil Code and other laws to immovable property.

municipal
adj. referring to localities or areas of subjects of the Russian Federation.

mutual
adj., adv. referring to anything in which both parties have reciprocal rights, understanding or agreement.

N

natural person (individual)
n. a real human being, as distinguished from a corporation, which is often treated at law as a fictitious person.

negatory
n. the right of the owner to file a lawsuit claiming that violations of his right be eliminated, even though these violations do not deprive the owner of the property.

negligence
n. failure to exercise the care toward others which a reasonable or prudent person would do in the circumstances, or taking action which such a reasonable person would not. Negligence is accidental as distinguished from "intentional torts" (assault or trespass, for example) or from crimes, but a crime can also constitute negligence, such as reckless driving. Negligence can result in all types of accidents causing physical and/or property damage, but can also include business errors and miscalculations, such as a sloppy land survey.

negotiable instrument
n. check, promissory note, bill of exchange, security or any document representing money payable which can be transferred to another by handing it over (delivery) and/or endorsing it (signing one's name on the back either with no instructions or directing it to another, such as "pay to the order of X").

net assets
n. a difference between total assets and current liabilities including non-capitalized long-term liabilities.

net profit
n. the company's total earnings, reflecting revenues adjusted for costs of doing business, depreciation, interest, taxes and other expenses. Same as Net Income.

next of kin
n. 1) the nearest blood relatives of a person who has died, including the surviving spouse. 2) anyone who would receive a portion of the estate by the laws of descent and distribution if there is no will.

nominal capital
n. total face value of authorized issuable capital.

non-grounded (unjust) enrichment (conversion)
n. 1) n. a benefit by chance, mistake or another's misfortune for which the one enriched has not paid or worked and morally and ethically should not keep. 2) the property acquired or saved groundlessly. A person who has acquired or saved property without grounds, established by law or by a contract for account of another person is obliged to return to the latter such property

notary public
n. a person authorized by the subject of the Russian Federation in which the person resides to administer oaths (swearings to truth of a statement), take acknowledgments, certify documents and to take depositions.

notice
n. 1) information, usually in writing in all legal proceedings, of all documents filed, decisions, requests, motions, petitions, and upcoming dates. 2) a writing informing a party to a contract, promissory note, lease, rental agreement or other legal relationship of a delinquency in payment, default, intent to foreclose, notice to pay rent or quit (leave) or other notice required by the agreement, mortgage, deed of trust or statute. 3) information. 4) being informed of a fact, or should have known based on the circumstances, as "he had notice that the roof was not water-tight."

novation
n. agreement of parties to a contract to substitute a new contract for the old one.

nullity
n. something which may be treated as nothing, as if it did not exist or never happened. This can occur by court ruling or enactment of a statute. The most common example is a nullity of a marriage by a court judgment.

O

obiter dicta
n. remarks of a judge which are not necessary to reaching a decision, but are made as comments.

object
1) v. to ask the court not to allow a particular question asked of a witness by the opposing lawyer on the basis that it is either legally not permitted, confusing in its wording or improper in its "form." 2) n. a particular thing. 3) n. an aim or purpose, as "the object of the contract..."

obligation
n. a legal duty to pay or do something.

offer
n. a specific proposal to enter into an agreement with another. An offer is essential to the formation of an enforceable contract. An offer and acceptance of the offer creates the contract.

official
1) adj. referring to an act, document or anything sanctioned or authorized by a public official or public agency. 2) n. a public officer or governmental employee who is empowered to exercise judgment. 3) n. an officer of a corporation or business.

ombudsman (ombudsmen)
n. an official, usually (but not always) appointed by the government or by parliament, who is charged with representing the interests of the public by investigating and addressing complaints reported by individual citizens. In some jurisdictions is referred to as the 'Parliamentary Commissioner'. Need not be appointed by government; may work for a corporation, a newspaper, a non-government organization or even for the general public.

omission
n. 1) failure to perform an act agreed to, where there is a duty to an individual or the public to act (including omitting to take care) or where it is required by law. Such an omission may give rise to a lawsuit in the same way as a negligent or improper act. 2) inadvertently leaving out a word, phrase or other language from a contract, deed, judgment or other document.

operation of law
n. a change or transfer which occurs automatically due to existing laws and not an agreement or court order. Example: a joint tenant obtains full title to real property when the other joint tenant dies.

overrule
v. 1) to reject an attorney's objection to a question to a witness or admission of evidence. 2) to decide that a prior decision on a legal issue was not correct.

own
v. to have legal title or right to something. Mere possession is not ownership.

ownership
n. legal title coupled with exclusive legal right to possession. Co-ownership, however, means that more than one person has a legal interest in the same thing.

P

paid-in capital
n. capital received from investors for stock, equal to capital stock plus paid-in capital, NOT that capital received from earnings or donations. Also called contributed capital.

par
n. 1) an equal level. 2) the face value of a stock or bond, printed on the certificate, which is the amount the original purchaser paid the issuing corporation.

par value
n. 1) the maturity value or face value, i.e., the amount that an issuer agrees to pay at the maturity date. 2) the official exchange rate between two countries' currencies. 3) the value of a security that is set by the company issuing it; unrelated to market value.

parent company
n. a company of which others are subsidiaries.

partial disability (restricted capability)
n. the result of an injury which permanently reduces a person's ability to function, but still permits some working or other activity.

participate
v. to invest and then receive a part or share, as in business profits, payments on a promissory note, title to land, or as one of the beneficiaries of the estate of a person who has died.

partner
n. one of the co-owners and investors in a "partnership" which is an on-going business enterprise entered into for profit.

party
n. 1) one of the participants in a lawsuit or other legal proceeding who has an interest in the outcome. Parties include plaintiff (person filing suit), defendant (person sued or charged with a crime), petitioner (files a petition asking for a court ruling), respondent (usually in opposition to a petition or an appeal), cross-complainant (a defendant who sues someone else in the same lawsuit), or cross-defendant (a person sued by a cross-complainant). 2) a person or entity involved in an agreement. 3) a common reference by lawyers to people or entities involved in lawsuits, transactions, contracts or accidents, as in "both parties knew what was expected," "he is a party to the contract," "he was not a party to the criminal conspiracy...."

passive legal capacity
n. the capability to possess civil rights and to perform duties.

patent
1) adj. obvious. 2) n. an exclusive right to the benefits of an invention or improvement granted by the Intellectual Property Service.

pay
v. to deliver money owed.

payable
1) adj. referring to a debt which is due. A debt may be owed, but not yet payable until a certain date or event. 2) n. a debt which is due. "Payables" are all the liabilities (debts) of a business.

payback period
n. in capital budgeting, is the length of time needed to recoup the cost of CAPITAL INVESTMENT. The payback period is the ratio of the initial investment (cash outlay, regardless of the source of the cash) to the annual cash inflows for the recovery period. The major shortcoming for the payback period method is that it does not take into account cash flows after the payback period and is therefore not a measure of the profitability of an investment project.

pecuniary
adj. relating to money, as in "pecuniary loss."

penalty
n. 1) in criminal law, a money fine or forfeiture of property ordered by the judge after conviction for a crime. 2) an amount agreed in advance if payment or performance is not made on time, such as a "late payment" on a promissory note or lease, or a financial penalty for each day a building contractor fails to complete a job.

per
prep. from Latin for "by means of" or simply, "by" as in "per day" (by day) or "per capita" (by head).

per se
adj. Latin for "by itself," meaning inherently.

perform
v. 1) to fulfill one's obligations under a contract. 2) to comply with requirements of a court order.

permanent disability
n. an injury which impairs the physical and/or mental ability of a person to perform his/her normal work or non-occupational activities supposedly for the remainder of his/her life.

permit
1) v. to allow by silence, agreement or giving a license. 2) n. a license or other document given by an authorized public official or agency (building inspector, department of motor vehicles) to allow a person or business to perform certain acts.

perpetuity
n. forever.

person
n. 1) a human being. 2) a corporation treated as having the rights and obligations of a person.

personal effects (belongings)
n. things which include clothes, cosmetics and items of adornment.

petition
1) n. a formal written request to a court for an order of the court. It is distinguished from a complaint in a lawsuit which asks for damages and/or performance by the opposing party. 2) n. a general term for a writing signed by a number of people asking for a particular result from a private governing body (such as a homeowners association, a political party, or a club). 3) in public law, a writing signed by a number of people which is required to place a proposition or ordinance on the ballot, nominate a person for public office, or demand a recall election. Such petitions for official action must be signed by a specified number of registered voters (such as five percent). 4) v. to make a formal request of a court; to present a written request to an organization's governing body signed by one or more members.

petty cash
n. is an account and location where tangible cash is stored for usage in purchasing or the reimbursing of inexpensive out-of-pocket expenditures.

place of residence
n. the place, where the individual resides permanently or most of the time.

plaintiff
n. the party who initiates a lawsuit by filing a complaint with the clerk of the court against the defendant(s) demanding damages, performance and/or court determination of rights.

pledge
v. to deposit personal property as security for a personal loan of money. If the loan is not repaid when due, the personal property pledged shall be forfeit to the lender. The property is known as collateral. To pledge is the same as to pawn. 2) to promise to do something.

possess
v. to own, have title to, occupy, physically hold or have under exclusive control.

power
n. the right, authority and ability to take some action or accomplish something, including demanding action, executing documents, contracting, taking title, transferring, exercising legal rights and many other acts.

power of attorney (proxy)
n. a written document signed by a person (individual or legal entity) giving another person the power to act in conducting the signer's business, including signing papers, checks, title documents, contracts, voting, handling bank accounts and other activities in the name of the person granting the power.

precedent
1) n. a prior reported opinion of an appeals court which establishes the legal rule (authority) in the future on the same legal question decided in the prior judgment. 2) adj. before, as in the term "condition precedent," which is a situation which must exist before a party to a contract has to perform.

preemptive (priority) right
n. the right of a shareholder in a corporation to have the first opportunity to purchase a new issue of stock of that corporation in proportion to the amount of stock already owned by the shareholder.

preference share capital
n. capital raised by an entity through the sale of preferred shares.

preferred (preference) dividend
n. a payment of a corporation's profits to holders of preferred (preference) shares of stock.

preferred (preference) stock
n. a class of shares of stock in a corporation which gives the holders priority in payment of dividends (and distribution of assets in case of dissolution of the corporation) over owners of "common" stock at a fixed rate.

premises
n. 1) in real estate, land and the improvements on it, a building, store, shop, apartment, or other designated structure. The exact premises may be important in determining if an outbuilding (shed, cabana, detached garage) is insured or whether a person accused of burglary has actually entered a structure. 2) in legal pleading, premises means "all that has hereinabove been stated," as in a prayer (request) at the end of a complaint asking for "any further order deemed proper in the premises" (an order based on what has been stated in the complaint).

prima facie
adj. Latin for "at first look," or "on its face," referring to a lawsuit or criminal prosecution in which the evidence before trial is sufficient to prove the case unless there is substantial contradictory evidence presented at trial.

priority
n. the right to be first or ahead of the rights or claims of others.

privacy
n. the right to be free of unnecessary public scrutiny or to be let alone.

privity
n. contact, connection or mutual interest between parties.

pro rata
adj. from Latin for "in proportion," referring to a share to be received or an amount to be paid based on the fractional share of ownership, responsibility or time used. Examples: an heir who receives one-quarter of an estate may be responsible for one-quarter of the estate taxes as his/her pro rata share. A buyer of a rental property will pay his/her pro rata share of the property taxes for that portion of the year in which he/she holds title.

prohibition
n. forbidding an act or activity.

promise
1) n. a firm agreement to perform an act, refrain from acting or make a payment or delivery. In contract law, if the parties exchange promises, each promise is "consideration" (a valuable item) for the other promise.

Failure to fulfill a promise in a contract is a breach of the contract, for which the other party may sue for performance and/or damages. 2) v. to make a firm agreement to act, refrain from acting or make a payment or delivery.

promissory note
n. a written promise by a person (variously called maker, obligor, payor, promisor) to pay a specific amount of money (called "principal") to another (payee, obligee, promisee), usually to include a specified amount of interest on the unpaid principal amount (what he/she owes).

proof
n. confirmation of a fact by evidence.

proper party
n. a person or entity who has an interest (financial or protection of some legal rights) in the subject matter of a lawsuit and, therefore, can join in the lawsuit as he/she/it wishes, or may be brought into the suit (as an unnecessary party) by one of the parties to the legal action.

property
n. anything that is owned by a person or entity.

prosecute
v. 1) in criminal law, to charge a person with a crime and thereafter pursue the case through trial on behalf of the government. 2) to conduct any legal action by a lawyer on behalf of a client, including both civil and criminal cases, but most commonly referring to prosecution for crimes.

public
1) n. the people of the nation, state, county, district or municipality which the government serves. 2) adj. referring to any agency, interest, property, or activity which is under the authority of the government or which belongs to the people. This distinguishes public from private interests as with public and private schools, public and private utilities, public and private hospitals, public and private lands and public and private roads.

public easement
n. the right of the general public to use certain streets, highways, paths or airspace.

puffing
n. the exaggeration of the good points of a product, a business, real property and the prospects for future rise in value, profits and growth. Since a certain amount of "puffing" can be expected of any salesman, it cannot be the basis of a lawsuit for fraud or breach of contract unless the exaggeration exceeds the reality.

Q

quantum meruit
n. Latin for "as much as he deserved," the actual value of services performed.

quasi
adj., adv. from Latin for "as if," almost, somewhat, to a degree (always used in combination with another word). Quasi refers to things and actions which are not exactly or fully what they might appear, but have to be treated "as if" they were.

query
n. common lawyer lingo for a question to be answered.

question of fact
n. in a lawsuit or criminal prosecution, an issue of fact in which the truth or falsity (or a mix of the two) must be determined by the "trier of fact" (the jury or the judge in a non-jury trial) in order to reach a decision in the case.

question of law
n. an issue arising in a lawsuit or criminal prosecution which only relates to determination of what the law is, how it is applied to the facts in the case, and other purely legal points in contention.

quit
v. to leave, used in a written notice to a tenant to leave the premises (notice to quit).

quorum
n. the number of people required to be present before a meeting can conduct business. Unless stated differently in laws, bylaws, articles,

regulations or other rules established by the organization, a quorum is usually a majority of members.

R

ratify
v. to confirm and adopt the act of another even though it was not approved beforehand.

real property
n. 1) all land, structures, firmly attached and integrated equipment (such as light fixtures or a well pump), anything growing on the land, and all "interests" in the property, which may include the right to future ownership (remainder), right to occupy for a period of time (tenancy or life estate), the right to drill for oil, the right to get the property back (a reversion) if it is no longer used for its current purpose (such as use for a hospital, school or city hall), use of airspace (condominium) or an easement across another's property.

reasonable care
n. the degree of caution and concern for the safety of himself/herself and others an ordinarily prudent and rational person would use in the circumstances. This is a subjective test of determining if a person is negligent, meaning he/she did not exercise reasonable care.

reasonable doubt
n. not being sure of a criminal defendant's guilt to a moral certainty.

reasonable wear and tear
n. commonly used in leases to limit the tenant's responsibility (and therefore liability to repair or repaint) upon leaving. It is subjective, but the considerations include the length of time of tenancy (the longer the occupancy the more wear and tear can be expected), the lack of unusual damage such as a hole in the wall or a broken window, and the condition of the premises when the tenant moved in. This is often a source of conflict between landlord and tenant, particularly when there is a deposit for any damages "beyond reasonable wear and tear."

receipt
n. a written and signed acknowledgment by the recipient of payment for goods, money in payment of a debt or receiving assets from the estate of someone who has died.

receiver
n. an arbitrazh manager appointed by Arbitrazh court to receive rents and profits coming to a debtor while a bankruptcy is being processed to pay creditors, so that funds will be paid for debts and possibly available for distribution to creditors.

receivership
n. bankruptcy procedure where the receiver appointment by Arbitrazh court aimed at the protection of rights of creditors, as its primary goal is to recover as much of the debtor's property as possible.

reckless
adj. in both negligence and criminal cases, careless to the point of being heedless of the consequences ("grossly" negligent). Most commonly this refers to the traffic misdemeanor "reckless driving."

record
1) v. to write down or tape the minutes, financial transactions, discussions and other happenings at meetings. 3) n. in trials, hearings or other legal proceedings the total of the proceedings which are transcribed by a court secretary and included in the minutes (protocol), as well as all the documents filed in the case.

recourse
n. the right to demand payment to the writer of a check or bill of exchange.

recover
v. to receive a money judgment in a lawsuit.

redeem
v. to buy back.

register
n. in corporations, the record of shareholders, and issuance and transfer of shares on the records of the corporation.

regulations
n. rules and administrative codes issued by governmental agencies at all levels.

reimbursement
n. to pay back to someone, e.g. to pay an employee for travel expenses that was paid by the employee out of that employee's own personal funds.

remainder (right of the inherited life possession; life annuity)
n. in real property law, the interest in real property that is left after another interest in the property ends, such as full title after a life estate (the right to use the property until one dies).

remedy
n. the means to achieve justice in any matter in which legal rights are involved.

reorganization
n. the implementation of a business plan to restructure a legal entity.

repeal
1) v. to annul an existing law, by passage of a repealing statute, or by public vote on a referendum. 2) n. the act of annulling a statute.

replevin
n. the right of the owner to bring a lawsuit for recovery of goods improperly taken by another.

res
n. Latin, "thing." In law lingo res is used in conjunction with other Latin words as "thing that."

rescind
v. to cancel a contract, putting the parties back to the position as if the contract had not existed. Both parties rescind a contract by mutual agreement, since a unilateral cancellation of a contract is a "breach" of the contract and could result in a lawsuit by the non-cancelling party.

reserve fund
n. a fund of money created to take care of maintenance, repairs or unexpected expenses of a business or a multi-unit housing development

(often condominiums or a housing cooperative) operated by a homeowners association or other governing body.

residence
n. 1) the place where one makes his/her home. 2) in corporation law, the state of incorporation.

resident
n. a person who lives in a particular place.

respondent
n. 1) the party who is required to answer a petition for a court order or writ requiring the respondent to take some action, halt an activity or obey a court's direction. 2) on an appeal, the party who must respond to an appeal by the losing party in the trial court (called "appellant") in the appeals court.

responsible
adj. 1) legally liable or accountable. 2) having the ability to pay or perform.

restitution
n. 1) returning to the proper owner property or the monetary value of loss. Sometimes restitution is made part of a judgment in negligence and/or contracts cases. 2) in criminal cases, one of the penalties imposed is requiring return of stolen goods to the victim or payment to the victim for harm caused.

restraint of trade
n. in antitrust law, any activity (including agreements among competitors or companies doing business with each other) which tends to limit trade, sales and transportation in interstate commerce or has a substantial impact on interstate commerce.

restriction
n. any limitation on activity, by statute, regulation or contract provision.

retroactive
adj. referring to a court's decision or a statute enacted by a legislative body which would result in application to past transactions and legal actions.

revenue
n. the inflows of assets from selling goods and providing services to customers; including the reduction of liabilities from selling goods and providing services to customers.

revocation
n. 1) mutual cancellation of a contract by the parties to it. 2) withdrawing an offer before it is accepted ("I revoke my offer"). 3) cancelling a document before it has come into legal effect or been acted upon, as revoking a will. 4) to recall a power or authority previously given, as cancelling a power of attorney.

right
1) n. an entitlement to something, whether to concepts like justice and due process or to ownership of property or some interest in property, real or personal. 2) adj. just, fair, correct.

risk
n. chances of danger or loss, particularly of property covered by an insurance policy or property being used or transported by another.

rule
1) v. to decide a legal question, by a court, as in: "I rule that the plaintiff is entitled to the goods and damages for delay in the sum of $10,000." 2) n. any regulation governing conduct.

ruling
n. court decision on a case or any legal question.

S

said
adj. a reference back to a thing that was previously mentioned or identified, popular in legal documents, as "the said driver drove said automobile in a negligent manner."

sanction
n. 1) a financial penalty imposed by a judge on a party or attorney for violation of a court rule, for receiving a special waiver of a rule, or as a fine for contempt of court. 2) v. to impose a fine or penalty as part of a judge's duty to maintain both order and fairness in court. 3) v. in

international law, to impose economic constraints on trade against a country that violates international law or is guilty of human rights violations. 4) v. to allow or approve. This meaning is ironically in contrast to the other definitions of "sanction."

satisfaction
n. receiving payment or performance of what is due.

securities
n. generic term for shares of stock, bonds and debentures issued by corporations and governments to evidence ownership and terms of payment of dividends or final pay-off.

seized
n. 1) having ownership, commonly used in wills as "I give all the property of which I die seized as follows:…." 2) having taken possession of evidence for use in a criminal prosecution. 3) having taken property or a person by force.

self-defense
n. the use of reasonable force to protect oneself or members of the family from bodily harm from the attack of an aggressor, if the defender has reason to believe he/she/they is/are in danger.

servitude (easement)
n. 1) the right of the limited use of the neighboring land plot. 2) the right to use the real property of another for a specific purpose.

set aside
v. to annul or negate a court order or judgment by another court order. Example: a court dismisses a complaint believing the case had been settled. Upon being informed by a lawyer's motion that the lawsuit was not settled, the judge will issue an order to "set aside" the original dismissal.

setoff (offset)
n. 1) n. the deduction by a debtor from a claim or demand of a debt or obligation. Such an offset is based upon a counterclaim against the party making the original claim. Example: Creditor makes a claim or files a lawsuit asking for $20,000 from Debtor as the final payment in purchase of a restaurant; as part of his defense Debtor claims an offset of $10,000 for alleged funds owed by Creditor for repairs Debtor made on property

owned by Creditor, thus reducing the claim of Creditor to $10,000. 2) v. to counterclaim an alleged debt owed by a claimant to reduce the demand of that claimant.

settle
v. to resolve a lawsuit without a final court judgment by negotiation between the parties.

severance
n. extra pay offered and made to a person to encourage him/her to resign, retire or settle a potential claim for discharge.

shall
v. an imperative command as in "you shall not kill."

share
n. 1) a portion of a benefit from a trust, estate, claim or business usually in equal division (or a specifically stated fraction) with others ("to my three daughters, in equal shares"). 2) a portion of ownership interest in a corporation, represented by a stock certificate stating the number of shares of an issue of the corporation's stock.

share capital
n. a portion of a corporation's equity obtained from issuing shares in return for cash or other considerations.

share ownership
n. an ownership with a defined share of each of the owners in the right of common ownership.

shareholder
n. the owner of one or more shares of stock in a corporation.

shareholders' agreement
n. an employment agreement among the shareholders of a small corporation permitting a shareholder to take a management position with the corporation without any claim of conflict of interest or self-dealing against the shareholder/manager. Such agreements are common when there are only three or four shareholders.

shareholders' meeting
n. a meeting, usually annual, of all shareholders of a corporation to elect the board of directors and hear reports on the company's business situation. In larger corporations top management people hold the proxies signed over to them by many of the shareholders to vote for them.

sign
v. 1) to write one's signature on a document, including an "X" by an illiterate or physically impaired person. 2) to communicate by sign language.

sole executive body (chief executive officer)
n. an officer of a legal entity, executing management of the company's current activity and elected by the general meeting of participants.

specific performance
n. the right of a party to a contract to demand that the defendant (the party who it is claimed breached the contract) be ordered in the judgment to perform the contract.

stake
n. a share or an interest in an enterprise (e.g. LLC).

standard of care
n. the watchfulness, attention, caution and prudence that a reasonable person in the circumstances would exercise.

state
n. 1) the federal government and any of its departments, agencies or components (such as a city, county or board). 2) a nation's government.

state of domicile
n. the state in which a person has his/her permanent residence or intends to make his/her residence, as compared to where the person is living temporarily.

statute
n. written law enacted by legislative bodies of the Russian Federation or its subjects.

stock
1) n. inventory (goods) of a business meant for sale (as distinguished from equipment and facilities). 2) share in the ownership of a corporation (called "shares of stock" or simply "shares").

strike
1) v. to remove a statement from the record of the court proceedings by order of the judge due to impropriety of a question, answer or comment to which there has been an objection. 2) n. the organized refusal of workers to remain on the job, usually accompanied by demands for a union contract, higher wages, better conditions or other employee desires, and possibly including a picket line to give voice to workers' demands and discourage or intimidate other workers and customers from entering the business, factory or store.

subject to
adj. referring to the acquisition of title to real property upon which there is an existing mortgage or deed of trust when the new owner agrees to take title with the responsibility to continue to make the payments on the promissory note secured by the mortgage or deed of trust.

subrogation
n. assuming the legal rights of a person for whom expenses or a debt has been paid.

subscribe
v. 1) to sign at the end of a document. 2) to order and agree to pay for an issue of stock, bonds, limited partnership interest, investment or periodical magazine or newspaper.

substantive law
n. law which establishes principles and creates and defines rights and limitations under which society is governed, as differentiated from "procedural law," which sets the rules and methods employed to obtain one's rights and, in particular, how the courts are conducted.

substitution
n. the power of attorney given from the attorney to sub-attorney.

suffering

n. the pain, hurt, inconvenience, embarrassment and/or inability to perform normal activities as a result of injury.

suit (lawsuit)

n. generic term for any filing of a complaint (or petition) asking for legal redress by judicial action. In common parlance a suit asking for a court order for action rather than a money judgment is often called a "petition," but technically it is a "suit in equity." The legal claims within a lawsuit are called "causes of action."

T

tangible property

n. physical articles (things) as distinguished from "incorporeal" assets such as rights, patents, copyrights and franchises. Commonly tangible property is called "personalty."

tax evasion

n. intentional and fraudulent attempt to escape payment of taxes in whole or in part.

taxable income

n. income that is reported to the government for the purposes of calculating income taxes.

temporary insanity

n. in a criminal prosecution, a defense by the accused that he/she was briefly insane at the time the crime was committed and therefore was incapable of knowing the nature of his/her alleged criminal act.

title

n. 1) ownership of real property or personal property, which stands against the right of anyone else to claim the property. 2) the name for one's position in a business or organization, such as president, general manager, mayor, governor, duke. 3) the name for a legal case, which is part of the "caption" of the case.

tort

n. a civil wrong arising from a breach of duty created not by agreement but by operation of law for which the normal remedy is an action for damages.

trade
1) n. a business or occupation for profit, particularly in retail or wholesale sales or requiring special mechanical skill. 2) v. to exchange one thing for another, which includes money for goods, goods for goods and favors for goods or money.

trade name
n. a name of a business or one of its products which, by use of the name and public reputation, identifies the product as that of the business.

trade secret
n. a process, method, plan, formula or other information unique to a manufacturer, which gives it an advantage over competitors.

trademark
n. a distinctive design, picture, emblem, logo or wording (or combination) affixed to goods for sale to identify the manufacturer as the source of the product.

transfer
n. 1) the movement of property from one person or entity to another. 2) passage of title to property from the owner to another person. 3) a piece of paper given to allow a person or shipment to continue travel.

treaty
n. a pact between nations.

trespass
n. entering another person's property without permission of the owner or his/her agent and without lawful authority and causing any damage, no matter how slight.

trial
n. the examination of facts and law presided over by a judge with authority to hear the matter (jurisdiction).

trust
n. an entity created to hold assets for the benefit of certain persons or entities, with a trustee managing the trust (and often holding title on behalf of the trust).

trusteeship
n. supervision over minors from 14 to 18 years of age and over individuals, who have been restricted in their active capacity as a result of their abuse of alcohol or drug addiction.

U

ultra vires
adj. Latin for "beyond powers," in the law of corporations, referring to acts of a corporation and/or its officers outside the powers and/or authority allowed a corporation by law.

unconstitutional
adj. referring to a statute, governmental conduct, court decision or private contract which violate one or more provisions of the Constitution.

under the influence
n. one of many phrases for being drunk on alcoholic beverages or high on drugs or a combination of alcohol and drugs.

underwrite
v. 1) to agree to pay an obligation which may arise from an insurance policy. 2) to guarantee purchase of all shares of stock or bonds being issued by a corporation, including an agreement to purchase by the underwriter if the public does not buy all the shares or bonds. 3) to guarantee by investment in a business or project.

undue influence
n. the amount of pressure which one uses to force someone to execute a will leaving assets in a particular way, to make a direct gift while alive or to sign a contract.

unexpired
n. means not having come to an end or been terminated by the passage of time.

unfair competition
n. wrongful and/or fraudulent business methods to gain an unfair advantage over competitors.

unlawful
adj. referring to any action which is in violation of a statute.

V

valuable consideration
n. a necessary element of a contract, which confers a benefit on the other party. Valuable consideration can include money, work, performance, assets, a promise or abstaining from an act.

value added tax (VAT)
n. a consumption tax where taxes are levied at each step of a manufacturing process where value is added to that product at that point in the manufacturing cycle; as well as at the point where the consumer purchases the end product.

venue
n. the proper or most convenient location for trial of a case.

viz
prep. to wit, or namely. Example: "There were several problems, viz: leaky roof, dangerous electrical system and broken windows."

void
adj. referring to a statute, contract, ruling or anything which is null and of no effect.

voidable
adj. capable of being made void.

W

wage
n. actual remuneration paid to an employee for services rendered.

waive
v. to voluntarily give up something, including not enforcing a term of a contract (such as insisting on payment on an exact date), or knowingly giving up a legal right such as a jury trial.

ward
n. a person (usually a minor) who has a guardian appointed by the court to care for and take responsibility for that person.

warrant
1) n. an order (writ) of a court which directs a law enforcement officer (usually a court bailiff) to arrest and bring a person before the judge. 2) v. to claim to a purchaser that merchandise is sound, of good quality or will perform as it should, or that title to real property belongs to the seller.

warranty
n. a written statement of good quality of merchandise, clear title to real estate or that a fact stated in a contract is true.

waste
n. 1) any damage to real property by a tenant which lessens its value to the landlord, owner or future owner. 2) garbage, which may include poisonous effluents.

wind up
v. to liquidate (sell or dispose of) assets of a legal entity.

winding up
n. liquidating the assets of a corporation or partnership, settling accounts, paying bills, distributing remaining assets to shareholders or partners, and then dissolving the business.

withholding tax
n. usually refers to those taxes that are withheld from an employee's compensation to account for that individuals tax liability on his/her compensation.

withdrawal
n. the removal of money from a bank account.

writ
n. a written order of a judge requiring specific action by the person or entity to whom the writ is directed.

writ of execution
n. a court order to a court bailiff to enforce a judgment by levying on real or personal property of a judgment debtor to obtain funds to satisfy the judgment amount (pay the winning plaintiff).